Best of Bridge Holiday Classics

225 Recipes
for Special Occasions

Robert
ROSE

Best of Bridge Holiday Classics
Text copyright © 2014 The Best of Bridge Publishing Ltd. and Robert Rose Inc. (see page 292)
Photographs copyright © 2014 Robert Rose Inc. (except as noted below)
Cover and text design copyright © 2014 Robert Rose Inc.

For complete cataloguing information, see page 292.

Disclaimer
The recipes in this book have been carefully tested by our kitchen and our tasters. To the best of our knowledge, they are safe and nutritious for ordinary use and users. For those people with food or other allergies, or who have special food requirements or health issues, please read the suggested contents of each recipe carefully and determine whether or not they may create a problem for you. All recipes are used at the risk of the consumer.

We cannot be responsible for any hazards, loss or damage that may occur as a result of any recipe use.

For those with special needs, allergies, requirements or health problems, in the event of any doubt, please contact your medical adviser prior to the use of any recipe.

Design and Production: Joseph Gisini/PageWave Graphics Inc.
Editor: Sue Sumeraj
Proofreader: Sheila Wawanash
Indexer: Gillian Watts
Photographer: Colin Erricson
Associate Photographer: Matt Johannsson
Food Stylist: Kathryn Robertson
Prop Stylist: Charlene Erricson
Other Images: Turkey (cover) © istockphoto.com/Liliboas; Turkey (inside) © istockphoto.com/LauriPatterson; Eggnog (cover and inside) © istockphoto.com/bhofack2

Cover Images (clockwise from top left): Roast Turkey with Sage-Bread Stuffing (page 148); Christmas Morning Wife Saver (page 21); Eggnog Supreme (page 85); Snowballs (page 235), Nanny's Real Scottish Shortbread (page 231) and Ginger Cookies (page 237)

The publisher gratefully acknowledges the financial support of our publishing program by the Government of Canada through the Canada Book Fund.

Published by Robert Rose Inc.
120 Eglinton Avenue East, Suite 800, Toronto, Ontario, Canada M4P 1E2
Tel: (416) 322-6552 Fax: (416) 322-6936
www.robertrose.ca

Printed and bound in China

1 2 3 4 5 6 7 8 9 PPLS 22 21 20 19 18 17 16 15 14

CONTENTS

INTRODUCTION

SINCE 1975, THE BEST OF BRIDGE "LADIES," AS THEIR CHILDREN NAMED THEM, HAVE BEEN DEVELOPING RECIPES THAT ARE EASY TO UNDERSTAND, WRITTEN WITH A SENSE OF HUMOR AND GUARANTEED TO WORK. NOT SURPRISINGLY, GIVEN THEIR MOTTO — "SIMPLE RECIPES WITH GOURMET RESULTS" — OVER THE COURSE OF FOUR DECADES, THEY HAVE COOKED UP COUNTLESS TREATS THAT ARE PERFECT FOR SHARING WITH FAMILY AND FRIENDS WHEN IT'S TIME FOR A CELEBRATION.

THIS NEW COLLECTION FOCUSES ON RECIPES THAT WILL MEET ALL OF YOUR HOLIDAY ENTERTAINING NEEDS, FROM CASUAL POTLUCK GET-TOGETHERS TO FESTIVE BRUNCHES AND BUFFETS TO ELEGANT SIT-DOWN DINNERS. OF COURSE, NO HOLIDAY BOOK WOULD BE COMPLETE WITHOUT LIBATIONS, SUCH AS HOT BUTTERED RUM (PAGE 80) OR EGGNOG SUPREME (PAGE 85), AND AN ABUNDANCE OF GREAT DIPS, SPREADS AND FINGER FOODS TO ANCHOR THE PERFECT COCKTAIL PARTY.

FOR HOLIDAY BAKERS, THERE ARE COOKIES AND SQUARES AND AN ABUNDANCE OF SHORTBREADS. THE LIP-SMACKING DESSERTS INCLUDE GOOD OLD-FASHIONED GINGERBREAD (PAGE 257) AND LITTLE STICKY TOFFEE PUDDINGS (PAGE 272). AND IN CASE YOU DIDN'T HAVE TIME TO SHOP, THERE IS EVEN A CHAPTER ON FOOD GIFTS.

'TIS THE SEASON FOR SOCIALIZING. HAVE FUN AND ENJOY YOUR PARTY!

SAMPLE MENUS

HOLIDAY BRUNCH

- EGGS BENEDICT WITH BLENDER HOLLANDAISE (PAGE 14)
- SCHWARTIES HASH BROWNS (PAGE 42)
- WARM SPINACH SALAD WITH APPLES AND BRIE (PAGE 91)
- "LAND OF NOD" CINNAMON BUNS (PAGE 48)

BUFFET PARTY

- CRABMEAT DIP (PAGE 62)
- ARTICHOKE NIBBLERS (PAGE 69)
- GREEN GODDESS SALAD (PAGE 97)
- RENÉ'S SANDWICH LOAF (PAGE 104)
- PARTY MEATBALLS WITH SWEET AND SOUR SAUCE (PAGE 121)
- POACHED SALMON (PAGE 176)
- CRANBERRY SQUARES (PAGE 242)
- CAJUN BREAD PUDDING WITH RUM SAUCE AND SOFT CREAM (PAGE 270)

TRADITIONAL HOLIDAY MEAL

- ROAST TURKEY WITH SAGE-BREAD STUFFING (PAGE 148)
- GOURMET CRANBERRY SAUCE (PAGE 210)
- CREAMY WHIPPED POTATOES (PAGE 203)
- SAUCY BRUSSELS SPROUTS (PAGE 189)
- JALAPEÑO CORN MUFFINS (PAGE 53)
- PUMPKIN PECAN PIE (PAGE 256)

A SNOWY CHRISTMAS EVE

- GLØGG (PAGE 82)
- SUMPTUOUS SPINACH AND ARTICHOKE DIP (PAGE 57)
- GUACAMOLE CHERRY TOMATO HALVES (PAGE 71)
- CHRISTMAS CHEESE BALLS (PAGE 72)
- TOURTIÈRE WITH RHUBARB RELISH (PAGE 168)
- SPINACH AND STRAWBERRY SALAD (PAGE 89)
- SHORTBREAD (PAGE 230)
- COFFEE BRANDY FREEZE (PAGE 255)

NEW YEAR'S EVE BANQUET

- WINTER PUNCH (PAGE 84)
- SMOKED SALMON HORS D'OEUVRE (PAGE 74)
- CAESAR SALAD (PAGE 92)
- ROAST BEEF WITH MUSTARD-PEPPERCORN CRUST (PAGE 160)
- YORKSHIRE PUDDING (PAGE 161)
- LEMON RISOTTO (PAGE 208)
- CHOCOLATE RASPBERRY TORTE (PAGE 262)

A VEGETARIAN CELEBRATION

- SUN-DRIED TOMATO DIP (PAGE 59)
- SPANAKOPITA (PAGE 73)
- BROCCOLI MANDARIN SALAD (PAGE 93)
- SPANISH VEGETABLE PAELLA (PAGE 206)
- LEMON BERRY CAKE (PAGE 266)

HOLIDAY BRUNCHES

THIS SECTION PROVIDES RECIPES THAT ARE PERFECT FOR EARLY OR MID-DAY ENTERTAINING IN THE HOLIDAY SEASON, AS WELL AS TRADITIONAL COMFORT FOOD DISHES THAT WILL HELP YOU START YOUR DAY IN A FESTIVE MOOD IF YOU HAVE SLEEPOVER GUESTS. FOR CONVENIENCE, SOME RECIPES CAN BE PREPARED AHEAD, CHILLED AND FROZEN, FOR FUSS-FREE COOKING WHEN YOU'RE READY TO SERVE; OTHERS CAN BE MADE IN YOUR SLOW COOKER.

MAINS

BREADS AND MUFFINS

SCOTTY'S NEST EGGS

*ONE OF OUR FAVORITE BACHELORS
LOVES TO WHIP THIS UP.*

EACH NEST

2 to 3	THIN SLICES BLACK FOREST HAM	2 to 3
1	LARGE EGG	1
1 TBSP	TABLE (18%) CREAM	15 ML
1½ TBSP	SHREDDED SWISS CHEESE	22 ML
	SPRINKLE OF BASIL	
½	ENGLISH MUFFIN	½

PREHEAT OVEN TO 350°F (180°C). GREASE LARGE MUFFIN CUPS. LINE WITH HAM AND BREAK EGG OVER TOP. ADD CREAM AND SPRINKLE WITH CHEESE AND BASIL. (PLACE WATER IN ANY UNUSED MUFFIN CUPS TO PREVENT DAMAGE.) BAKE 12 TO 15 MINUTES. SERVE ON HALF A TOASTED ENGLISH MUFFIN.

*THE BEST PLACE TO GO WITH A CHILD
IS THEIR IMAGINATION.*

EGGS OLÉ!

EASY, COLORFUL AND, OF COURSE, DELICIOUS! CARAMBA!

12	EGGS	12
1/4 CUP	WATER	60 ML
	SALT AND BLACK PEPPER TO TASTE	
6 TBSP	BUTTER, DIVIDED	90 ML
1 CUP	SLICED MUSHROOMS	250 ML
1/2 CUP	CHOPPED GREEN ONION	125 ML
1/2 CUP	COARSELY CHOPPED GREEN BELL PEPPER	125 ML
1/2 CUP	COARSELY CHOPPED RED BELL PEPPER	125 ML
1/2 CUP	COARSELY CHOPPED ZUCCHINI	125 ML
1/2 CUP	COARSELY CHOPPED TOMATOES	125 ML
1/4 CUP	GREEN CHILES (OPTIONAL)	60 ML
8 OZ	MONTEREY JACK CHEESE, SHREDDED	250 G
	SALSA, MILD OR HOT	

BEAT EGGS AND WATER TOGETHER. SEASON WITH SALT AND PEPPER. MELT HALF THE BUTTER IN A FRYING PAN AND ADD EGG MIXTURE. SCRAMBLE JUST UNTIL MOIST. PLACE IN A LARGE OVENPROOF DISH; KEEP WARM IN 150°F (70°C) OVEN. MELT THE REMAINING BUTTER IN FRYING PAN; SAUTÉ ALL VEGGIES TILL TENDER. SEASON WITH SALT AND PEPPER. SPOON OVER EGGS, SPRINKLE WITH CHEESE AND BAKE AT 300°F (150°C) UNTIL CHEESE MELTS. SERVE WITH LOTS OF SALSA. SERVES 6.

HUEVOS RANCHEROS

POACHED EGGS — SOUTHWESTERN STYLE

CHILI SAUCE

2 TBSP	VEGETABLE OIL	30 ML
1 CUP	FINELY CHOPPED ONION	250 ML
1 CUP	FINELY CHOPPED RED OR ANAHEIM PEPPER	250 ML
2	CLOVES GARLIC, MINCED	2
1	CAN (28 OZ/796 ML) CHOPPED TOMATOES	1
1 TSP	SUGAR	5 ML
	SALT AND BLACK PEPPER TO TASTE	
1/4 TSP	CRUSHED HOT PEPPER FLAKES (OPTIONAL)	1 ML
1 CUP	GRATED CHEDDAR CHEESE	250 ML
4	8-INCH (20 CM) FLOUR OR CORN TORTILLAS	4
8	EGGS (FOR POACHING)	8

GARNISH

SALSA, SOUR CREAM, GRATED CHEDDAR, GUACAMOLE, CANNED BLACK BEANS, RINSED AND DRAINED

TO PREPARE SAUCE: IN A DEEP FRYING PAN, HEAT OIL; SAUTÉ ONION, PEPPER AND GARLIC UNTIL SOFT. ADD TOMATOES AND SEASONINGS; SIMMER 20 MINUTES. ADD CHEESE; HEAT AND STIR UNTIL MELTED AND WELL BLENDED.

WRAP TORTILLAS IN FOIL AND HEAT IN OVEN. HEAT BEANS.

TO POACH EGGS: BREAK EGGS INTO BUBBLING SAUCE AND POACH 3 TO 5 MINUTES TO DESIRED DONENESS. PLACE EGGS AND CHILI SAUCE ON TORTILLAS AND PASS THE GARNISHES. SERVES 4.

EGGS FLORENTINE

I	PACKAGE (10 OZ/300 G) FROZEN CHOPPED SPINACH	I
2 TBSP	BUTTER	30 ML
2 TSP	LEMON JUICE	10 ML
1/4 TSP	CELERY SALT	I ML
	SALT AND BLACK PEPPER TO TASTE	
2 TBSP	ALL-PURPOSE FLOUR	30 ML
2 TBSP	BUTTER	30 ML
I CUP	MILK	250 ML
1 1/2 TSP	GRATED ONION	7 ML
PINCH	GROUND NUTMEG	PINCH
6	EGGS	6
I CUP	SHREDDED SWISS CHEESE	250 ML
3	ENGLISH MUFFINS, HALVED AND TOASTED	3

COOK SPINACH AND DRAIN WELL. SEASON WITH BUTTER, LEMON JUICE, CELERY SALT, SALT AND PEPPER. IN A DOUBLE BOILER, COMBINE FLOUR, BUTTER, SALT AND PEPPER TO TASTE. ADD MILK SLOWLY; STIR AND COOK UNTIL THICK, ABOUT 10 MINUTES. ADD SAUCE, ONION AND NUTMEG TO SPINACH MIXTURE AND MIX THOROUGHLY. PLACE IN SHALLOW BAKING DISH. BREAK EGGS OVER SPINACH MIXTURE. SPRINKLE CHEESE OVER EGGS. BAKE AT 325°F (160°C) FOR 15 TO 20 MINUTES OR UNTIL EGGS ARE SET. SERVE ON HALVED ENGLISH MUFFINS. SERVES 6.

EGGS BENEDICT WITH BLENDER HOLLANDAISE

THIS CLASSIC DISH WAS CREATED AT NEW YORK'S FAMED DELMONICO'S IN THE 1920S FOR MR. AND MRS. LEGRAND BENEDICT, WHO COMPLAINED THERE WAS NOTHING NEW ON THE LUNCH MENU.

1 TSP	WHITE VINEGAR	5 ML
1 TSP	SALT	5 ML
1 TBSP	BUTTER	15 ML
8	SLICES CANADIAN BACON	8
4	ENGLISH MUFFINS, SPLIT	4
8	EGGS	8
	BLENDER HOLLANDAISE (SEE RECIPE, OPPOSITE)	

PREHEAT OVEN TO 250°F (120°C). IN A LARGE DEEP SKILLET, BRING ABOUT 2 INCHES (5 CM) OF WATER, VINEGAR AND SALT TO A SIMMER OVER HIGH HEAT. REDUCE HEAT TO MEDIUM-LOW AND KEEP WATER SIMMERING UNTIL READY TO POACH EGGS. IN A LARGE NONSTICK SKILLET, MELT BUTTER OVER MEDIUM-HIGH HEAT. COOK BACON FOR 1 TO 2 MINUTES PER SIDE OR UNTIL LIGHTLY BROWNED. TOAST ENGLISH MUFFINS. ARRANGE ON A RIMMED BAKING SHEET AND TOP EACH HALF WITH A SLICE OF BACON. PLACE IN PREHEATED OVEN TO KEEP WARM.

BREAK EACH EGG INTO A SMALL DISH OR MEASURING CUP AND SLIP INTO SIMMERING WATER. (BY ALL MEANS USE A POACHING RING IF YOU HAVE ONE.) COOK UNTIL WHITES AND YOLKS ARE SET TO DESIRED DONENESS, ABOUT 4 TO 5 MINUTES FOR MEDIUM-SET YOLKS. REMOVE

EGGS USING A SLOTTED SPOON AND PLACE ON A DOUBLE
PAPER TOWEL-LINED PLATE TO BLOT MOISTURE.

   PLACE 2 ENGLISH MUFFIN HALVES ON SERVING PLATES
AND TOP EACH WITH A POACHED EGG. SPOON WARM
HOLLANDAISE SAUCE OVER EGGS AND SERVE IMMEDIATELY.
SERVES 4.

VARIATION: INSTEAD OF HOLLANDAISE, LAYER THINLY
SLICED CHEDDAR CHEESE OVER POACHED EGGS AND PLACE
UNDER PREHEATED BROILER FOR 2 MINUTES OR UNTIL
CHEESE IS MELTED.

VARIATION: SUBSTITUTE THICKLY SLICED SMOKED HAM
FOR THE CANADIAN BACON.

VARIATION: *EGGS BENEDICT FLORENTINE:* STEAM 8 OZ
(250 G) BABY SPINACH LEAVES UNTIL WILTED; DRAIN WELL.
LAYER OVER ENGLISH MUFFINS AND TOP WITH POACHED
EGGS AND HOLLANDAISE SAUCE.

BLENDER HOLLANDAISE

4	EGG YOLKS, AT ROOM TEMPERATURE	4
I TBSP	FRESHLY SQUEEZED LEMON JUICE	15 ML
1/4 TSP	SALT	I ML
PINCH	CAYENNE PEPPER	PINCH
1/2 CUP	BUTTER, CUT INTO PIECES	125 ML

IN A BLENDER, COMBINE EGG YOLKS, LEMON JUICE, SALT
AND CAYENNE. BLEND ON HIGH FOR A FEW SECONDS
UNTIL FROTHY. PLACE BUTTER IN A 2-CUP (500 ML) GLASS

CONTINUED ON NEXT PAGE...

MEASURE AND MICROWAVE ON HIGH FOR 1 TO $1\frac{1}{2}$ MINUTES
OR UNTIL MELTED AND BUBBLY. TURN BLENDER ON HIGH
AND ADD HOT BUTTER TO EGG YOLK MIXTURE IN A THIN
STEADY STREAM UNTIL THICKENED. SERVE IMMEDIATELY.
MAKES $\frac{2}{3}$ CUP (150 ML).

TIP: TO HELP KEEP HOLLANDAISE SAUCE HOT, HALF FILL
THE BLENDER CONTAINER WITH HOT WATER TO WARM IT;
DRAIN WELL JUST BEFORE USING.

TIP: HOLLANDAISE SAUCE CAN BE MADE UP TO 4 HOURS
AHEAD; COVER AND REFRIGERATE. TO REHEAT, PLACE IN
THE TOP OF A DOUBLE BOILER OR IN A STAINLESS STEEL
BOWL SET OVER A SAUCEPAN OF SIMMERING WATER;
WHISK CONSTANTLY UNTIL WARM.

POPEYE'S SOUFFLÉ

1	EGG	1
2	PACKAGES (EACH 10 OZ/300 G) CHOPPED SPINACH, COOKED AND DRAINED	2
$1\frac{1}{2}$ CUPS	SOUR CREAM	375 ML
$\frac{1}{2}$	PACKAGE ONION SOUP MIX	$\frac{1}{2}$
$\frac{1}{4}$ CUP	BREAD CRUMBS	50 ML
1 CUP	GRATED CHEDDAR CHEESE	250 ML

ADD EGG TO SPINACH, THEN MIX IN SOUR CREAM AND
SOUP MIX. POUR INTO CASSEROLE DISH. COVER WITH BREAD
CRUMBS AND CHEDDAR CHEESE. BAKE 40 MINUTES AT 350°F
(180°C). SERVES 6 TO 8.

SUNDAY EGGS AND HAM

24	EGGS	24
1/2 CUP	MILK	125 ML
1/2 CUP	BUTTER	125 ML
2 LBS	CANNED HAM	1 KG
1	CAN (10 OZ/284 ML) SLICED MUSHROOMS	1
2	CANS (EACH 10 OZ/284 ML) CREAM OF MUSHROOM SOUP	2
1/2 CUP	SHERRY	125 ML
8 OZ	SHARP (OLD) CHEDDAR CHEESE	250 G

BEAT EGGS; ADD MILK. MELT BUTTER IN A FRYING PAN AND SCRAMBLE EGGS. PLACE EGGS IN 13- BY 9-INCH (33 BY 23 CM) PAN. CHOP HAM AND SPRINKLE ON EGGS. NEXT, LAYER THE MUSHROOMS ON TOP OF HAM. WARM THE MUSHROOM SOUP WITH SHERRY AND SPREAD OVER ALL. GRATE CHEDDAR CHEESE ON TOP. COVER WITH FOIL AND REFRIGERATE UNTIL REQUIRED. BAKE AT 250°F (120°C) FOR 50 MINUTES, UNCOVERED. GREAT WITH COFFEE CAKE OR FRESH FRUIT. SERVES 12.

THE OLDER YOU GET, THE BETTER YOU GET,
UNLESS YOU ARE A BANANA.

CHILLED SALMON SOUFFLÉ

1 1/2 TBSP	UNFLAVORED GELATIN	22 ML
1/2 CUP	COLD TOMATO JUICE	125 ML
1	CAN (10 OZ/284 ML) CREAM OF SHRIMP SOUP	1
3/4 CUP	MILK	175 ML
4	EGGS, SEPARATED	4
1/4 CUP	LEMON JUICE	60 ML
1 1/2 TSP	PREPARED HORSERADISH	7 ML
1 1/2 TSP	SALT	7 ML
1 CUP	HEAVY OR WHIPPING (35%) CREAM	250 ML
1	CAN (15 1/2 OZ/440 G) SALMON, DRAINED AND FLAKED	1
1 TBSP	SNIPPED PARSLEY	15 ML

SPRINKLE GELATIN OVER TOMATO JUICE AND LET STAND 5 MINUTES TO SOFTEN. ADD SOUP AND MILK AND HEAT TO A SIMMER, STIRRING CONSTANTLY, UNTIL GELATIN IS DISSOLVED. STIR A LITTLE OF THE HOT MIXTURE INTO WELL-BEATEN EGG YOLKS. RETURN TO SAUCEPAN AND COOK 2 MINUTES LONGER. ADD LEMON JUICE, HORSERADISH AND SALT. CHILL UNTIL PARTIALLY SET. BEAT EGG WHITES UNTIL STIFF BUT NOT DRY. WHIP CREAM UNTIL SOFTLY STIFF. FOLD EGG WHITES, CREAM AND SALMON INTO CHILLED MIXTURE. TURN INTO A 4-CUP (1 L) SOUFFLÉ DISH THAT HAS BEEN EXTENDED WITH A 2-INCH (5 CM) PAPER COLLAR. CHILL UNTIL SET. REMOVE COLLAR AND GARNISH WITH PARSLEY. SERVES 6 TO 8.

WEEKENDER SPECIAL

*BECAUSE YOU DON'T HAVE TO
SPEND YOUR MORNING IN THE KITCHEN.*

10	SLICES BACON	10
1/2 CUP	CHOPPED GREEN BELL PEPPER	125 ML
8	GREEN ONIONS, FINELY CHOPPED	8
1 LB	MUSHROOMS, SLICED INTO T'S	500 G
3 TBSP	CHOPPED PIMENTO	45 ML
3 TBSP	SHERRY	45 ML
12	EGGS	12
1 1/2 CUPS	MILK	375 ML
1 TSP	SEASONED SALT	5 ML
1 TSP	DRY MUSTARD	5 ML
1 TSP	DRIED THYME	5 ML
4 CUPS	SHREDDED GRUYÈRE CHEESE	1 L

FRY BACON UNTIL CRISP. DRAIN AND CHOP. IN SAME PAN, SAUTÉ GREEN PEPPER, ONIONS AND MUSHROOMS UNTIL LIMP. ADD PIMENTO AND SHERRY, HEATING UNTIL SHERRY EVAPORATES. IN A BOWL, BEAT EGGS, MILK, SALT, MUSTARD AND THYME. ADD BACON, MUSHROOM MIXTURE AND 3 CUPS (750 ML) OF CHEESE. POUR MIXTURE INTO EITHER A GREASED 13- BY 9-INCH (33 BY 23 CM) BAKING PAN OR TWO GREASED 8-INCH (20 CM) SQUARE BAKING PANS. COVER AND REFRIGERATE OVERNIGHT.

BAKE UNCOVERED AT 350°F (180°C) FOR 40 MINUTES. SPRINKLE REMAINING CUP (250 ML) OF CHEESE AND BAKE FOR 5 MINUTES OR UNTIL CHEESE MELTS AND AN INSERTED KNIFE COMES OUT CLEAN. LET STAND FOR 20 MINUTES BEFORE SERVING. SERVES 8.

SOUTHWEST BRUNCH BAKE

4 CUPS	FROZEN SHREDDED-STYLE HASH BROWN POTATOES	1 L
1	CAN (15 OZ/425 ML) BLACK BEANS, RINSED AND DRAINED	1
1 CUP	FROZEN WHOLE KERNEL CORN	250 ML
1	RED PEPPER, CHOPPED	1
1/2 CUP	CHOPPED ONION	125 ML
2 CUPS	SHREDDED MONTEREY JACK CHEESE	500 ML
2 TBSP	CHOPPED FRESH CILANTRO	30 ML
8	EGGS	8
1 1/4 CUPS	MILK	300 ML
1/2 TSP	SALT	2 ML
1/4 TSP	CAYENNE PEPPER	1 ML

SPRAY 11- BY 7-INCH (28 BY 18 CM) BAKING DISH WITH COOKING SPRAY. MIX POTATOES, BEANS, CORN, RED PEPPER AND ONION IN BAKING DISH. SPRINKLE WITH CHEESE AND CILANTRO. BEAT EGGS, MILK, SALT AND CAYENNE PEPPER UNTIL WELL BLENDED. POUR EVENLY OVER POTATO MIXTURE. COVER AND REFRIGERATE AT LEAST 2 HOURS BUT NO LONGER THAN 24 HOURS. HEAT OVEN TO 350°F (180°C) AND BAKE, UNCOVERED, 55 TO 60 MINUTES OR UNTIL KNIFE INSERTED IN CENTER COMES OUT CLEAN. LET STAND 5 MINUTES BEFORE CUTTING. SERVES 6 TO 8. SERVE WITH SLICED FRESH TOMATOES OR SALSA AND JALAPEÑO CORN MUFFINS (PAGE 53).

CHRISTMAS MORNING WIFE SAVER

A CANADIAN TRADITION — DON'T WAIT FOR CHRISTMAS!
MAKE BREAKFAST THE NIGHT BEFORE
AND ENJOY YOUR MORNING.

16	SLICES WHITE BREAD, CRUSTS REMOVED	16
	SLICES OF CANADIAN BACK BACON OR HAM	
	SLICES OF SHARP (OLD) CHEDDAR CHEESE	
6	EGGS	6
1/2 TSP	PEPPER	2 ML
1/2 to 1 TSP	DRY MUSTARD	2 to 5 ML
1/4 CUP	MINCED ONION	60 ML
1/4 CUP	FINELY CHOPPED GREEN PEPPER	60 ML
1 to 2 TSP	WORCESTERSHIRE SAUCE	5 to 10 ML
3 CUPS	MILK	750 ML
	DASH TABASCO	
1/2 CUP	BUTTER	125 ML
	CRUSHED CORN FLAKES CEREAL	

PUT 8 PIECES OF BREAD IN A 13- BY 9-INCH (33 BY 23 CM)
BUTTERED GLASS BAKING DISH. ADD PIECES TO COVER
DISH ENTIRELY. COVER BREAD WITH THINLY SLICED BACON.
TOP WITH SLICES OF CHEDDAR CHEESE. COVER WITH
SLICES OF BREAD. IN A BOWL, BEAT EGGS AND PEPPER. ADD
MUSTARD, ONION, GREEN PEPPER, WORCESTERSHIRE, MILK
AND TABASCO. POUR OVER BREAD, COVER AND REFRIGERATE
OVERNIGHT. IN THE MORNING, MELT BUTTER AND POUR
OVER TOP. COVER WITH CEREAL. BAKE AT 350°F (180°C),
UNCOVERED, 1 HOUR. LET SIT 10 MINUTES BEFORE SERVING.
SERVE WITH FRESH FRUIT. SERVES 8.

WEEKEND SPOUSE SAVER

HAVE THE SEÑOR MAKE THIS MEXICAN
MARVEL — THE NEXT BRUNCH FAVORITE.

3	CANS (EACH 4½ OZ/127 ML) CHOPPED GREEN CHILES, DRAINED	3
6	CORN TORTILLAS, CUT INTO 1-INCH (2.5 CM) STRIPS	6
2 LBS	HOT ITALIAN SAUSAGE, CASINGS REMOVED, COOKED, DRAINED	1 KG
2½ CUPS	SHREDDED MONTEREY JACK CHEESE	625 ML
½ CUP	MILK	125 ML
8	LARGE EGGS	8
½ TSP	SALT	2 ML
½ TSP	GARLIC SALT	2 ML
½ TSP	ONION SALT	2 ML
½ TSP	GROUND CUMIN	2 ML
½ TSP	FRESHLY GROUND BLACK PEPPER	2 ML
	PAPRIKA TO SPRINKLE	
2	LARGE RIPE TOMATOES, SLICED	2
	SALSA AND SOUR CREAM	

THE NIGHT BEFORE, GREASE A 13- BY 9-INCH (33 BY
23 CM) CASSEROLE AND LAYER HALF THE CHILES, HALF
THE CORN TORTILLAS, HALF THE COOKED SAUSAGE, AND
HALF THE CHEESE. REPEAT LAYERS. IN A MEDIUM BOWL,
BEAT MILK, EGGS, SALT, GARLIC SALT, ONION SALT,
CUMIN AND PEPPER. POUR OVER CASSEROLE INGREDIENTS.
SPRINKLE WITH PAPRIKA. COVER WITH PLASTIC WRAP
AND REFRIGERATE OVERNIGHT.

HOORAY — IT'S THE FOLLOWING DAY, AND YOU'RE READY! PREHEAT OVEN TO 350°F (180°C). PLACE TOMATOES OVER TOP OF CASSEROLE. BAKE 1 HOUR, OR UNTIL SET IN CENTER AND SLIGHTLY BROWNED AT EDGES. LET SIT 5 MINUTES BEFORE SERVING. PASS THE SALSA AND SOUR CREAM. SERVE WITH A TRAY OF SLICED FRESH FRUIT. ¡MAGNIFICO! SERVES 10.

BAKED EGGS

NICE LUNCHEON DISH OR A DAY WHEN YOU WANT TO SKIP MEAT AT DINNER. SERVE WITH A SALAD.

1/4 CUP	MILK OR CREAM	60 ML
1 TSP	SALT	5 ML
18	EGGS	18
1	CAN (10 OZ/284 ML) MUSHROOM SOUP	1
2	CANS (EACH 10 OZ/284 ML) MUSHROOMS	2
1/4 LB	CHEDDAR CHEESE	125 G

ADD MILK AND SALT TO EGGS. BEAT AND SCRAMBLE UNTIL SOFT. DON'T OVERCOOK! MIX SOUP AND MUSHROOMS TOGETHER. SPRAY A 13- BY 9-INCH (33 BY 23 CM) CASSEROLE DISH WITH COOKING SPRAY OR GREASE WITH BUTTER. PUT EGGS IN PAN AND POUR SOUP MIXTURE OVER. SPRINKLE GRATED CHEESE OR LAY SLICES ON TOP. BAKE AT 350°F (180°C) FOR 30 MINUTES. CUT INTO SQUARES AND SERVE HOT. SERVES 8 TO 10.

ARTICHOKE AND ONION STRATA

THIS IS A GREAT DISH FOR BRUNCH
BECAUSE YOU CAN ASSEMBLE IT THE NIGHT BEFORE,
THEN PUT IT IN THE SLOW COOKER IN THE MORNING
TO BE READY AS YOUR GUESTS ARRIVE.

1 TBSP	OLIVE OIL	15 ML
1	LARGE SPANISH ONION, THINLY SLICED ON THE VERTICAL	1
4	CLOVES GARLIC, MINCED	4
1 TBSP	DRIED ITALIAN SEASONING	15 ML
1/2 TSP	SALT	2 ML
1/2 TSP	CRACKED BLACK PEPPERCORNS	2 ML
1	CAN (14 OZ/398 ML) ARTICHOKES, DRAINED AND QUARTERED	1
1 1/2 CUPS	SHREDDED CHEDDAR CHEESE	375 ML
3	SLICES WHITE OR LIGHT WHOLE WHEAT BREAD (ABOUT 1 INCH/2.5 CM THICK), CUBED	3
4	EGGS	4
1	CAN (12 OZ OR 370 ML) EVAPORATED MILK	1
2 TBSP	GRATED PARMESAN CHEESE	30 ML

IN A SKILLET, HEAT OIL OVER MEDIUM HEAT. ADD
ONION AND COOK, STIRRING, UNTIL SOFTENED, ABOUT
3 MINUTES. ADD GARLIC, ITALIAN SEASONING, SALT AND
PEPPERCORNS AND COOK, STIRRING, FOR 1 MINUTE. ADD
ARTICHOKES AND TOSS TO COAT. REMOVE FROM HEAT
AND STIR IN CHEESE. TRANSFER TO A LARGE MIXING
BOWL. ADD BREAD AND TOSS WELL. IN A BOWL, BEAT EGGS
AND EVAPORATED MILK. POUR MIXTURE OVER BREAD AND
STIR WELL. COVER WITH PLASTIC WRAP AND, USING YOUR

HANDS, PUSH THE BREAD DOWN SO IT IS SUBMERGED IN THE LIQUID. REFRIGERATE OVERNIGHT, PUSHING THE BREAD DOWN INTO THE LIQUID ONCE OR TWICE, IF POSSIBLE.

TRANSFER TO A LIGHTLY GREASED 8-CUP (2 L) SOUFFLÉ DISH. COVER WITH FOIL AND TIE TIGHTLY WITH A STRING. PLACE DISH IN A LARGE (MINIMUM 5-QUART) OVAL SLOW COOKER AND ADD BOILING WATER TO COME 1 INCH (2.5 CM) UP THE SIDES. COVER AND COOK ON HIGH FOR 3 HOURS, UNTIL STRATA IS PUFFED.

PREHEAT BROILER. REMOVE FOIL AND SPRINKLE PARMESAN EVENLY OVER TOP OF STRATA. PLACE UNDER BROILER UNTIL MELTED AND NICELY BROWNED. SERVE IMMEDIATELY. SERVES 6.

TIP: USE WHITE OR LIGHT WHOLE WHEAT BREAD IN THIS RECIPE. HEAVIER BREAD SUCH AS MULTIGRAIN WILL OVERWHELM THE FLAVORS.

TIP: THE BREAD CONDENSES AS IT ABSORBS THE LIQUID, SO IT WILL FIT INTO THE BAKING DISH.

BABIES ARE SUCH A NICE WAY TO START PEOPLE.

BAKED CHEESE AND TOMATO STRATA

2/3 CUP	SOFT MARGARINE	150 ML
I	CLOVE GARLIC, MINCED	I
I TSP	DRY MUSTARD	5 ML
I	LOAF ITALIAN STYLE WHITE BREAD, SLICED	I
12 OZ	SHREDDED SWISS CHEESE (OR HALF CHEDDAR, HALF SWISS)	375 G
3 TBSP	GRATED ONION	45 ML
1 1/2 TSP	SALT	7 ML
I TSP	PAPRIKA	5 ML
PINCH	BLACK PEPPER	PINCH
1/3 CUP	ALL-PURPOSE FLOUR	75 ML
3 CUPS	MILK	750 ML
I	CAN (19 OZ/540 ML) STEWED TOMATOES	I
3	EGGS, BEATEN	3

IN A SMALL BOWL, CREAM 1/3 CUP (75 ML) MARGARINE, GARLIC AND 1/2 TSP (2 ML) MUSTARD. REMOVE BREAD CRUSTS AND SPREAD ONE SIDE OF EACH SLICE WITH MARGARINE MIXTURE. LINE A 13- BY 9-INCH (33 BY 23 CM) BAKING DISH WITH BREAD TO COVER BOTTOM AND SIDES, MARGARINE SIDE DOWN.

IN A LARGE BOWL, COMBINE CHEESE, ONION, SALT, PAPRIKA, PEPPER AND REMAINING MUSTARD. TOSS UNTIL WELL BLENDED. IN A MEDIUM SAUCEPAN, MELT REMAINING MARGARINE. REMOVE FROM HEAT AND STIR IN FLOUR, THEN GRADUALLY STIR IN MILK. HEAT TO BOILING, THEN

STIR IN TOMATOES. ADD A LITTLE HOT MIXTURE TO EGGS, STIRRING, AND POUR BACK INTO SAUCEPAN. STIR.

SET ASIDE $\frac{1}{2}$ CUP (125 ML) CHEESE MIXTURE. IN THE LINED DISH, ALTERNATE LAYERS OF REMAINING CHEESE MIXTURE AND BREAD, MARGARINE SIDE UP. POUR TOMATO SAUCE OVER ALL. SPRINKLE WITH REMAINING CHEESE. REFRIGERATE, COVERED, OVERNIGHT. PREHEAT OVEN TO 375°F (190°C). BAKE FOR 45 MINUTES OR UNTIL PUFFY AND GOLDEN ON TOP. SERVES 8.

DEAR NOAH: WE COULD HAVE SWORN THAT YOU SAID THE ARK WASN'T LEAVING UNTIL 5. YOURS SINCERELY, THE UNICORNS.

MEXICAN STRATA

¡OLÉ! ANOTHER WIFE SAVER AND A GREAT MAKE-AHEAD!

16	SLICES WHITE BREAD, TRIMMED	16
4	LARGE, RIPE TOMATOES, SLICED	4
1	MEDIUM ONION, SLICED AND SEPARATED	1
2	CANS (EACH 4 1/2 OZ/127 ML) CHOPPED GREEN CHILES, DRAINED	2
1 1/2 CUPS	SHREDDED CHEDDAR OR MONTEREY JACK CHEESE	375 ML
7	LARGE EGGS	7
3 1/2 CUPS	MILK	875 ML
1 TSP	SALT	5 ML
1/2 TSP	GARLIC SALT	2 ML
1/2 TSP	GROUND CUMIN	2 ML
1/2 TSP	CHILI POWDER	2 ML

PLACE 8 SLICES OF BREAD IN BOTTOM OF BUTTERED 13- BY 9-INCH (33 BY 23 CM) PAN. ARRANGE TOMATO SLICES, ONION RINGS AND GREEN CHILES OVER BREAD. SPRINKLE TWO-THIRDS OF THE CHEESE OVER ALL. TOP WITH REMAINING SLICES OF BREAD. BEAT EGGS, MILK AND SEASONINGS; POUR OVER BREAD (LIQUID SHOULD COME TO TOP OF PAN). IF MORE LIQUID IS NEEDED, ADD MIXTURE OF 1 EGG AND 1/2 CUP (125 ML) MILK. SPRINKLE REMAINING CHEESE OVER TOP. COVER WITH FOIL AND REFRIGERATE OVERNIGHT. REMOVE FROM REFRIGERATOR 1 HOUR BEFORE BAKING FOR A LIGHTER AND FLUFFIER DISH. PREHEAT OVEN TO 350°F (180°C). BAKE, UNCOVERED, FOR 1 TO 1 1/2 HOURS OR UNTIL KNIFE INSERTED IN CENTER COMES OUT CLEAN. LET STAND 5 MINUTES BEFORE SERVING. SERVE WITH SALSA. SERVES 8.

ZUCCHINI CHEESE PIE

A GREAT CASUAL DISH FOR BARBECUE OR BRUNCH.
SERVE WITH A SALAD ON THE SIDE.

½ CUP	SHREDDED CHEDDAR CHEESE	125 ML
3 CUPS	SHREDDED ZUCCHINI	750 ML
1 CUP	BISCUIT MIX	250 ML
½ CUP	VEGETABLE OIL	125 ML
1 TBSP	CHOPPED FRESH PARSLEY	15 ML
4	EGGS	4
	SALT AND BLACK PEPPER TO TASTE	

MIX CHEESE, ZUCCHINI, BISCUIT MIX, OIL AND PARSLEY
TOGETHER. IN A BOWL, BEAT EGGS, SALT AND PEPPER AND
MIX WITH OTHER INGREDIENTS. POUR INTO 9-INCH (23 CM)
PIE PLATE AND BAKE AT 375°F (190°C) FOR 40 MINUTES.
CUT INTO WEDGES. SERVES 6 TO 8.

I GET PLENTY OF EXERCISE JUMPING TO CONCLUSIONS
AND PUSHING MY LUCK.

BREAKFAST HASH BROWN AND SAUSAGE BAKE

MAKE-AHEAD DISHES ARE ALWAYS APPRECIATED
FOR A HOLIDAY BREAKFAST OR BRUNCH. LEFTOVERS
THE NEXT DAY ARE JUST AS DELICIOUS!

8 OZ	LEAN PORK OR CHICKEN SAUSAGES, CASINGS REMOVED	250 G
1 TBSP	VEGETABLE OIL	15 ML
3 CUPS	FROZEN DICED HASH BROWN POTATOES	750 ML
1	ONION, CHOPPED	1
1/2 TSP	DRIED CRUMBLED SAGE	2 ML
1/4 TSP	DRIED THYME LEAVES	1 ML
1 CUP	SHREDDED CHEDDAR CHEESE	250 ML
4	EGGS	4
1 CUP	MILK	250 ML
2 TBSP	FRESHLY GRATED PARMESAN CHEESE	30 ML
1	GREEN ONION, FINELY SLICED	1
	FRESHLY GROUND BLACK PEPPER	

IN A LARGE NONSTICK SKILLET OVER MEDIUM-HIGH HEAT, COOK SAUSAGE, BREAKING UP MEAT WITH BACK OF A WOODEN SPOON, FOR 5 MINUTES OR UNTIL NO LONGER PINK. TRANSFER TO A PLATE LINED WITH PAPER TOWEL TO ABSORB ANY FAT. LET COOL. CHOP SAUSAGE MEAT, USING A KNIFE OR PULSING IN A FOOD PROCESSOR.

PREHEAT OVEN TO 350°F (180°C) AND GREASE AN 8-INCH (20 CM) SQUARE BAKING DISH WELL. RETURN SKILLET TO MEDIUM-HIGH HEAT AND ADD OIL. COOK POTATOES, ONION, SAGE AND THYME, STIRRING OFTEN, FOR 10 MINUTES

OR UNTIL POTATOES ARE NICELY BROWNED. ARRANGE POTATO MIXTURE IN PREPARED DISH. TOP WITH SAUSAGE AND CHEDDAR CHEESE. IN A BOWL, BEAT TOGETHER EGGS, MILK, PARMESAN CHEESE AND GREEN ONION. SEASON WITH PEPPER. POUR OVER CHEESE LAYER. (CAN BE PREPARED AHEAD. COVER AND REFRIGERATE FOR UP TO I DAY.) BAKE FOR 35 TO 40 MINUTES (10 MINUTES LONGER IF REFRIGERATED) OR UNTIL TOP IS GOLDEN AND A KNIFE INSERTED IN THE CENTER COMES OUT CLEAN. TRANSFER TO A WIRE RACK AND LET STAND FOR 10 MINUTES BEFORE SERVING. SERVES 4.

TIP: THIS RECIPE CAN BE DOUBLED AND BAKED IN A 13- BY 9-INCH (33 BY 23 CM) BAKING DISH FOR 45 TO 50 MINUTES.

VARIATION: FOR A VEGETARIAN VERSION, OMIT SAUSAGE AND ADD I DICED RED BELL PEPPER ALONG WITH HASH BROWNS AND ONION IN SKILLET.

FRIENDSHIP MUST BE BUILT ON A SOLID FOUNDATION OF ALCOHOL, SARCASM, INAPPROPRIATENESS AND SHENANIGANS.

SAUSAGE PIE

ONCE AGAIN, IT'S AN EASY MAKE-AHEAD. LOOKS FANTASTIC AND, BEST OF ALL, IT'S DELICIOUS! SERVE WITH A SALAD.

1	CAN (28 OZ/796 ML) TOMATOES, WELL DRAINED AND PRESSED (NO IRONING BOARD NECESSARY)	1
1/2 TSP	DRIED BASIL	2 ML
1/4 TSP	BLACK PEPPER	1 ML
1 LB	SAUSAGE MEAT	500 G
1/2 TSP	CHILI POWDER	2 ML
1/2 TSP	DRIED OREGANO	2 ML
1/2 TSP	DRIED BASIL	2 ML
1 1/2 CUPS	SHREDDED MOZZARELLA CHEESE	375 ML
3	GREEN ONIONS, THINLY SLICED	3
1/2 CUP	FINELY CHOPPED RED BELL PEPPER	125 ML
2	PACKAGES (EACH 8 OZ/235 G) REFRIGERATED CRESCENT DINNER ROLLS	2

PREHEAT OVEN TO 350°F (180°C). IN A BOWL, COMBINE TOMATOES WITH BASIL AND BLACK PEPPER. SET ASIDE. BROWN SAUSAGE MEAT, STIRRING WITH A FORK TO KEEP SEPARATED. DRAIN OFF FAT. ADD CHILI POWDER, OREGANO, BASIL, 1/2 CUP (125 ML) CHEESE, GREEN ONION AND RED PEPPER. STIR AND SET ASIDE. THE NEXT PART IS EASY!

OPEN ONE PACKAGE OF DINNER ROLLS AND UNROLL. CUT RECTANGLE OF DOUGH IN HALF ALONG THE PERFORATED LINE. MOLD HALF IN THE BOTTOM OF A 9-INCH (23 CM) SPRINGFORM PAN, COVERING THE BASE COMPLETELY. PINCH TOGETHER ANY SECTIONS THAT HAVE SEPARATED.

DIVIDE THE REMAINING SQUARE OF DOUGH ALONG THE PERFORATED LINES AND FIT THESE AROUND THE SIDES OF THE PAN, TRIMMING OFF ANY EDGES THAT PROJECT ABOVE TOP OF PAN. PINCH ALL SEAMS TOGETHER. SPOON SAUSAGE MIXTURE OVER DOUGH AND PRESS DOWN FIRMLY. SPREAD TOMATO MIXTURE OVER MEAT AND SPRINKLE WITH REMAINING CUP (250 ML) OF MOZZARELLA CHEESE. USING THE SECOND PACKAGE OF ROLLS, SEPARATE DOUGH INTO TRIANGLES AND CUT INTO $\frac{1}{2}$-INCH (1 CM) STRIPS. FORM THESE INTO A LATTICE PATTERN OVER TOP OF THE FILLING. DON'T WORRY ABOUT "JOINS"; IT ALL BAKES TOGETHER. GENTLY ROLL THE DOUGH ALONG THE RIM DOWN TO COVER THE EDGES OF THE LATTICE STRIPS. BAKE FOR 35 TO 45 MINUTES OR UNTIL GOLDEN BROWN. REMOVE FROM OVEN AND COOL 5 MINUTES. RUN A KNIFE AROUND THE EDGE TO LOOSEN CRUST. REMOVE FROM PAN. CUT INTO WEDGES. SERVES 8.

STICK AROUND. I MAY NEED SOMEONE TO BLAME.

SAUSAGE 'N' JOHNNY CAKE

GREAT BRUNCH DISH!

16	LINK PORK SAUSAGES	16
1 CUP	CORNMEAL	250 ML
2 CUPS	BUTTERMILK	500 ML
1 1/3 CUPS	ALL-PURPOSE FLOUR	325 ML
1/2 TSP	BAKING SODA	2 ML
2 TSP	BAKING POWDER	10 ML
1/4 CUP	GRANULATED SUGAR	60 ML
1/2 TSP	SALT	2 ML
1/3 CUP	LARD	75 ML
1	EGG	1
1/2 TSP	VANILLA EXTRACT	2 ML

COOK SAUSAGES AND DRAIN FAT. ARRANGE IN PINWHEEL FASHION IN BOTTOM OF A WELL-GREASED 10-INCH (25 CM) ROUND PAN. SOAK CORNMEAL IN BUTTERMILK FOR 10 MINUTES. SIFT FLOUR, BAKING SODA, BAKING POWDER, SUGAR AND SALT. CUT IN LARD TO FORM A CRUMBLY MIXTURE. BEAT EGG AND VANILLA AND STIR INTO CORNMEAL MIXTURE. ADD TO DRY INGREDIENTS, STIRRING JUST TO MOISTEN. POUR OVER SAUSAGES AND BAKE AT 400°F (200°C) FOR 30 MINUTES. SERVE WARM WITH BUTTER AND MAPLE SYRUP. THIS RECIPE FREEZES WELL.

SERVES 8.

SHRIMP AND CRAB QUICHE

THIS IS GREAT FOR AN AFTER-FOOTBALL GATHERING. SERVE WITH A SALAD.

2 TBSP	CHOPPED GREEN ONION	30 ML
2 TBSP	BUTTER	30 ML
1	PACKAGE (6 OZ/175 G) FROZEN COOKED SHRIMP	1
1	LARGE CAN CRABMEAT	1
1/4 TSP	SALT	1 ML
1/4 TSP	BLACK PEPPER	1 ML
3	EGGS	3
1 CUP	HEAVY OR WHIPPING (35%) CREAM	250 ML
1 to 2 TBSP	KETCHUP	15 to 30 ML
1/4 TSP	SALT	1 ML
1	9-INCH (23 CM) PARTIALLY COOKED PASTRY SHELL	1
1/4 CUP	GRATED SWISS CHEESE	50 ML

PREHEAT OVEN TO 375°F (190°C). COOK ONIONS IN BUTTER. ADD SHRIMP AND CRAB; STIR 2 MINUTES. SPRINKLE WITH SALT AND PEPPER. ALLOW TO COOL. BEAT EGGS WITH CREAM, KETCHUP AND SALT. SLOWLY ADD SHRIMP AND CRAB. POUR INTO PASTRY SHELL AND SPRINKLE WITH CHEESE. BAKE IN UPPER PART OF OVEN FOR 25 TO 35 MINUTES, UNTIL QUICHE IS PUFFED AND BROWNED.

SERVES 6 TO 8.

CRAB OR CHICKEN CRÊPES

CRÊPES MAY BE MADE AHEAD OF TIME AND STORED FROZEN BETWEEN LAYERS OF WAXED PAPER.

CRÊPE BATTER

1 CUP	COLD WATER	250 ML
1 CUP	COLD MILK	250 ML
4	EGGS	4
1/2 TSP	SALT	2 ML
2 CUPS	FLOUR	500 ML
2 TBSP	BUTTER	25 ML

WHIRL CRÊPE INGREDIENTS IN BLENDER FOR 2 MINUTES. REFRIGERATE 2 HOURS. USING 6-INCH (15 CM) CRÊPE PAN OR SMALL NONSTICK FRYING PAN, MELT A LITTLE BUTTER AND POUR ABOUT 1/4 CUP (50 ML) BATTER INTO PAN, TIPPING UNTIL BATTER COVERS THE BOTTOM. COOK AND TURN UNTIL CRÊPE IS GOLDEN ON BOTH SIDES. TRANSFER TO PLATE. REPEAT METHOD UNTIL ALL BATTER IS USED.

FILLING

1/4 CUP	CHOPPED GREEN ONION	50 ML
1 TBSP	BUTTER	15 ML
1/2 CUP	SHERRY	125 ML
3 CUPS	CRAB OR COOKED DICED CHICKEN	750 ML
	SALT AND FRESHLY GROUND BLACK PEPPER TO TASTE	

SWISS CHEESE SAUCE

1/4 CUP	BUTTER	50 ML
1/3 CUP	FLOUR	75 ML
2 CUPS	MILK, HEATED	500 ML
	SALT AND FRESHLY GROUND BLACK PEPPER TO TASTE	
2	EGG YOLKS	2
1/2 CUP	HEAVY OR WHIPPING (35%) CREAM	125 ML
3/4 CUP	GRATED SWISS CHEESE	175 ML

TO MAKE FILLING: SAUTÉ ONION IN BUTTER; ADD SHERRY AND MIX IN CRAB, SALT AND PEPPER. SET ASIDE.

TO MAKE SAUCE: IN A SAUCEPAN, MELT BUTTER AND ADD FLOUR. BLEND. GRADUALLY ADD MILK, SALT AND PEPPER, STIRRING CONSTANTLY. BOIL FOR 1 MINUTE, THEN REMOVE FROM HEAT. BEAT YOLKS AND CREAM TOGETHER. ADD EGG MIXTURE TO SAUCEPAN, STIRRING CONSTANTLY. FOLD IN CHEESE (SAUCE SHOULD BE THICK). SET ONE-THIRD OF THE SAUCE ASIDE. POUR REMAINING SAUCE INTO THE FILLING. FILL AND ROLL CRÊPES AND PLACE IN A SHALLOW 13- BY 9-INCH (33 BY 23 CM) BAKING DISH. DRIZZLE WITH RESERVED SAUCE. HEAT IN WARM OVEN UNTIL SERVING TIME. SERVES 6 TO 8.

NOTE: THIN SAUCE WITH CREAM IF NECESSARY.

SAVORY BREAD-AND-BUTTER PUDDING

SERVED HOT FROM THE SLOW COOKER, THIS DISH IS A FABULOUS COMBINATION OF SOOTHING FOODS. MAKE IT WITH OLIVE BREAD FOR SOME MEDITERRANEAN FLAIR.

3	THICK SLICES BREAD (ABOUT 1 INCH/2.5 CM THICK)	3
1/4 CUP	SOFTENED BUTTER (APPROX.)	60 ML
2 CUPS	BABY SPINACH	500 ML
1 1/2 CUPS	SHREDDED OLD CHEDDAR CHEESE	375 ML
1 CUP	CHOPPED GREEN ONIONS	250 ML
4	EGGS	4
2	EGG YOLKS	2
1 CUP	EVAPORATED MILK	250 ML
2 TSP	DIJON MUSTARD	10 ML
1 TSP	SALT	5 ML
1 TSP	CRACKED BLACK PEPPERCORNS	5 ML
1	CAN (28 OZ/796 ML) DICED TOMATOES, WITH JUICE	1
1/4 CUP	GRATED PARMESAN CHEESE	60 ML

BUTTER THE BREAD ON BOTH SIDES AND CUT INTO 1-INCH (2.5 CM) CUBES. PLACE IN A LARGE MIXING BOWL. ADD SPINACH, CHEESE AND GREEN ONIONS AND TOSS WELL. IN A SEPARATE BOWL, WHISK TOGETHER EGGS, EGG YOLKS, EVAPORATED MILK, MUSTARD, SALT AND PEPPERCORNS UNTIL BLENDED. WHISK IN TOMATOES WITH JUICE. POUR OVER BREAD MIXTURE, STIRRING UNTIL WELL COVERED. COVER WITH PLASTIC WRAP AND, USING YOUR HANDS, PUSH THE BREAD DOWN SO IT IS SUBMERGED IN THE

LIQUID. REFRIGERATE OVERNIGHT (OR FOR UP TO 2 DAYS), PUSHING THE BREAD DOWN INTO THE LIQUID ONCE OR TWICE, IF POSSIBLE.

TRANSFER TO A LIGHTLY GREASED 8-CUP (2 L) BAKING OR SOUFFLÉ DISH. COVER WITH FOIL AND TIE TIGHTLY WITH A STRING. PLACE DISH IN A LARGE (MINIMUM 5-QUART) OVAL SLOW COOKER AND ADD BOILING WATER TO COME 1 INCH (2.5 CM) UP THE SIDES. COVER AND COOK ON HIGH FOR 3 TO 4 HOURS, UNTIL PUDDING IS PUFFED.

PREHEAT BROILER. REMOVE FOIL AND SPRINKLE PARMESAN EVENLY OVER TOP OF PUDDING. PLACE UNDER BROILER UNTIL MELTED AND NICELY BROWNED. SERVES 6.

TIP: USE WHITE OR LIGHT WHOLE WHEAT BREAD IN THIS RECIPE. OLIVE BREAD IS ALSO A GOOD CHOICE. DO NOT USE A HEAVY WHOLE WHEAT OR MULTIGRAIN BREAD; IT WOULD OVERWHELM THE OTHER FLAVORS.

TIP: DON'T WORRY ABOUT THE LARGE QUANTITY — THIS REHEATS IN THE MICROWAVE VERY WELL AND IS EVEN GOOD COLD.

WE'VE BEEN THROUGH A LOT TOGETHER,
AND MOST OF IT WAS YOUR FAULT.

MIDNIGHT FRENCH TOAST

WHAT A WAY TO END THE DAY — AND START THE NEXT!
SERVE WITH FRUIT OR MAPLE SYRUP.

12	EGGS	12
1/2 CUP	TABLE (18%) CREAM	125 ML
1/2 TSP	VANILLA EXTRACT	2 ML
	GRATED ZEST OF 1 ORANGE	
2 TBSP	ORANGE LIQUEUR OR ORANGE JUICE	30 ML
1	LOAF FRENCH BREAD, SLICED 1 INCH (2.5 CM) THICK	1

MIX EGGS, CREAM, VANILLA, ORANGE ZEST AND LIQUEUR IN 13- BY 9-INCH (33 BY 23 CM) PAN. PLACE SLICED BREAD IN PAN, MAKING SURE SLICES ARE WELL COATED. COVER WITH LID OR PLASTIC WRAP. PLACE IN FRIDGE OVERNIGHT.

NEXT MORNING, PLACE BREAD SLICES ON A WELL-GREASED COOKIE SHEET. BAKE AT 375°F (190°C) FOR 20 TO 25 MINUTES. SERVES 6.

ANYONE CAN BE COOL, BUT AWESOME TAKES PRACTICE.

POTATO LATKES

OY VEY! POTATO PANCAKES AND TASTY TOO! CAN BE MADE THE NIGHT BEFORE AND REFRIED OR MICROWAVED FOR BRUNCH. IF YOU HAVE LEFTOVERS, JUST FREEZE BETWEEN LAYERS OF WAXED PAPER.

3	LARGE POTATOES, PEELED AND GRATED	3
1/2	MEDIUM ONION, GRATED	1/2
	JUICE OF 1 LEMON	
6	EGGS	6
1/2 CUP	ALL-PURPOSE FLOUR	125 ML
1/2 CUP	VEGETABLE OIL	125 ML
2 TBSP	CHOPPED FRESH PARSLEY	30 ML
1 TSP	SALT	5 ML
1/2 TSP	BLACK PEPPER	2 ML
1/8 TSP	GARLIC POWDER	0.5 ML
	APPLESAUCE AND SOUR CREAM	

PLACE POTATOES AND ONION IN A BOWL AND TOSS WITH LEMON JUICE; COVER WITH COLD WATER. BEAT TOGETHER EGGS, FLOUR, OIL, PARSLEY, SALT, PEPPER AND GARLIC POWDER. ADD WELL-DRAINED POTATO MIXTURE AND MIX WELL. BATTER WILL BE SOUPY! DROP BY TABLESPOONS ONTO A LIGHTLY BUTTERED FRYING PAN, SPREADING OUT SLIGHTLY. FRY OVER MEDIUM HEAT UNTIL GOLDEN BROWN ON EACH SIDE. SERVE WITH APPLESAUCE AND SOUR CREAM. DEE-LISH! MAKES AT LEAST 30.

SCHWARTIES HASH BROWNS

GREAT FOR BUFFETS! FREEZES WELL.

2 LBS	FROZEN HASH BROWNS	1 KG
2 CUPS	FAT-FREE SOUR CREAM	500 ML
2	CANS (EACH 10 OZ/284 ML) MUSHROOM SOUP	2
1/4 CUP	MELTED BUTTER	60 ML
	GRATED ONION AND SALT TO TASTE	
2 CUPS	GRATED LIGHT CHEDDAR CHEESE	500 ML
2 TBSP	PARMESAN CHEESE	30 ML

THAW POTATOES SLIGHTLY. MIX FIRST SIX INGREDIENTS IN A 13- BY 9-INCH (33 BY 23 CM) BAKING DISH. SPRINKLE PARMESAN ON TOP. BAKE AT 350°F (180°C) FOR 1 HOUR. SERVES 8 TO 10.

WHAT DO YOU LOOK FOR FIRST IN A MAN?
THAT ALL HIS TATTOOS ARE SPELLED CORRECTLY.

BREAKFAST FRUIT KABOBS

ADDS A SPECIAL TOUCH TO A BRUNCH MENU!

	WATERMELON	
	CANTALOUPE	
	HONEYDEW MELON	
	PINEAPPLE	
	STRAWBERRIES	
	SEEDLESS GRAPES	
6 to 8	WOODEN SKEWERS	6 to 8
1/2 CUP	PLAIN YOGURT	125 ML
1 TSP	LIQUID HONEY	5 ML
1/4 TSP	FRESHLY GRATED NUTMEG	1 ML
2 TSP	LIME JUICE	10 ML
1	LIME, THINLY SLICED	

PREPARE FRUIT IN BALLS OR CHUNKS AND THREAD ON
SKEWERS. ARRANGE ON A PLATTER. COMBINE YOGURT,
HONEY, NUTMEG AND LIME JUICE. DRIZZLE OVER KABOBS.
GARNISH WITH LIME SLICES.

CHRISTMAS BRUNCH CARROT LOAF

SAVE YOUR 16-OZ (455 ML) AND
48-OZ (1.4 L) FRUIT JUICE CANS TO USE AS MOLDS.

2½ CUPS	SIFTED FLOUR	625 ML
1 CUP	GRANULATED SUGAR	250 ML
1 TSP	BAKING POWDER	5 ML
1 TSP	BAKING SODA	5 ML
2 TSP	CINNAMON	10 ML
1 TSP	EACH NUTMEG AND GINGER (OPTIONAL)	5 ML
½ TSP	SALT	2 ML
3	BEATEN EGGS	3
½ CUP	COOKING OIL	125 ML
½ CUP	MILK	125 ML
2 CUPS	SHREDDED CARROT	500 ML
1½ CUPS	SHREDDED COCONUT	375 ML
½ CUP	CHOPPED MARASCHINO CHERRIES (DRAINED)	125 ML
½ CUP	RAISINS	125 ML
½ CUP	CHOPPED PECANS	125 ML

IN LARGE BOWL, SIFT TOGETHER DRY INGREDIENTS.
COMBINE EGGS, OIL AND MILK AND ADD TO FIRST MIXTURE.
WHEN WELL COMBINED, ADD ADDITIONAL INGREDIENTS.
TURN INTO FOUR 16-OZ (455 ML) GREASED CANS,
LOAF PANS OR LARGE JUICE CANS. (LINE GREASED CANS
WITH WAXED PAPER.) BAKE AT 350°F (150°C) FOR 50 TO
60 MINUTES. REMOVE FROM CANS AND COOL. THIS MAY
BE KEPT IN REFRIGERATOR FOR SEVERAL WEEKS. SERVE
BUTTERED SLICES AT BRUNCH INSTEAD OF TOAST.

MAKES 4 LOAVES; EACH SERVES 4 TO 6.

BEST-EVER BANANA BREAD

DAY-O! HEY, MISTER TALLYMAN, TALLY THIS ONE!

1 CUP	BUTTER	250 ML
2 CUPS	GRANULATED SUGAR	500 ML
2 1/2 CUPS	MASHED RIPE BANANAS (ABOUT 5)	625 ML
4	EGGS, WELL BEATEN	4
2 1/2 CUPS	ALL-PURPOSE FLOUR	625 ML
2 TSP	BAKING SODA	10 ML
1 TSP	SALT	5 ML
1 TSP	GROUND NUTMEG	5 ML

PREHEAT OVEN TO 350°F (180°C). CREAM BUTTER AND SUGAR UNTIL LIGHT AND FLUFFY. ADD BANANAS AND EGGS AND BEAT UNTIL WELL MIXED. MIX DRY INGREDIENTS AND BLEND WITH BANANA MIXTURE, BUT DO NOT OVERMIX. POUR INTO TWO LIGHTLY GREASED LOAF PANS OR A 10-INCH (25 CM) BUNDT PAN. BAKE FOR 55 TO 60 MINUTES; TEST FOR DONENESS (TOOTHPICK INSERTED IN MIDDLE COMES OUT CLEAN) AND COOL ON RACK FOR 10 MINUTES BEFORE REMOVING FROM PANS. FREEZES BEAUTIFULLY. MAKES 2 LOAVES.

TIP: FREEZE OVERRIPE BANANAS IN THEIR SKINS IN A PLASTIC BAG.

SPENDING TIME WITH CHILDREN IS MORE IMPORTANT THAN SPENDING MONEY ON CHILDREN.

CRANBERRY SCONES

3/4 CUP	BUTTERMILK OR PLAIN YOGURT	175 ML
1	LARGE EGG	1
2 3/4 CUPS	ALL-PURPOSE FLOUR	675 ML
4 TSP	BAKING POWDER	20 ML
1/2 TSP	BAKING SODA	2 ML
1/2 TSP	SALT	2 ML
1/2 CUP	MARGARINE	125 ML
1 CUP	COARSELY CHOPPED CRANBERRIES (FRESH OR FROZEN)	250 ML
1/2 CUP	GRANULATED SUGAR	125 ML
	GRATED ZEST OF 1 ORANGE	
1 TBSP	BUTTER, MELTED	15 ML
1/4 CUP	CONFECTIONERS' (ICING) SUGAR	60 ML

PREHEAT OVEN TO 375°F (190°C). BEAT BUTTERMILK AND EGG IN SMALL BOWL AND SET ASIDE. IN LARGE BOWL, COMBINE FLOUR, BAKING POWDER, BAKING SODA AND SALT. CUT IN MARGARINE UNTIL MIXTURE RESEMBLES SMALL PEAS. MIX IN CRANBERRIES, SUGAR AND ORANGE ZEST. ADD BUTTERMILK MIXTURE AND STIR UNTIL SOFT DOUGH FORMS. USING YOUR HANDS, FORM DOUGH INTO A LARGE BALL AND PLACE ON FLOURED SURFACE. PAT OUT TO 1-INCH (2.5 CM) THICKNESS. CUT IN 4-INCH (20 CM) ROUNDS. PLACE ON UNGREASED COOKIE SHEET AND BAKE SCONES FOR 15 TO 20 MINUTES. WHILE STILL WARM, BRUSH WITH BUTTER AND SPRINKLE WITH CONFECTIONERS' SUGAR.

MAKES 8 LARGE SCONES.

FLAKY FREEZER BISCUITS

THESE WONDERFUL BISCUITS CAN BE BAKED IMMEDIATELY OR FROZEN AND BAKED AS NEEDED.

1	PACKAGE YEAST (1 TBSP/15 ML)	1
2 TBSP	GRANULATED SUGAR	30 ML
1/4 CUP	WARM WATER	60 ML
5 CUPS	ALL-PURPOSE FLOUR	1.25 L
3 TBSP	GRANULATED SUGAR	45 ML
1 TBSP	BAKING POWDER	15 ML
1 TSP	BAKING SODA	5 ML
1 TSP	SALT	5 ML
1 CUP	BUTTER OR MARGARINE	250 ML
2 CUPS	BUTTERMILK	500 ML

IN A SMALL BOWL, COMBINE YEAST AND SUGAR IN WATER. SET ASIDE FOR 10 MINUTES. IN A LARGE BOWL, MIX FLOUR, SUGAR, BAKING POWDER, BAKING SODA AND SALT. CUT IN BUTTER TO FORM A CRUMBLY MIXTURE. STIR IN YEAST MIXTURE AND BUTTERMILK. MIX JUST ENOUGH TO HOLD DOUGH TOGETHER. ROLL DOUGH 3/4 INCH (2 CM) THICK ON FLOURED SURFACE. CUT OUT BISCUITS WITH THE TOP OF A GLASS OR A CUTTER. PRICK TOPS WITH FORK. FREEZE SEPARATELY ON COOKIE SHEET. AFTER BISCUITS ARE FROZEN, STACK AND WRAP WELL. BEFORE BAKING, LET RISE UNTIL DOUBLED IN SIZE. BAKE AT 425°F (220°C) FOR 15 MINUTES ON A LIGHTLY GREASED COOKIE SHEET. MAKES 3 TO 4 DOZEN.

VARIATION: SHREDDED CHEDDAR CHEESE MAY BE ADDED TO SOFT DOUGH FOR FLAKY CHEESE BISCUITS.

"LAND OF NOD" CINNAMON BUNS

WHO WOULD THINK YOU COULD BE
THIS ORGANIZED SO EARLY IN THE A.M.!!

20	FROZEN DOUGH ROLLS	20
I CUP	BROWN SUGAR	250 ML
1/4 CUP	VANILLA INSTANT PUDDING POWDER	60 ML
I to 2 TBSP	GROUND CINNAMON	15 to 30 ML
3/4 CUP	RAISINS (OPTIONAL)	175 ML
1/4 to 1/2 CUP	MELTED BUTTER	60 to 125 ML

BEFORE YOU TURN OFF THE LIGHTS, GREASE A 10-INCH (25 CM) BUNDT PAN AND ADD FROZEN ROLLS. SPRINKLE WITH BROWN SUGAR, PUDDING POWDER, CINNAMON AND RAISINS. POUR MELTED BUTTER OVER ALL. COVER WITH A CLEAN, DAMP CLOTH. (LEAVE OUT AT ROOM TEMPERATURE.) TURN OUT THE LIGHTS AND SAY GOODNIGHT!

IN THE MORNING, PREHEAT OVEN TO 350°F (180°C) AND BAKE FOR 25 MINUTES. LET SIT FOR 5 MINUTES AND THEN TURN OUT ON A SERVING PLATE. NOW, AREN'T YOU CLEVER?

CHRISTMAS COFFEE CAKE

PRETTY AND DECORATIVE — MAKES A NICE LITTLE GIFT.

1/3 CUP	BUTTER	75 ML
1/3 CUP	BROWN SUGAR	75 ML
18 to 20	PECAN HALVES	18 to 20
12 to 14	CHERRY HALVES	12 to 14
1/4 CUP	BUTTER	60 ML
1 CUP	BROWN SUGAR	250 ML
1 TSP	VANILLA	5 ML
2	EGGS	2
1 CUP	SOUR CREAM	250 ML
1 1/2 CUPS	FLOUR	375 ML
1 1/2 TSP	BAKING POWDER	7 ML
1 TSP	BAKING SODA	5 ML

MELT 1/3 CUP (75 ML) BUTTER. ADD 1/3 CUP (75 ML) BROWN SUGAR AND STIR. PLACE IN THE BOTTOM OF A 10-INCH (25 CM) TUBE PAN OR BUNDT PAN. DECORATE THE BOTTOM WITH PECAN AND CHERRY HALVES. CREAM 1/4 CUP (50 ML) BUTTER AND 1 CUP (250 ML) BROWN SUGAR. ADD VANILLA AND EGGS. BEAT UNTIL FLUFFY. BLEND IN SOUR CREAM. MIX FLOUR, BAKING POWDER AND BAKING SODA AND SIFT. MAKE A WELL IN CENTER OF DRY INGREDIENTS, ADD LIQUIDS AND STIR GENTLY. POUR INTO GREASED PAN AND BAKE AT 350°F (180°C) FOR 30 MINUTES. SERVES 10 TO 12.

CRANAPPLE COFFEE CAKE

MOIST AND PERFECT FOR BRUNCH.

2 CUPS	ALL-PURPOSE FLOUR	500 ML
1 1/2 TSP	BAKING SODA	7 ML
1 TSP	GROUND CINNAMON	5 ML
1/2 TSP	BAKING POWDER	2 ML
1/2 TSP	SALT	2 ML
1 1/4 CUPS	UNSWEETENED APPLESAUCE	300 ML
1 CUP	PACKED BROWN SUGAR	250 ML
2	LARGE EGG WHITES	2
1/2 CUP	VEGETABLE OIL	125 ML
1 CUP	HALVED FRESH OR FROZEN CRANBERRIES	250 ML
1 CUP	COARSELY GRATED RED APPLE	250 ML

ICING

	GRATED ZEST AND JUICE OF 1 ORANGE	
1 CUP	CONFECTIONERS' (ICING) SUGAR	250 ML

PREHEAT OVEN TO 325°F (160°C). GREASE AND FLOUR A BUNDT PAN. COMBINE FLOUR, BAKING SODA, CINNAMON, BAKING POWDER AND SALT. IN A LARGE BOWL, BEAT APPLESAUCE, BROWN SUGAR, EGG WHITES AND OIL THOROUGHLY. BEAT IN FLOUR MIXTURE UNTIL SMOOTH. FOLD IN CRANBERRIES AND APPLE. POUR BATTER IN BUNDT PAN; BAKE 45 TO 55 MINUTES, OR UNTIL CAKE TESTER COMES OUT CLEAN. COOL IN PAN ON A RACK FOR 10 MINUTES. INVERT PAN AND PLACE CAKE ON RACK TO COOL.

TO MAKE ICING: BRING ORANGE ZEST AND ORANGE JUICE TO A BOIL AND SIMMER FOR 1 MINUTE. BEAT IN CONFECTIONERS' SUGAR UNTIL SMOOTH. DRIZZLE OVER CAKE. MAKES 16 SLICES.

APPLE CINNAMON MUFFINS

A PLEASANT CHANGE FOR YOUR FAMILY BREAKFAST OR AN AFTER-SCHOOL TREAT!

2 CUPS	FLOUR	500 ML
1/2 CUP	GRANULATED SUGAR	125 ML
1 TBSP	BAKING POWDER	15 ML
1/2 TSP	CINNAMON	2 ML
1/2 TSP	SALT	2 ML
1/2 CUP	BUTTER	125 ML
1	LARGE APPLE, PEELED AND DICED	1
1/4 CUP	WALNUTS, FINELY CHOPPED	60 ML
1	EGG	1
2/3 CUP	MILK	150 ML
1 TSP	CINNAMON	5 ML
1 TBSP	BROWN SUGAR	15 ML

SIFT FLOUR, SUGAR, BAKING POWDER, 1/2 TSP (2 ML) CINNAMON AND SALT INTO LARGE BOWL. CUT IN BUTTER WITH PASTRY BLENDER. MEASURE OUT 1/4 CUP (60 ML) AND RESERVE FOR TOPPING. ADD APPLE AND NUTS TO FLOUR MIXTURE. BEAT EGG IN SMALL BOWL AND ADD MILK. POUR INTO FLOUR MIXTURE AND STIR UNTIL JUST MIXED (BATTER WILL BE LUMPY). SPOON INTO LIGHTLY GREASED MUFFIN PANS TWO-THIRDS FULL. ADD 1 TSP (5 ML) CINNAMON AND BROWN SUGAR TO RESERVED TOPPING MIXTURE. SPRINKLE OVER EACH MUFFIN. BAKE AT 425°F (220°C) FOR 15 TO 20 MINUTES. MAKES 16 LARGE OR 32 SMALL MUFFINS.

CRANBERRY MUFFINS

2 CUPS	CRANBERRIES, FRESH OR FROZEN, COARSELY CHOPPED	500 ML
1/3 CUP	GRANULATED SUGAR	75 ML
1 TBSP	GRATED ORANGE ZEST	15 ML
1/2 CUP	ORANGE JUICE	125 ML
2 CUPS	ALL-PURPOSE FLOUR	500 ML
1 TSP	BAKING POWDER	5 ML
1/2 TSP	BAKING SODA	2 ML
1/2 TSP	SALT	2 ML
1/2 CUP	MARGARINE	125 ML
1 CUP	GRANULATED SUGAR	250 ML
1	LARGE EGG	1

PREHEAT OVEN TO 375°F (190°C). LIGHTLY GREASE MUFFIN CUPS. COMBINE CRANBERRIES, 1/3 CUP (75 ML) SUGAR, ORANGE ZEST AND ORANGE JUICE. SET ASIDE. MIX DRY INGREDIENTS TOGETHER. SET ASIDE. CREAM MARGARINE, 1 CUP (250 ML) SUGAR AND EGG IN LARGE BOWL. ADD CRANBERRY MIXTURE AND DRY INGREDIENTS. MIX UNTIL JUST BLENDED AND SPOON INTO MUFFIN CUPS. BAKE FOR 20 MINUTES. MAKES 18 MEDIUM MUFFINS.

JALAPEÑO CORN MUFFINS

1/2 CUP	ALL-PURPOSE FLOUR	125 ML
1 TBSP	BAKING POWDER	15 ML
1/2 TSP	SALT	2 ML
1 1/2 CUPS	YELLOW CORNMEAL	375 ML
2	EGGS	2
1 CUP	FAT-FREE SOUR CREAM	250 ML
1 CUP	SHREDDED LIGHT CHEDDAR CHEESE	250 ML
1	CAN (10 OZ/284 G) CREAMED CORN	1
1/4 CUP	CHOPPED SEEDED JALAPEÑO PEPPERS	60 ML
1/2 CUP	BUTTER OR MARGARINE, MELTED	125 ML

SIFT FLOUR, BAKING POWDER AND SALT TOGETHER. ADD CORNMEAL, EGGS, SOUR CREAM, CHEESE, CREAMED CORN, JALAPEÑO PEPPERS AND BUTTER; MIX WELL. SPRAY MEDIUM MUFFIN TINS OR USE PAPER LINERS AND FILL WITH MIXTURE. BAKE AT 450°F (230°C) FOR 15 TO 20 MINUTES. MAKES ABOUT 18 MEDIUM MUFFINS.

A STATUS SYMBOL IS ANYTHING YOU CAN'T AFFORD BUT DID.

PUMPKIN PECAN MUFFINS

1 1/2 CUPS	ALL-PURPOSE FLOUR	375 ML
3/4 CUP	BROWN SUGAR	175 ML
2 TSP	BAKING POWDER	10 ML
1/4 TSP	BAKING SODA	1 ML
1/4 TSP	SALT	1 ML
1/2 TSP	GROUND CINNAMON	2 ML
1/4 TSP	GROUND ALLSPICE	1 ML
1/4 TSP	GROUND GINGER	1 ML
1/4 TSP	GROUND CLOVES	1 ML
1 CUP	COOKED MASHED OR CANNED PUMPKIN	250 ML
1/2 CUP	MILK	125 ML
1/3 CUP	VEGETABLE OIL	75 ML
1	LARGE EGG	1
1/2 CUP	CHOPPED DATES	125 ML
1/2 CUP	CHOPPED PECANS	125 ML

PREHEAT OVEN TO 375°F (190°C). COMBINE DRY INGREDIENTS AND SPICES IN MEDIUM BOWL. IN A LARGE BOWL, BEAT PUMPKIN, MILK, OIL AND EGG. ADD DRY INGREDIENTS AND MIX UNTIL MOISTENED. FOLD IN DATES AND NUTS AND SPOON INTO GREASED MUFFIN CUPS. BAKE ABOUT 20 MINUTES OR UNTIL TOPS ARE GOLDEN AND SPRING BACK WHEN TOUCHED. MAKES 20 MEDIUM MUFFINS.

Christmas Morning Wife Saver (page 21)

Midnight French Toast (page 40)

Cranberry Scones (page 46)

Nippy Cheddar Rabbit (page 63)

COCKTAIL PARTIES PLUS

IN THIS CHAPTER YOU WILL FIND A WIDE SELECTION OF DIPS AND VARIOUS OTHER KINDS OF FINGER FOODS, PLUS SOME OF OUR FAVORITE LIBATIONS. HERE, THEIR USE IS FOCUSED ON COCKTAIL PARTIES, BUT MANY ALSO WORK AS STARTERS FOR A SIT-DOWN HOLIDAY MEAL, AS A POTLUCK CONTRIBUTION OR AS A SELECTION ON A BUFFET TABLE.

HOT ARTICHOKE DIP

SERVE WITH CRACKERS.

I	CAN (14 OZ/398 ML) ARTICHOKE HEARTS, DRAINED AND CHOPPED	398 ML
1/2 CUP	FRESHLY GRATED PARMESAN CHEESE	125 ML
I CUP	MAYONNAISE	250 ML
I	CLOVE GARLIC, MINCED	I
DASH	LEMON JUICE	DASH

MIX ALL INGREDIENTS. BAKE AT 350°F (180°C) FOR 10 MINUTES. IF YOU LOVE IT, SERVES I! OTHERWISE, SERVES 6.

YEAR-ROUND SPINACH DIP

I CUP	MAYONNAISE	250 ML
I CUP	SOUR CREAM	250 ML
10 OZ	PKG. FROZEN CHOPPED SPINACH (WELL SQUEEZED!)	300 G
8 OZ	CAN WATER CHESTNUTS, CHOPPED	236 ML
1 1/2 OZ	KNORRS VEGETABLE SOUP MIX (I PKG.)	40 G
1/2 CUP	CHOPPED GREEN ONION	125 ML
I	ROUND LOAF OF BREAD, RYE, PUMPERNICKEL OR WHITE	I

COMBINE ALL INGREDIENTS EXCEPT BREAD AND MIX WELL. CHILL SEVERAL HOURS OR OVERNIGHT. SERVE IN A HOLLOWED-OUT ROUND LOAF OF BREAD. CUT SCOOPED OUT BREAD INTO CUBES AND SERVE WITH DIP. YOU'LL NEED SOME CRACKERS TOO!

SUMPTUOUS SPINACH AND ARTICHOKE DIP

THIS CHUNKY DIP, SIMPLICITY ITSELF, ALWAYS DRAWS RAVE REVIEWS AND DISAPPEARS TO THE LAST DROP.

I CUP	SHREDDED MOZZARELLA CHEESE	250 ML
8 OZ	CREAM CHEESE, CUBED	250 G
1/4 CUP	FRESHLY GRATED PARMESAN CHEESE	60 ML
I	CLOVE GARLIC, MINCED	I
I	CAN (14 OZ/398 ML) ARTICHOKES, DRAINED AND FINELY CHOPPED	I
I LB	FRESH SPINACH LEAVES, STEMS REMOVED, FINELY CHOPPED	500 G
1/4 TSP	FRESHLY GROUND BLACK PEPPER	I ML
	TOSTADAS OR TORTILLA CHIPS	

IN A SMALL (MAXIMUM 3 1/2-QUART) SLOW COOKER, COMBINE MOZZARELLA, CREAM CHEESE, PARMESAN, GARLIC, ARTICHOKES, SPINACH AND PEPPER. COVER AND COOK ON HIGH FOR 2 HOURS, UNTIL HOT AND BUBBLY. STIR WELL AND SERVE WITH TOSTADAS OR OTHER TORTILLA CHIPS. SERVES 6 TO 8.

TIP: IF YOU PREFER, SUBSTITUTE I PACKAGE (10 OZ/300 G) FRESH SPINACH LEAVES OR FROZEN SPINACH, THAWED AND SQUEEZED DRY.

TIP: FOR A SMOOTHER DIP, PLACE SPINACH AND ARTICHOKES IN A FOOD PROCESSOR, IN SEPARATE BATCHES, AND PULSE UNTIL DESIRED DEGREE OF FINENESS IS ACHIEVED. THEN COMBINE WITH REMAINING INGREDIENTS IN SLOW COOKER STONEWARE.

CHARRED PEPPER AND FETA DIP

MAKE THIS THE DAY BEFORE YOU NEED IT!

3	LARGE RED BELL PEPPERS	3
6 OZ	FETA CHEESE	175 G
2 TBSP	PINE NUTS	30 ML
I TBSP	OLIVE OIL	15 ML

CUT PEPPERS IN HALF AND REMOVE SEEDS. PLACE CUT SIDE DOWN ON COOKIE SHEET. BROIL UNTIL SKINS ARE BLACKENED AND PUFFED. PUT PEPPERS IN PLASTIC BAG AND LET STAND FOR 10 MINUTES TO STEAM. REMOVE AND PEEL. PLACE ALL INGREDIENTS IN FOOD PROCESSOR AND BLEND. SERVE WITH WATER BISCUITS OR UNSALTED CRACKERS OR FRESH VEGETABLES.

THE ONLY REASON SOME PEOPLE GET LOST IN THOUGHT IS BECAUSE THEY'RE IN UNFAMILIAR TERRITORY.

SUN-DRIED TOMATO DIP

*KEEP THESE INGREDIENTS ON HAND
AND PRESTO — AN INSTANT APPETIZER!*

8 OZ	LIGHT SPREADABLE CREAM CHEESE	250 G
2 TBSP	MAYONNAISE	30 ML
1 TSP	LEMON JUICE	5 ML
1/4 CUP	FINELY CHOPPED SUN-DRIED TOMATOES (RECONSTITUTED IF DRIED)	60 ML
1/4 CUP	FRESH BASIL, CHOPPED	60 ML
2	GARLIC CLOVES, MINCED	2

MIX CREAM CHEESE, MAYONNAISE AND LEMON JUICE
TOGETHER IN A BOWL. ADD TOMATOES, BASIL AND GARLIC
AND MIX WELL. LET SIT FOR AT LEAST 1 HOUR BEFORE
SERVING. SERVE WITH CRACKERS OR BAGEL CHIPS.

CURRY DIP FOR VEGETABLE PLATTER

1 CUP	MAYONNAISE	250 ML
1/2 CUP	KETCHUP	125 ML
1 TBSP	CURRY POWDER (MORE OR LESS, TO YOUR TASTE)	15 ML
1 TBSP	WORCESTERSHIRE SAUCE	15 ML
1 TSP	SALT	5 ML
1 TSP	BLACK PEPPER	5 ML

MIX ALL TOGETHER AND CHILL FOR A COUPLE OF HOURS.
THIS WILL KEEP IN COVERED CONTAINER FOR A FEW DAYS.
MAKES 1 1/2 CUPS (375 ML).

BUBBLING BACON AND HORSERADISH DIP

ON A COLD WINTER DAY, THERE'S NOTHING MORE
INVITING THAN A BUBBLING POT OF THIS SAVORY DIP.
OPEN A BIG BAG OF POTATO CHIPS TO ACCOMPANY
IT OR, FOR A MORE ELEGANT PRESENTATION,
SERVE ON CRISP SPEARS OF BELGIAN ENDIVE.

2	SLICES BACON, FINELY CHOPPED	2
8 OZ	CREAM CHEESE, CUBED	250 G
$\frac{1}{4}$ CUP	SOUR CREAM	60 ML
2 TBSP	MAYONNAISE	30 ML
2 TBSP	PREPARED HORSERADISH	30 ML
2 TBSP	FINELY CHOPPED GREEN ONION	30 ML
1	CLOVE GARLIC, MINCED	1
$\frac{3}{4}$ CUP	SHREDDED CHEDDAR CHEESE, PREFERABLY SHARP (OLD)	175 ML
	FRESHLY GROUND BLACK PEPPER	

IN A SKILLET OVER MEDIUM-HIGH HEAT, COOK BACON
UNTIL CRISP. REMOVE WITH A SLOTTED SPOON AND DRAIN
THOROUGHLY ON PAPER TOWEL. IN A SMALL (MAXIMUM
$3\frac{1}{2}$-QUART) SLOW COOKER, COMBINE CREAM CHEESE,
SOUR CREAM, MAYONNAISE, HORSERADISH, GREEN ONION,
GARLIC, CHEDDAR CHEESE AND RESERVED BACON. SEASON
TO TASTE WITH PEPPER. STIR WELL. COVER AND COOK ON
HIGH FOR 1 HOUR. STIR AGAIN AND COOK ON HIGH FOR AN
ADDITIONAL 30 MINUTES, UNTIL HOT AND BUBBLY. SERVE
IMMEDIATELY OR SET TEMPERATURE AT LOW OR WARM
UNTIL READY TO SERVE. SERVES 6.

TIP: IF YOU WANT TO AVOID STIRRING THE DIP AFTER AN HOUR, PLACE ALL THE INGREDIENTS IN A FOOD PROCESSOR AND PULSE TWO OR THREE TIMES UNTIL WELL COMBINED. TRANSFER TO SLOW COOKER STONEWARE AND COOK AS DIRECTED.

ANYONE WHO THINKS THE ART OF CONVERSATION IS DEAD OUGHT TO TELL A CHILD TO GO TO BED.

CRABMEAT DIP

1	CAN (6 1/2 OZ/184 G) DRAINED CRABMEAT	1
1/2 CUP	MAYONNAISE	125 ML
2 TBSP	KETCHUP OR CHILI SAUCE	30 ML
2 to 3 TBSP	LEMON JUICE	30 to 45 ML
	SEASONED BLACK PEPPER TO TASTE	
	GARLIC SALT OR POWDER TO TASTE	
1/2 TSP	HORSERADISH	2 ML

COMBINE ALL INGREDIENTS, MIXING WELL. SERVE AS AN APPETIZER WITH COLD FRESH VEGETABLE TRAY, INCLUDING ZUCCHINI STICKS, CAULIFLOWER CHUNKS, CARROT AND CELERY STICKS, CHERRY TOMATOES. MAKES ABOUT 1 1/2 CUPS (375 ML).

IN EVERY FAT BOOK THERE IS A THIN BOOK
TRYING TO GET OUT.

NIPPY CHEDDAR RABBIT

MADE WITH BEER, THIS ADULT VERSION OF
WELSH RAREBIT IS A GREAT NIBBLER FOR GUESTS.
SET OUT FONDUE FORKS AND A PLATE OF TOASTED
BREAD CUBES SO THEY CAN DIP THE BREAD IN THE
CHEESE, AND MAKE SURE THEY HAVE NAPKINS
OR PLATES TO CATCH ANY DRIPPING SAUCE.

8 OZ	SHARP (OLD) CHEDDAR CHEESE, SHREDDED	250 G
1 CUP	BEER	250 ML
2	EGG YOLKS, BEATEN	2
1/4 TSP	DRY MUSTARD	1 ML
1 TSP	WORCESTERSHIRE SAUCE	5 ML
1 TSP	PACKED BROWN SUGAR	5 ML
PINCH	CAYENNE PEPPER	PINCH

IN A SMALL (MAXIMUM 3 1/2-QUART) SLOW COOKER,
COMBINE CHEESE AND BEER. COVER AND COOK ON
LOW FOR 30 MINUTES, OR UNTIL CHEESE MELTS. IN
A BOWL, WHISK TOGETHER EGG YOLKS, MUSTARD,
WORCESTERSHIRE SAUCE, BROWN SUGAR AND CAYENNE.
POUR MIXTURE INTO SLOW COOKER STONEWARE AND STIR
UNTIL THICKENED. SERVES 6.

TIP: A SPOONFUL OF WORCESTERSHIRE SAUCE ADDS
WELCOME ZEST TO MANY GRAVIES AND SAUCES. THE
REGULAR VERSION CONTAINS ANCHOVIES, BUT THERE ARE
BRANDS THAT ARE SUITABLE FOR VEGANS.

TIP: NIPPY CHEDDAR RABBIT CAN ALSO BE SERVED AS A
LIGHT LUNCHEON DISH, OVER HOT TOAST.

BRIE WITH SUN-DRIED TOMATOES

4 OZ	SUN-DRIED TOMATOES IN OIL, FINELY CHOPPED	125 G
3 to 4	CLOVES GARLIC, MINCED	3 to 4
6 OZ	BRIE CHEESE	175 G
2 TBSP	CHOPPED FRESH PARSLEY	30 ML

MIX TOMATOES AND GARLIC AND PILE GENEROUSLY ON CHEESE. SPRINKLE WITH PARSLEY. (IT'S NOT NECESSARY TO REMOVE RIND FROM CHEESE.) HEAT IN OVEN AT 350°F (180°C) FOR A FEW MINUTES UNTIL CHEESE IS SOFT. SERVE WITH BAGEL CHIPS OR CRACKERS.

STILTON PÂTÉ

A FAVE!! SERVE WITH CRUSTY BREAD OR CRACKERS.

8 OZ	STILTON CHEESE	250 G
1/4 CUP	BUTTER	60 ML
4 OZ	CREAM CHEESE	125 G
2 TBSP	BRANDY	30 ML
	FRESHLY GROUND BLACK PEPPER TO TASTE	

BRING STILTON, BUTTER AND CREAM CHEESE TO ROOM TEMPERATURE. ADD ALL INGREDIENTS TO FOOD PROCESSOR AND MIX. PLACE IN SMALL BOWL AND REFRIGERATE UNTIL SERVING TIME.

LIVER PÂTÉ

I LB	CHICKEN LIVERS	500 G
I	ONION, SLICED	I
1/4 CUP	GRATED ONION	60 ML
I TSP	DRY MUSTARD	5 ML
2 TBSP	DRY SHERRY	30 ML
1/2 to	SOFT BUTTER	125 to
3/4 CUP		175 ML
PINCH	MACE	PINCH
	SALT AND PEPPER	

SIMMER CHICKEN LIVERS IN WATER WITH ONION FOR ABOUT 20 MINUTES. DRAIN LIVERS AND REMOVE ONION. GRIND LIVERS VERY FINE. ADD REMAINING INGREDIENTS AND MIX WELL. SERVE AS AN HORS D'OEUVRE WITH THINLY SLICED BROWN BREAD OR MELBA TOAST. MAKES 2 TO 3 CUPS (500 TO 750 ML).

HOUSEKEEPING IS LIKE STRINGING BEADS WITH NO KNOT IN THE END OF THE THREAD.

COCKTAIL CRISPS

*OUR FAVORITE COCKTAIL COOKIE — AND
IT FREEZES WELL.*

1 CUP	BUTTER	250 ML
1	PACKAGE (8 OZ/250 G) IMPERIAL CHEESE (SHARP COLD-PACK CHEDDAR CHEESE)	1
PINCH	SALT	PINCH
1/4 TSP	CAYENNE PEPPER OR HOT PEPPER SAUCE	1 ML
1/4 TSP	WORCESTERSHIRE SAUCE	1 ML
1 1/2 CUPS	ALL-PURPOSE FLOUR	375 ML
4 CUPS	RICE KRISPIES	1 L

CREAM BUTTER AND CHEESE TOGETHER. ADD SEASONINGS. BEAT IN FLOUR, THEN ADD RICE KRISPIES. MIX WELL. SHAPE INTO BALLS. PRESS DOWN WITH A FORK WHICH HAS BEEN DIPPED IN COLD WATER. BAKE AT 350°F (180°C) FOR 15 TO 20 MINUTES, UNTIL LIGHTLY BROWNED. MAKES ABOUT 4 DOZEN.

*HOME IS A PLACE WHERE, WHEN YOU GO THERE,
THEY HAVE TO TAKE YOU IN.*

PARMESAN CRISPS

GREAT TO SERVE WITH SOUP OR SALAD!

3/4 CUP	COARSELY SHREDDED FRESH PARMESAN CHEESE	175 ML
I TSP	FLOUR	5 ML

PREHEAT OVEN TO 350°F (180°C). LINE A COOKIE SHEET
WITH PARCHMENT PAPER OR COAT WITH VEGETABLE OIL.
IN A SMALL BOWL, STIR CHEESE AND FLOUR TOGETHER.
SPOON I ROUNDED TEASPOON (7 ML) CHEESE MIXTURE
ONTO BAKING SHEET. GENTLY SPREAD MIXTURE TO FORM
SMALL CIRCLES, ABOUT 2 INCHES (5 CM) IN DIAMETER.
FILL SHEET WITH 4 OR 5 CIRCLES, LEAVING AT LEAST
2 INCHES (5 CM) BETWEEN EACH ONE. BAKE IN CENTER
OF OVEN UNTIL GOLDEN, ABOUT 5 TO 7 MINUTES.
COOL CRISPS COMPLETELY ON BAKING SHEET BEFORE
REMOVING. REPEAT UNTIL ALL CHEESE MIXTURE IS USED.
CRISPS CAN BE MADE UP TO I DAY BEFORE SERVING.
STORE AT ROOM TEMPERATURE IN AN AIRTIGHT
CONTAINER. MAKES IO TO I2 CRISPS.

ANTIPASTO

A DELICIOUS APPETIZER TO SERVE DURING THE
FESTIVE SEASON. IT'S A LOT OF CHOPPING,
BUT DON'T USE A FOOD PROCESSOR!

I CUP	OLIVE OIL	250 ML
I	LARGE CAULIFLOWER, CUT INTO BITE-SIZE PIECES	I
2	LARGE GREEN PEPPERS, CHOPPED	2
2	CANS (EACH 10½ OZ/294 ML) SLICED RIPE OLIVES, CHOPPED	2
I	JAR (16 OZ/454 ML) GREEN OLIVES WITH PIMIENTO, CHOPPED	I
2	JARS (EACH 13 OZ/370 ML) PICKLED ONIONS, CHOPPED	2
2	CANS (EACH 10 OZ/284 ML) MUSHROOM STEMS AND PIECES	2
I	JAR (48 OZ/1.4 L) MIXED PICKLES, CHOPPED	I
2	BOTTLES (EACH 48 OZ/1.4 L) KETCHUP	2
I	BOTTLE (15 OZ/426 ML) HOT KETCHUP	I
2	CANS (EACH 2 OZ/56 G) ANCHOVIES, CHOPPED (OPTIONAL)	2
3	CANS (EACH 4½ OZ/128 G) SOLID TUNA, CHOPPED	3
3	CANS (EACH 4 OZ/114 G) SMALL SHRIMP	3

DRAIN ALL JARS AND CANS. PUT ALL INGREDIENTS, EXCEPT
THE FISH, INTO A LARGE DUTCH OVEN. BRING TO A BOIL,
THEN SIMMER FOR 20 MINUTES, STIRRING OFTEN. POUR
BOILING WATER OVER ALL THE FISH TO RINSE. DRAIN
AND ADD TO MIXTURE. GENTLY STIR AND SIMMER FOR
ANOTHER 10 MINUTES.

ARTICHOKE NIBBLERS

2	JARS (EACH 6 OZ/170 ML) MARINATED ARTICHOKE HEARTS	2
1	SMALL ONION, FINELY CHOPPED	1
1	CLOVE GARLIC, MINCED	1
4	EGGS, BEATEN	4
1/4 CUP	FINE DRY BREAD CRUMBS	60 ML
1/4 TSP	SALT	1 ML
1/4 TSP	EACH BLACK PEPPER, OREGANO AND TABASCO SAUCE	1 ML
2 CUPS	GRATED SHARP (OLD) CHEDDAR CHEESE	500 ML
1	JAR (4 OZ/113 ML) PIMENTOS	1
2 TBSP	SNIPPED PARSLEY	30 ML

DRAIN LIQUID FROM 1 JAR OF ARTICHOKE HEARTS AND
DISCARD. DRAIN LIQUID FROM THE OTHER JAR INTO
FRYING PAN. ADD ONION AND GARLIC AND SAUTÉ. CHOP
ARTICHOKES INTO QUARTERS. COMBINE EGGS, CRUMBS,
SALT, PEPPER, OREGANO AND TABASCO. STIR IN CHEESE,
PIMIENTO AND ARTICHOKES. ADD ONION MIXTURE. POUR
INTO 9-INCH (23 CM) SQUARE BUTTERED BAKING DISH.
SPRINKLE WITH PARSLEY AND BAKE AT 325°F (160°C) FOR
30 MINUTES, OR UNTIL LIGHTLY SET. CUT INTO 1-INCH
(2.5 CM) SQUARES. MAKES 81 PIECES.

STUFFED MUSHROOM CAPS

18	LARGE WHOLE FRESH MUSHROOMS	18
2 TBSP	VEGETABLE OIL	30 ML
1	SMALL ONION FINELY CHOPPED	1
1/4 LB	GROUND BEEF	125 G
2	SLICES HAM, COARSELY CHOPPED	2
1/3 CUP	DRY SHERRY	75 ML
1/4 CUP	FINE BREAD CRUMBS	60 ML
1 TSP	GARLIC POWDER	5 ML
1 TSP	SALT	5 ML
1/2 TSP	BLACK PEPPER	2 ML
1/4 CUP	GRATED PARMESAN CHEESE	60 ML

CAREFULLY REMOVE STEMS FROM THE MUSHROOMS. CHOP STEMS FINELY AND RESERVE. PLACE MUSHROOM CAPS ON A COOKIE SHEET. HEAT OIL IN A LARGE SKILLET OVER MODERATE HEAT, COOK ONION AND BEEF UNTIL LIGHTLY BROWNED, STIRRING FREQUENTLY. ADD THE CHOPPED STEMS, HAM AND SHERRY TO ONION-BEEF MIXTURE AND COOK 5 MINUTES. ADD BREAD CRUMBS, GARLIC POWDER, SALT AND PEPPER AND MIX WELL. STUFF MIXTURE INTO CAPS. SPRINKLE WITH CHEESE. BROIL MUSHROOMS IN PREHEATED BROILER, 3 INCHES (7.5 CM) FROM SOURCE OF HEAT, 2 TO 5 MINUTES. SERVE HOT. MAKES 18.

GUACAMOLE CHERRY TOMATO HALVES

TOMATO LOVERS WILL BE HAPPY TO SEE THESE SAVORY LITTLE APPETIZERS.

1	SMALL BASKET CHERRY TOMATOES	1
1	LARGE RIPE AVOCADO	1
4 TSP	LEMON JUICE	20 ML
1 TBSP	FINELY CHOPPED ONION	15 ML
1	CLOVE GARLIC, MINCED	1
1/2 TSP	SALT	2 ML
6	STRIPS BACON, COOKED AND CRUMBLED	6

REMOVE STEMS FROM TOMATOES; CUT EACH IN HALF CROSSWISE. SCOOP OUT AND DISCARD SEED FILLING. LAY CUT SIDE DOWN ON PAPER TOWELS FOR ABOUT HALF AN HOUR. PREPARE GUACAMOLE FILLING BY PEELING AND REMOVING PIT FROM AVOCADO. IN A SMALL BOWL, MASH THE AVOCADO COARSELY WITH A FORK. STIR IN LEMON JUICE, ONION, GARLIC AND SALT. BLEND WELL. FILL TOMATOES. SPRINKLE WITH BACON. SERVES 8.

A SUBURBAN MOTHER'S ROLE IS TO DELIVER CHILDREN OBSTETRICALLY ONCE, AND BY CAR FOR EVER AFTER.

CHRISTMAS CHEESE BALLS

A "MUST" AT OUR CHRISTMAS EXCHANGE.

2	PACKAGES (EACH 8 OZ/250 G) CREAM CHEESE	2
2 TBSP	GRATED ONION	30 ML
I LB	INGERSOLL CHEESE	500 G
I	PACKAGE (8 OZ/250 G) IMPERIAL CHEESE	250 G
3 OZ	BLUE CHEESE	90 G
2 TSP	WORCESTERSHIRE SAUCE	IO ML
4 OZ	SHARP (OLD) CHEDDAR CHEESE, SHREDDED	I25 G
I CUP	CHOPPED PECANS	250 ML
I CUP	DRIED PARSLEY	250 ML

COMBINE ALL INGREDIENTS, EXCEPT PECANS AND PARSLEY, IN DOUBLE BOILER OR LARGE PAN OVER VERY LOW HEAT. STIR UNTIL WELL BLENDED, THEN COOL. IF MAKING DOUBLE QUANTITIES, COMBINE IN A ROASTING PAN OR DUTCH OVEN AND HEAT IN SLOW OVEN TO MELT. WHEN COOL, SHAPE INTO BALLS OR LOGS, THEN ROLL IN PECANS AND PARSLEY. TO STORE, WRAP IN PLASTIC AND REFRIGERATE. SERVES 24.

"NEVER GO TO BED MAD. STAY UP AND FIGHT."
— PHYLLIS DILLER

SPANAKOPITA

A SHORTCUT ROUTE TO GREEK GOURMET.

2	BUNCHES SPINACH	2
1 1/3 CUPS	FINELY CHOPPED ONIONS	325 ML
1/2 CUP	DICED MUSHROOMS	125 ML
	SALT AND BLACK PEPPER TO TASTE	
2	EGGS, BEATEN	2
8 OZ	FETA CHEESE, CRUMBLED	250 G
1/3 CUP	BREAD CRUMBS	75 ML
1 TSP	DRIED DILLWEED	5 ML
PINCH	GROUND NUTMEG	PINCH
1/2 CUP	BUTTER, MELTED	125 ML
12	SHEETS PHYLLO DOUGH	12

WASH, STEM AND STEAM SPINACH UNTIL WILTED; CHOP. SAUTÉ ONIONS, MUSHROOMS, SALT AND PEPPER UNTIL LIQUID HAS EVAPORATED (ABOUT 5 MINUTES). ADD TO SPINACH. ADD EGGS, CHEESE, BREAD CRUMBS, DILL AND SPICES. FOLLOW PACKAGE INSTRUCTIONS FOR KEEPING PHYLLO MOIST. BRUSH EACH SHEET WITH BUTTER, LAYERING 4 SHEETS ON TOP OF EACH OTHER. PUT FILLING ALONG LENGTH OF TOP LAYER, LEAVING 1-INCH (2.5 CM) MARGIN AT EACH EDGE. SEAL BY FOLDING AND ROLLING UP LIKE A JELLY ROLL. BRUSH TOPS WITH BUTTER AND BAKE AT 425°F (220°C) FOR 20 MINUTES. COOL 10 MINUTES. SLICE AND SERVE. MESSY BUT MARVELOUS! MAY BE REHEATED IN MICROWAVE. MAKES 3 ROLLS.

SMOKED SALMON HORS D'OEUVRE

1	PACKAGE (8 OZ/250 G) CREAM CHEESE	1
1 TSP	CAPERS	5 ML
1 TSP	CAPER JUICE	5 ML
1 TSP	FINELY CHOPPED GREEN ONION	5 ML
1 TSP	MAYONNAISE	5 ML
1/2 LB	SMOKED SALMON OR LOX, CUT INTO 1-INCH (2.5 CM) STRIPS	250 G

CREAM FIRST FIVE INGREDIENTS. SPOON SMALL AMOUNT ONTO SALMON STRIP AND ROLL. FASTEN WITH COCKTAIL TOOTHPICKS. SERVES 6.

CRAB-STUFFED ARTICHOKE HEARTS

3	GREEN ONIONS, FINELY CHOPPED	3
1/4 CUP	BUTTER	60 ML
1	CAN (6 1/2 OZ/185 G) CRABMEAT	1
1/2 CUP	WHITE WINE	125 ML
1	CAN (14 OZ/398 ML) ARTICHOKE HEARTS, DRAINED (6 TO 8 COUNT IS BEST)	1
1 CUP	HOLLANDAISE SAUCE (SUCH AS KNORR'S, OR HOMEMADE)	125 ML

SAUTÉ ONION IN BUTTER UNTIL SOFT. ADD CRAB AND WINE. SIMMER FOR 3 MINUTES AND SET ASIDE. CUT ARTICHOKE HEARTS IN HALF LENGTHWISE AND PLACE IN SHALLOW OVENPROOF CASSEROLE OR INDIVIDUAL SCALLOP SHELLS. TOP WITH CRABMEAT MIXTURE AND COVER WITH HOLLANDAISE SAUCE. PLACE UNDER BROILER UNTIL BUBBLY; WATCH CAREFULLY! MAKES 12 TO 16.

CURRIED SEAFOOD COCKTAIL PUFFS

THESE ELEGANT PUFFS CAN BE MADE AHEAD, FROZEN, THEN FILLED AT SERVING TIME.

PUFFS (CHOUX PASTRY)

I CUP	WATER	250 ML
1/2 CUP	BUTTER	125 ML
I CUP	FLOUR	250 ML
1/2 TSP	SALT	2 ML
4	EGGS	4

SEAFOOD FILLING

7 OZ	CRAB OR SHRIMP	200 G
1/3 CUP	MAYONNAISE	75 ML
I TSP	CURRY POWDER	5 ML
2 TBSP	CHOPPED GREEN ONION	30 ML

PREHEAT OVEN TO 400°F (200°C).

TO MAKE PUFFS: IN A MEDIUM SAUCEPAN, BOIL WATER. ADD BUTTER AND STIR UNTIL MELTED. TURN HEAT TO LOW, ADD FLOUR AND SALT, STIRRING VIGOROUSLY UNTIL MIXTURE FORMS A SMOOTH BALL. REMOVE FROM HEAT. ADD EGGS ONE AT A TIME, BEATING WELL WITH A SPOON AFTER EACH ADDITION. DROP BY TEASPOONFULS (5 ML) ONTO LIGHTLY GREASED COOKIE SHEET; BAKE 20 TO 25 MINUTES, UNTIL GOLDEN. COOL; CUT IN HALF.

TO MAKE FILLING: MIX FILLING INGREDIENTS TOGETHER. FILL PUFFS, REPLACING TOPS. HEAT BEFORE SERVING. MAKES ABOUT 24.

SAMOSAS IN PHYLLO

THESE LOW-FAT APPETIZERS FREEZE WELL. NOW YOU'RE READY FOR LAST-MINUTE GUESTS!

FILLING

1 CUP	PEELED AND FINELY CHOPPED POTATOES	250 ML
1 TSP	VEGETABLE OIL	5 ML
1	ONION, FINELY CHOPPED	1
2 TSP	CURRY POWDER	10 ML
2 TSP	CUMIN	10 ML
1 TSP	TURMERIC	5 ML
1/4 TSP	SALT	1 ML
	PINCH CAYENNE PEPPER	
1/2 LB	LEAN GROUND BEEF	250 G
1/2 CUP	SMALL FROZEN PEAS	125 ML
3 TBSP	BEEF BROTH	45 ML
1 TBSP	CURRANTS	15 ML
1 TBSP	LEMON JUICE	15 ML
2 TSP	LIQUID HONEY	10 ML
9	SHEETS PHYLLO PASTRY	9
1/4 CUP	BUTTER, MELTED	60 ML

TO MAKE FILLING: COOK POTATOES IN BOILING WATER UNTIL TENDER BUT STILL FIRM; DRAIN AND SET ASIDE. IN NONSTICK PAN, HEAT OIL OVER MEDIUM HEAT AND COOK ONION, STIRRING, UNTIL SOFTENED. STIR IN CURRY POWDER, CUMIN, TURMERIC, SALT AND CAYENNE. STIR AND COOK FOR 2 MINUTES. ADD BEEF, BREAKING UP INTO SMALL PIECES; COOK UNTIL NO LONGER PINK. STIR IN POTATOES, PEAS, BEEF BROTH, CURRANTS, LEMON JUICE AND HONEY.

COOK, GENTLY STIRRING, UNTIL PEAS ARE THAWED. COOL. PLACE 1 SHEET OF PHYLLO ON WORK SURFACE (KEEP A SLIGHTLY DAMP CLEAN CLOTH OVER THE OTHER SHEETS SO THEY WILL NOT DRY OUT.) LIGHTLY BRUSH PHYLLO WITH SOME OF THE BUTTER. USING A SHARP KNIFE, CUT THE PHYLLO INTO FOUR 3-INCH (8 CM) WIDE STRIPS. SPOON 1 TBSP (15 ML) FILLING ONTO PHYLLO ABOUT 1 INCH (2.5 CM) FROM BOTTOM ON THE RIGHT SIDE. FOLD THE LEFT SIDE OVER FILLING AND CONTINUE FOLDING IN A TRIANGULAR SHAPE (FLAG-FASHION) TO THE END OF THE STRIP. PRESS EDGES TOGETHER AND PLACE ON BAKING SHEET. REPEAT WITH REMAINING STRIPS. BRUSH TOPS LIGHTLY WITH BUTTER. (THESE MAY BE FROZEN ON A COOKIE SHEET AND STORED IN A FREEZER BAG. DO NOT THAW.) BAKE AT 375°F (190°C) FOR 20 MINUTES OR UNTIL SAMOSAS ARE GOLDEN. MAKES 36 APPETIZERS.

SERVE WITH CORIANDER CHUTNEY OR A HOT MANGO CHUTNEY OR GINGER PICKLE RELISH — ALL AVAILABLE AT LARGE GROCERIES OR EASTERN SPECIALTY STORES — EXPERIMENT!

SOMEONE ONCE TOLD ME THAT THERE IS MORE TO LIFE THAN GOLF. I THINK IT WAS MY EX-WIFE.

HAM AND CHEESE PUFFS

THEY FREEZE WELL. IF YOU'VE GOT TENNIS ELBOW,
YOU'LL NEED HELP BEATING THESE.

1 CUP	WATER	250 ML
1/3 CUP	BUTTER	75 ML
1 CUP	ALL-PURPOSE FLOUR	250 ML
4	EGGS	4
1 1/2 CUPS	SHREDDED SHARP (OLD) CHEDDAR CHEESE	375 ML
1 CUP	HAM OR CRISP BACON, FINELY CHOPPED	250 ML
1/2 to 1 TSP	DRY MUSTARD	2 to 5 ML
1	CAN (4 OZ/114 ML) CHOPPED JALAPEÑOS, DRAINED (OPTIONAL)	1

COMBINE WATER AND BUTTER IN A HEAVY SAUCEPAN AND BRING TO A BOIL. REMOVE FROM HEAT AND ADD FLOUR ALL AT ONCE. BEAT WITH A WOODEN SPOON UNTIL WELL MIXED. RETURN TO MEDIUM HEAT AND BEAT UNTIL MIXTURE LEAVES SIDES OF PAN AND FORMS A BALL. REMOVE FROM HEAT AND BEAT IN EGGS ONE AT A TIME TO FORM A SMOOTH MIXTURE (BE PATIENT AND BEAT THOROUGHLY). STIR IN CHEESE, HAM, MUSTARD AND JALAPEÑOS (IF USING). DROP BY SMALL TEASPOONFULS (5 ML) ONTO GREASED COOKIE SHEET. BAKE AT 400°F (200°C) FOR 15 TO 20 MINUTES. REHEAT IF FROZEN IN 350°F (180°C) OVEN FOR 5 TO 10 MINUTES.

MAKES ABOUT 64 PUFFS.

ASPARAGUS CHICKEN PUFFS

1	LARGE BONELESS CHICKEN BREAST, COOKED AND CUBED	1
2 TBSP	MAYONNAISE	30 ML
1/2 to 1 TSP	CURRY POWDER	2 to 5 ML
	SALT AND BLACK PEPPER TO TASTE	
1	PACKAGE (14 OZ/400 G) PUFF PASTRY	1
1	CAN (12 OZ/341 ML) ASPARAGUS, WELL-DRAINED (OR 12 FRESH SMALL ASPARAGUS, BLANCHED)	1
1	EGG, BEATEN	1
	SESAME SEEDS	

IN A FOOD PROCESSOR, PURÉE CHICKEN, MAYONNAISE, CURRY, SALT AND PEPPER UNTIL SMOOTH. ROLL PASTRY INTO A 14- BY 10-INCH (35 BY 25 CM) RECTANGLE. CUT LENGTHWISE INTO 3 EVEN STRIPS. SPREAD CHICKEN MIXTURE ALONG ONE SIDE OF EACH STRIP OF PASTRY. PLACE ASPARAGUS SPEARS LENGTHWISE BESIDE CHICKEN MIXTURE. BRUSH EDGES OF PASTRY WITH EGG. ROLL PASTRY OVER TO CLOSE COMPLETELY. BRUSH TOP WITH EGG, CUT ROLLS DIAGONALLY INTO 1-INCH (2.5 CM) PIECES AND SPRINKLE WITH SESAME SEEDS. PLACE ON GREASED COOKIE SHEET AND BAKE AT 450°F (230°C) FOR 10 MINUTES. LOWER TEMPERATURE TO 350°F (180°C); BAKE FOR ANOTHER 10 MINUTES OR UNTIL GOLDEN BROWN.

MAKES 4 DOZEN.

HOT BUTTERED RUM

*STORE IN YOUR FREEZER IN SMALL CONTAINERS.
GREAT FOR GIFTS.*

HOT RUM BASE

1 LB	BUTTER, ROOM TEMPERATURE	500 G
4 CUPS	VANILLA ICE CREAM, SOFTENED	1 L
3 1/2 CUPS	CONFECTIONERS' (ICING) SUGAR	875 ML
2 CUPS	BROWN SUGAR	500 ML
1 1/2 TSP	GROUND CINNAMON	7 ML
1/2 TSP	GROUND ALLSPICE	2 ML

IN A LARGE BOWL, MIX BUTTER AND ICE CREAM TOGETHER.
BLEND IN ALL OTHER INGREDIENTS. STORE IN FREEZER.
MAKES ABOUT 9 CUPS (2.25 L).

HOT BUTTERED RUM

2 TBSP	HOT RUM BASE	30 ML
1 1/2 OZ	DARK RUM	45 ML
	CINNAMON STICK	

IN A LARGE MUG, ADD HOT RUM BASE AND DARK RUM. FILL
MUG WITH BOILING WATER AND STIR WITH CINNAMON
STICK UNTIL MIXTURE IS BLENDED. SERVES 1.

NEVER TEST THE DEPTH OF THE WATER WITH BOTH FEET.

HOT RUM CANADIENNE

*MARVELOUS AFTER SKIING, AFTER FOOTBALL GAMES,
AFTER TOBOGGANING, AFTER ANYTHING!*

2 OZ	DARK RUM	60 ML
2 TBSP	MAPLE SYRUP	25 ML
	SQUIRT OF LEMON JUICE	
	NUTMEG	
	CINNAMON (A CINNAMON STICK IS BEST)	
	BOILING WATER	
	DAB OF BUTTER	

COMBINE FIRST FIVE INGREDIENTS; TOP OFF WITH
BOILING WATER AND A SMALL DAB OF BUTTER. MAKES
1 STEAMING MUG.

FALLEN ANGELS

*TO BE A "FALLEN ANGEL" YOU HAVE TO
OWN A CAPPUCCINO MAKER.*

1/4 CUP	FRANGELICO LIQUEUR	60 ML
1/4 CUP	VODKA	60 ML
1/4 CUP	MILK, STEAMED	60 ML

MIX EQUAL PORTIONS OF FRANGELICO AND VODKA. ADD
STEAMED MILK. ADD MORE MILK IF YOU DON'T WANT TO
GO TO THE DEVIL! THIS IS ONE DRINK — THE REST IS UP
TO YOU!

GLØGG

OUR DANISH FRIEND SERVES THIS WONDERFUL
SPICED WINE AT SKATING PARTIES.

3	CINNAMON STICKS	3
I TBSP	WHOLE CLOVES	15 ML
I	BOTTLE (750 ML) RED WINE	I
I CUP	BRANDY	250 ML
I	BOTTLE (12 OZ/341 ML) BEER	I
I	ORANGE, THINLY SLICED WITH RIND ON	I
I	SLICE LEMON	I
3/4 CUP	GRANULATED SUGAR	175 ML
I CUP	RAISINS	250 ML
1/3 CUP	SLIVERED ALMONDS	75 ML

MAKE A SPICE BAG WITH CINNAMON AND CLOVES. COMBINE
EVERYTHING IN A LARGE POT; BRING TO A BOIL; SIMMER
FOR 1 1/2 HOURS, COVERED. REMOVE ORANGE AND LEMON
SLICES AND SPICE BAG BEFORE SERVING. SERVES 12 TO 16.

NEVER ARGUE WITH A SPOUSE
WHO IS PACKING YOUR PARACHUTE.

SPICED TEA

THIS MIXTURE CAN BE STORED IN A PLASTIC CONTAINER INDEFINITELY. GREAT WITH LATE SNACKS, ON THE SKI TRAIL, AT MEETINGS, ANY TIME!

1/2 CUP	INSTANT TEA	125 ML
1 1/2 CUPS	GRANULATED SUGAR	375 ML
2	PACKAGES (3 1/2 OZ/100 G) ORANGE TANG	2
1 TSP	GROUND CINNAMON	5 ML
1/2 TSP	GROUND CLOVES	2 ML

USE 2 TO 3 TSP (10 TO 15 ML) PER CUP, ADD BOILING WATER.

WINTER PUNCH

FUN TO SERVE THE GALS WHEN THEY ARRIVE FOR
BRIDGE ON THOSE COLD WINTER NIGHTS. YOU MAY
WANT TO DOUBLE THIS RECIPE BECAUSE
THEY'LL WANT MORE.

2	CINNAMON STICKS	2
16	CLOVES	16
6 CUPS	APPLE JUICE	1.5 L
2 CUPS	CRANBERRY COCKTAIL	500 ML
1 TSP	BITTERS	5 ML
4 OZ	CINNAMON RED HOTS	125 G
1 CUP	RUM (LIGHT)	250 ML

TIE CINNAMON STICKS AND CLOVES IN A CHEESECLOTH
BAG. MIX REST OF INGREDIENTS, EXCEPT RUM, TOGETHER
AND PLACE CHEESECLOTH BAG IN MIXTURE. SIMMER IN A
LARGE POT FOR 45 MINUTES. ADD 1 CUP (250 ML) RUM OR
MORE. SERVES 8.

WHEN IN DOUBT, MUMBLE. WHEN IN TROUBLE, DELEGATE.

EGGNOG SUPREME

THIS IS A BEST OF BRIDGE CHRISTMAS TRADITION.

12	EGG YOLKS	12
1 CUP	SUGAR	250 ML
7/8 CUP	BRANDY (OKAY! USE THE WHOLE CUP)	210 ML
1 1/3 CUPS	RYE OR RUM	325 ML
2 CUPS	HALF-AND-HALF (10%) CREAM	500 ML
12	EGG WHITES	12
3 CUPS	HEAVY OR WHIPPING (35%) CREAM	750 ML
	NUTMEG FOR GARNISH	

IN A LARGE BOWL, BEAT EGG YOLKS AND SUGAR TOGETHER UNTIL LEMON-COLORED AND THICK. ADD BRANDY, RYE AND HALF-AND-HALF. BLEND WELL. CHILL FOR SEVERAL HOURS. BEAT EGG WHITES UNTIL STIFF. BEAT WHIPPING CREAM IN LARGE BOWL AND FOLD IN EGG WHITES. FOLD INTO EGG YOLK MIXTURE. POUR INTO A LARGE PUNCH BOWL. SPRINKLE WITH GRATED NUTMEG. ENJOY! SERVES 24.

NOTE: THIS RECIPE CONTAINS RAW EGGS. IF THE FOOD SAFETY OF RAW EGGS IS A CONCERN FOR YOU, SUBSTITUTE PASTEURIZED EGGS IN THE SHELL.

BUFFETS AND POTLUCKS

BUFFET PARTIES, PARTICULARLY IF THEY HAVE A POTLUCK COMPONENT, ARE PROBABLY THE EASIEST WAY TO ENTERTAIN A LARGE NUMBER OF PEOPLE. PLAN TO SERVE PLENTY OF COLD DISHES, INCLUDING SALADS, BECAUSE THEY CAN BE MADE AHEAD AND REFRIGERATED UNTIL NEEDED. BUT HOT DISHES STRIKE A SIGNIFICANT "COMFORT FOOD" NOTE AND, IF MADE AND KEPT WARM IN A SLOW COOKER, ARE EQUALLY CONVENIENT. THE RECIPES IN THIS CHAPTER ARE EASILY SUPPLEMENTED BY SMALL-PLATE RECIPES, SUCH THOSE IN CHAPTER 2. FINISH OFF WITH SWEET TREATS, SUCH AS THE RECIPES IN CHAPTERS 6 AND 7.

POMEGRANATE AND FETA SALAD

THE POMEGRANATE SEEDS ADD SPARKLE TO THIS SALAD!

1	HEAD ROMAINE LETTUCE, WASHED AND TORN	1
1	BUNCH SPINACH, STEMS REMOVED, WASHED AND TORN	1
1/2 CUP	DRIED CRANBERRIES OR SEEDS OF 1 POMEGRANATE	125 ML
1/4 CUP	TOASTED PINE NUTS	60 ML
1/2 CUP	CRUMBLED FETA CHEESE	125 ML

DRESSING

1/3 CUP	OLIVE OIL	75 ML
1 TBSP	RED WINE VINEGAR	15 ML
2 TBSP	PURE MAPLE SYRUP	30 ML
1 TSP	DIJON MUSTARD	5 ML
1/2 TSP	DRIED OREGANO	2 ML
	SALT AND FRESHLY GROUND BLACK PEPPER	

TOSS LETTUCE AND SPINACH TOGETHER IN A LARGE SALAD BOWL. ADD DRIED CRANBERRIES OR POMEGRANATE SEEDS, PINE NUTS AND FETA. WHISK DRESSING INGREDIENTS TOGETHER; STORE IN REFRIGERATOR. TOSS WITH SALAD INGREDIENTS JUST BEFORE SERVING. SERVES 6.

SPINACH AND STRAWBERRY SALAD

SPINACH — ENOUGH FOR YOUR CREW.
STRAWBERRIES — SAME AS ABOVE!

POPPYSEED WORCESTERSHIRE DRESSING

1/3 CUP	GRANULATED SUGAR	75 ML
1/2 CUP	OIL	125 ML
1/4 CUP	WHITE VINEGAR	60 ML
2 TBSP	SESAME SEEDS	30 ML
2 TBSP	POPPY SEEDS	30 ML
1/4 TSP	PAPRIKA	1 ML
1/2 TSP	WORCESTERSHIRE SAUCE	2 ML
1 1/2 TSP	MINCED ONION	7 ML

TEAR SPINACH INTO BITE-SIZE PIECES. CUT STRAWBERRIES IN HALF. COMBINE DRESSING INGREDIENTS AND MIX WELL. TOSS WITH SPINACH AND STRAWBERRIES.

NEVER ASK A TWO-YEAR-OLD TO HOLD A TOMATO.

COMMITTEE SALAD

WE ALL WORKED ON IT AND WE ALL LOVE IT.

DRESSING

1/2 CUP	VEGETABLE OIL	125 ML
3 TBSP	RED WINE VINEGAR	45 ML
1 TBSP	LEMON JUICE	15 ML
2 TSP	GRANULATED SUGAR	10 ML
1/2 TSP	SALT	2 ML
1/2 TSP	DRY MUSTARD	2 ML
1	CLOVE GARLIC, MINCED	1

SALAD

2 TBSP	BUTTER	30 ML
1/2 CUP	SUNFLOWER SEEDS, SHELLED	125 ML
1/2 CUP	SLIVERED ALMONDS	125 ML
1	HEAD LEAF LETTUCE	1
2	GREEN ONIONS, FINELY CHOPPED	2
1	CAN (10 OZ/284 ML) MANDARIN ORANGES, DRAINED	1
1	RIPE AVOCADO, PEELED AND SLICED	1

COMBINE ALL DRESSING INGREDIENTS IN A JAR; SHAKE TO BLEND. MELT BUTTER IN A FRYING PAN AND SAUTÉ SUNFLOWER SEEDS AND ALMONDS UNTIL GOLDEN BROWN. PREPARE REMAINING INGREDIENTS. ADD COOLED SEEDS AND ALMONDS. TOSS WITH DRESSING JUST BEFORE SERVING. SERVES 6.

A COMMITTEE IS A GROUP THAT
KEEPS MINUTES AND LOSES HOURS.

Brie with Sun-Dried Tomatoes (page 64)

Guacamole Cherry Tomato Halves (page 71)
and Christmas Cheese Balls (page 72)

Eggnog Supreme (page 85)

Senate Salad Bowl (page 96)

WARM SPINACH SALAD
WITH APPLES AND BRIE

THIS IS A WINNER!

4	LARGE GRANNY SMITH APPLES	4
1/4 CUP	PURE MAPLE SYRUP	60 ML
8 CUPS	WASHED SPINACH LEAVES	2 L
8 OZ	BRIE CHEESE, CUT IN SMALL PIECES	250 G
1/2 CUP	TOASTED PECANS	125 ML

DRESSING

1/4 CUP	APPLE CIDER OR APPLE JUICE	60 ML
3 TBSP	CIDER VINEGAR	45 ML
1 TSP	DIJON MUSTARD	5 ML
1	CLOVE GARLIC, MINCED	1
1/4 CUP	OLIVE OIL	60 ML
	SALT AND BLACK PEPPER TO TASTE	

PEEL AND CORE APPLES; CUT INTO 1/2-INCH (1 CM) SLICES.
ARRANGE ON BAKING SHEET AND BRUSH WITH SYRUP.
BROIL UNTIL GOLDEN; TURN, BRUSH SYRUP ON OTHER
SIDE AND BROIL. PLACE SPINACH IN LARGE BOWL. WHISK
DRESSING INGREDIENTS TOGETHER IN A SMALL SAUCEPAN
AND HEAT UNTIL SIMMERING. POUR OVER SPINACH,
TOSS AND ADD CHEESE, APPLES AND NUTS. DEE-LISH!

CAESAR SALAD

YOU'LL DESERVE THE "HAILS" WHEN YOU
SERVE THIS CLASSIC.

1	LARGE HEAD ROMAINE LETTUCE	1
1	CLOVE GARLIC, MINCED	1
$1/3$ CUP	OIL	75 ML
	SALT AND FRESHLY GROUND BLACK PEPPER TO TASTE	
$1/4$ TSP	DRY MUSTARD	1 ML
$1^1/_2$ TSP	WORCESTERSHIRE SAUCE	7 ML
3 (OR MORE)	ANCHOVY FILLETS, DRAINED	3 (OR MORE)
1	EGG	1
1 to 2 TBSP	FRESH LEMON JUICE	15 to 30 ML
2 TBSP	FRESHLY GRATED PARMESAN CHEESE	30 ML
	CROUTONS	

WASH AND TEAR ROMAINE INTO BITE-SIZE PIECES. BLEND
REMAINING INGREDIENTS IN A BLENDER, EXCEPT PARMESAN
AND CROUTONS. TOSS LETTUCE AND DRESSING. SPRINKLE
ON PARMESAN AND CROUTONS. TOSS AGAIN. SERVES 6.

NOTE: THIS RECIPE CONTAINS A RAW EGG. IF THE
FOOD SAFETY OF RAW EGGS IS A CONCERN FOR YOU,
SUBSTITUTE A PASTEURIZED EGG IN THE SHELL OR $1/4$ CUP
(60 ML) PASTEURIZED LIQUID WHOLE EGGS.

NEVER UNDERESTIMATE THE POWER OF
STUPID PEOPLE IN LARGE GROUPS.

BROCCOLI MANDARIN SALAD

DRESSING

2	LARGE EGGS	2
1/2 CUP	GRANULATED SUGAR	125 ML
1 TSP	CORNSTARCH	5 ML
1 TSP	DRY MUSTARD	5 ML
1/4 CUP	WHITE WINE VINEGAR	60 ML
1/4 CUP	WATER	60 ML
1/2 CUP	MAYONNAISE	125 ML

SALAD

4 CUPS	FRESH BROCCOLI FLORETS	1 L
1/2 CUP	RAISINS	125 ML
8	SLICES BACON, COOKED AND CHOPPED	8
2 CUPS	SLICED FRESH MUSHROOMS	500 ML
1/2 CUP	SLIVERED TOASTED ALMONDS	125 ML
1	10-OZ (284 ML) CAN MANDARIN ORANGES, DRAINED	1
1/2	RED ONION, SLICED	1/2

TO MAKE DRESSING: IN A SAUCEPAN, WHISK TOGETHER EGGS, SUGAR, CORNSTARCH AND DRY MUSTARD. ADD VINEGAR AND WATER AND COOK SLOWLY UNTIL THICKENED. REMOVE FROM HEAT AND STIR IN MAYONNAISE. COOL.

TO MAKE SALAD: MARINATE BROCCOLI IN DRESSING FOR SEVERAL HOURS. ADD REMAINING INGREDIENTS AND TOSS WELL. SERVES 6.

CANLIS' SPECIAL SALAD

ORIGINATED BY CANLIS RESTAURANT IN HONOLULU.

SALAD

2	HEADS ROMAINE LETTUCE	2
2	PEELED TOMATOES	2
1	CLOVE GARLIC	1
	SALT	
2 TBSP	OLIVE OIL	30 ML

CONDIMENTS

1/4 CUP	GREEN ONION, CHOPPED	60 ML
1/2 CUP	ROMANO CHEESE, GRATED	125 ML
1 LB	COOKED BACON, FINELY CHOPPED	500 G

DRESSING

6 TBSP	OLIVE OIL	90 ML
	JUICE OF 2 LEMONS	
1/2 TSP	FRESHLY GROUND BLACK PEPPER	2 ML
1/2 TSP	FRESH MINT, CHOPPED	2 ML
1/4 TSP	DRIED OREGANO	1 ML
1	CODDLED EGG	1
1 CUP	CROUTONS	250 ML

INTO A LARGE BOWL (WOODEN), POUR APPROXIMATELY
2 TBSP (30 ML) OF GOOD OLIVE OIL, SPRINKLE WITH SALT
AND RUB WITH A LARGE CLOVE OF GARLIC. (THE OIL WILL
ACT AS A LUBRICANT AND THE SALT AS AN ABRASIVE.)
REMOVE GARLIC. IN THE BOTTOM OF THE BOWL, FIRST
PLACE TOMATOES CUT IN EIGHTHS; ADD ROMAINE LETTUCE,
SLICED IN 1-INCH (2.5 CM) STRIPS.

DRESSING: POUR THE OLIVE OIL INTO A BOWL; ADD LEMON JUICE AND SEASONINGS. ADD CODDLED EGG AND WHIP VIGOROUSLY. WHEN READY TO SERVE, POUR DRESSING OVER SALAD. ADD CROUTONS LAST. TOSS GENEROUSLY. SERVES 6 TO 8.

NOTE: YOU MAY ADD OTHER VEGETABLES TO THIS SALAD IF YOU CHOOSE, BUT REMEMBER TO PUT THE HEAVY VEGETABLES IN FIRST WITH ROMAINE LETTUCE ON TOP. ADD CONDIMENTS.

MY WIFE GIVES SOUND ADVICE, ALTHOUGH MOST OF IT TENDS TO BE SOUND RATHER THAN ADVICE.

SENATE SALAD BOWL

I CUP	TORN ICEBERG LETTUCE LEAVES	250 ML
I CUP	TORN ROMAINE LETTUCE	250 ML
1/2 CUP	WATERCRESS, STEMS REMOVED	125 ML
I CUP	DICED CELERY	250 ML
1/4 CUP	CHOPPED GREEN ONION	60 ML
1 1/2 CUPS	CUBED COOKED LOBSTER OR SHRIMP	375 ML
2	MEDIUM TOMATOES, DICED	2
1	AVOCADO, PEELED AND SLICED	1
1/2	MEDIUM GRAPEFRUIT, SECTIONED	1/2
5	LARGE PITTED RIPE OLIVES, SLICED	5
1/4 CUP	LEMON JUICE, FRESH, FROZEN OR CANNED	60 ML

CREAM DRESSING

I CUP	CREAMED COTTAGE CHEESE	250 ML
1/4 TSP	SALT	I ML
1/4 CUP	SOUR CREAM	50 ML
PINCH	BLACK PEPPER	PINCH

TOSS TOGETHER FIRST FIVE INGREDIENTS IN LARGE SALAD BOWL. COMBINE NEXT FIVE INGREDIENTS, SPRINKLE ALL WITH LEMON JUICE AND ADD TO GREENS. GARNISH WITH ADDITIONAL TOMATO SLICES AND RIPE OLIVES. REFRIGERATE UNTIL WELL CHILLED. MEANWHILE, MAKE DRESSING: COMBINE ALL INGREDIENTS IN BLENDER OR MIXING BOWL AND BEAT UNTIL CREAMY SMOOTH. POUR OVER SALAD JUST BEFORE SERVING. SERVES 4.

GREEN GODDESS SALAD

THE NAME SAYS IT ALL!

DRESSING

1	CLOVE GARLIC, MINCED	1
1/2 TSP	SALT	2 ML
1/2 TSP	DRY MUSTARD	2 ML
1 TSP	WORCESTERSHIRE SAUCE	5 ML
1 TBSP	GREEN ONION, CHOPPED	15 ML
1 CUP	MAYONNAISE	250 ML
1/2 CUP	SOUR CREAM	125 ML
PINCH	BLACK PEPPER	PINCH

SALAD

1	HEAD LETTUCE	1
2 TSP	ANCHOVIES, CHOPPED	10 ML
1 TBSP	CHOPPED PARSLEY	15 ML
1 CUP	SHRIMP OR CRAB, COOKED	250 ML
2	TOMATOES, QUARTERED	2

MIX INGREDIENTS FOR DRESSING TOGETHER AND CHILL.
PREPARE SALAD AND TOSS GENTLY. POUR DRESSING OVER
SALAD AND TOSS AGAIN, COATING WELL. DELICIOUS SERVED
WITH A BUFFET OR LUNCHEON ALONG WITH WARM ROLLS.
SERVES 4 TO 6.

FROSTED WALDORF SALAD

2 CUPS	MINIATURE MARSHMALLOWS	500 ML
3 to 4 CUPS	GREEN GRAPES, SEEDLESS IF AVAILABLE; IF NOT, REMOVE SEEDS	750 ML to 1 L
2 to 3	UNPEELED CHOPPED RED APPLES	2 to 3
1	PEELED ORANGE, OR 1 CAN (10 OZ/284 ML) MANDARIN ORANGES, DRAINED (RESERVE JUICE TO COAT APPLES)	1
1 TBSP	ORANGE JUICE	15 ML

TOSS TOGETHER TO PREVENT APPLES FROM DISCOLORING, THEN ADD:

1/2 CUP	CHOPPED CELERY	125 ML
1/2 CUP	CHOPPED WALNUTS OR PECANS	125 ML
1/2 CUP	SEEDLESS RAISINS, OR SNIPPED DATES (OPTIONAL)	125 ML

IN A BOWL, COMBINE:

1 CUP	HEAVY OR WHIPPING (35%) CREAM, WHIPPED (OR WHIPPED TOPPING)	250 ML
1/2 CUP	MAYONNAISE	125 ML
1 TBSP	GRANULATED SUGAR	15 ML

COMBINE ALL INGREDIENTS. SERVE IN LETTUCE-LINED GLASS BOWL OR ON INDIVIDUAL SERVING PLATES, ALONG WITH WARM BUTTERED ROLLS. GARNISH WITH ADDITIONAL GREEN GRAPE CLUSTERS, WASHED, AND WHILE DAMP, DIP IN GRANULATED SUGAR. SERVES 8 TO 10.

SHRIMP LOUIS SALAD

LADIES LOVE SALADS AT NOON AND THIS
SHOULD PROVE TO BE A POPULAR ONE.

CREAMY MAKE-AHEAD DRESSING

1 CUP	CREAM-STYLE COTTAGE CHEESE	250 ML
1	HARD-COOKED EGG, PEELED AND HALVED	1
1/4 CUP	TOMATO JUICE	60 ML
1 TSP	PREPARED MUSTARD	5 ML

SALAD

1 LB	SHRIMP, COOKED, PEELED AND DEVEINED	500 G
1	LARGE RIPE AVOCADO, PEELED AND SLICED	1
1	CUCUMBER, WASHED AND UNPEELED, SLICED	1
1	LARGE HEAD OF ROMAINE LETTUCE	1
1	CAN (7 1/2 OZ/213 ML) RIPE OLIVES, HALVED	1

DRESSING: COMBINE COTTAGE CHEESE, EGG, TOMATO JUICE AND MUSTARD IN CONTAINER OF ELECTRIC BLENDER. WHIRL UNTIL SMOOTH. COVER AND CHILL UNTIL SERVING TIME. MAKES 1 1/3 CUPS (325 ML).

SALAD: COMBINE SHRIMP, AVOCADO, CUCUMBER, OLIVES AND LETTUCE IN LARGE SALAD BOWL. TOSS GENTLY AND POUR CHILLED DRESSING OVER. TOSS AGAIN UNTIL WELL MIXED. ACCOMPANY SALAD WITH A LIGHT CHILLED WHITE WINE AND HOT ROLLS. YUMMY! SERVES 8.

COBB SALAD

THIS SUBSTANTIAL SALAD, MADE FAMOUS AT HOLLYWOOD'S BROWN DERBY IN THE 1930S, HAS REMAINED A FAVORITE OVER THE YEARS.

DRESSING

1/3 CUP	OLIVE OIL	75 ML
2 TBSP	RED WINE VINEGAR	30 ML
2 TSP	WHOLE-SEED MUSTARD	10 ML
1/2 TSP	DRIED TARRAGON LEAVES	2 ML
1/2 TSP	SALT	2 ML
1/4 TSP	FRESHLY GROUND BLACK PEPPER	1 ML

SALAD

8 CUPS	BABY SALAD GREENS	2 L
1 1/2 CUPS	DICED COOKED CHICKEN	375 ML
2	RIPE BUT FIRM TOMATOES, SEEDED AND DICED	2
1	HASS AVOCADO, PEELED AND CUT INTO SLICES	1
2	HARD-COOKED EGGS, SLICED (SEE TIP, OPPOSITE)	2
6	SLICES BACON, COOKED CRISP AND CRUMBLED	6
3/4 CUP	CRUMBLED BLUE CHEESE	175 ML
2 TBSP	CHOPPED FRESH CHIVES	30 ML

DRESSING: IN A BOWL, WHISK TOGETHER OLIVE OIL, VINEGAR, MUSTARD, TARRAGON, SALT AND PEPPER.

SALAD: PLACE SALAD GREENS IN A LARGE, WIDE, SHALLOW SALAD OR SERVING BOWL. POUR HALF OF THE DRESSING OVER GREENS AND TOSS TO COAT WELL. LAYER WITH CHICKEN, TOMATO, AVOCADO, EGG, BACON BITS AND

BLUE CHEESE. SPRINKLE WITH CHIVES AND DRIZZLE WITH REMAINING DRESSING. SERVE IMMEDIATELY. SERVES 4.

TIP: TO HARD-COOK EGGS, PLACE EGGS IN A SAUCEPAN AND ADD COLD WATER TO COVER EGGS BY 1 INCH (2.5 CM). BRING TO A GENTLE ROLLING BOIL OVER MEDIUM-HIGH HEAT. BOIL FOR 2 MINUTES, THEN COVER AND REMOVE FROM HEAT. LET STAND FOR 10 MINUTES. DRAIN AND CHILL EGGS IN COLD WATER.

CRAB AND DEVILED EGG SANDWICHES

1	CAN (6$\frac{1}{2}$ OZ/184 G) CRABMEAT	1
2	HARD-COOKED EGGS	2
$\frac{1}{2}$ TSP	PREPARED MUSTARD	2 ML
2 TBSP	MAYONNAISE	30 ML
1 TBSP	LEMON JUICE	15 ML
$\frac{1}{2}$ TSP	CURRY POWDER	2 ML

DRAIN CRABMEAT. MIX WITH OTHER INGREDIENTS. LOBSTER OR CHICKEN MAY BE USED. SERVE IN SMALL BUNS.
SERVES 2 TO 4.

DON'T BITE YOUR NAILS, ESPECIALLY IF YOU'RE A CARPENTER.

SMOKED SALMON AND WATERCRESS TEA SANDWICHES

5 OZ	SMOKED SALMON, COARSELY CHOPPED	150 G
4 OZ	LIGHT CREAM CHEESE, SOFTENED	125 G
2 TSP	FRESHLY SQUEEZED LEMON JUICE	10 ML
1 TSP	WORCESTERSHIRE SAUCE	5 ML
	HOT PEPPER SAUCE	
8	THIN SLICES PUMPERNICKEL OR WHOLE-GRAIN BREAD	8
2 TBSP	BUTTER (APPROX.), SOFTENED	30 ML
1	BUNCH WATERCRESS, LARGE STEMS REMOVED	1

IN A FOOD PROCESSOR, COMBINE SALMON, CREAM CHEESE, LEMON JUICE, WORCESTERSHIRE SAUCE AND HOT PEPPER SAUCE TO TASTE. PROCESS UNTIL SMOOTH. (IF PREPARING AHEAD, TRANSFER TO A BOWL, COVER AND REFRIGERATE.) SPREAD BREAD LIGHTLY WITH BUTTER. SPREAD SALMON MIXTURE THINLY ON BREAD SLICES. ARRANGE WATERCRESS SPRIGS ON TOP OF THE SALMON. TOP WITH REMAINING BREAD SLICES, PRESSING TOGETHER LIGHTLY. TRIM OFF CRUSTS AND CUT SANDWICHES INTO QUARTERS (EITHER SQUARES OR TRIANGLES). ARRANGE ON A SERVING PLATTER AND GARNISH WITH WATERCRESS. MAKES 16 SANDWICH PIECES.

VARIATION: INSTEAD OF WATERCRESS, USE CUCUMBER SLICES AND FRESH DILL SPRIGS.

SHRIMP SANDWICHES

*THESE ARE ALWAYS A HIT AND REALLY FILLING.
(HAVE YOU TRIED ALFALFA SPROUTS ON A
PEANUT BUTTER SANDWICH?)*

2	SLICES 7-GRAIN BREAD, BUTTERED	2
1/2 CUP	COOKED FROZEN BABY SHRIMP, THAWED AND RINSED	125 ML
1/4 CUP	ALFALFA SPROUTS	50 ML
1/2	AVOCADO, SLICED	1/2
	LEMON JUICE	
	MAYONNAISE	

PLACE SHRIMP ON ONE BUTTERED BREAD SLICE. TOP WITH
SPROUTS AND PLACE AVOCADO SLICES OVER ALL. SPRINKLE
LIBERALLY WITH FRESHLY SQUEEZED LEMON JUICE.
SPREAD MAYONNAISE ON SECOND SLICE OF BREAD AND
PLACE ON TOP OF AVOCADO. SLICE DIAGONALLY. SERVES 1.

SEAFOOD SALAD SANDWICHES

1	PACKAGE (8 OZ/250 G) CREAM CHEESE	1
1	CAN (6 1/2 OZ/184 G) SMALL SHRIMP	1
1	CAN (6 1/2 OZ/184 G) CRABMEAT	1

SOFTEN CHEESE AND ADD SEAFOOD. SPREAD ON
WARM HOLLAND RUSKS. TOP WITH SLICE OF TOMATO
AND CHEDDAR CHEESE. HEAT IN MODERATE OVEN UNTIL
CHEESE IS MELTED (15 TO 20 MINUTES). SERVES 8.

RENÉ'S SANDWICH LOAF

PUTTIN' ON THE RITZ!

1	PACKAGE (8 OZ/250 G) CREAM CHEESE	1
1 TBSP	MILK	15 ML
	UNSLICED SANDWICH LOAF, SLIGHTLY FROZEN	

HAM FILLING

1 CUP	GROUND COOKED HAM	250 ML
2 TBSP	PICKLE RELISH, DRAINED	30 ML
1/2 TSP	HORSERADISH	2 ML
1/3 CUP	FINELY CHOPPED CELERY	75 ML
1/4 CUP	MAYONNAISE	50 ML

ASPARAGUS TIP FILLING

	CHEEZ WHIZ	
1	CAN ASPARAGUS TIPS, DRAINED	1

EGG FILLING

4	HARD-COOKED EGGS, CHOPPED	4
2 TBSP	FINELY CHOPPED GREEN ONIONS	25 ML
1/2 TSP	PREPARED MUSTARD	2 ML
1/4 CUP	MAYONNAISE	60 ML
	SALT AND BLACK PEPPER TO TASTE	
	CHOPPED FRESH PARSLEY	
	PIMENTO-STUFFED OLIVES	

IN A SMALL BOWL, BEAT CREAM CHEESE WITH MILK UNTIL FLUFFY. SET ASIDE. TRIM CRUSTS FROM SANDWICH LOAF AND SLICE BREAD LENGTHWISE IN 4 EQUAL LAYERS. BUTTER EACH SLICE. SPREAD FIRST LAYER WITH HAM FILLING, SECOND LAYER WITH CHEEZ WHIZ; TOP WITH ASPARAGUS, AND THIRD LAYER WITH EGG FILLING. FROST

TOP SLICE AND SIDES OF LOAF WITH CREAM CHEESE.
SPRINKLE WITH PARSLEY AND GARNISH WITH OLIVES.
SERVES 8 TO 10.

STUFFED HAM LOAF

1	LOAF UNSLICED ITALIAN BREAD	1
1/4 CUP	MAYONNAISE OR SALAD DRESSING	60 ML
1/3 CUP	CHOPPED PARSLEY	75 ML
1	PACKAGE (8 OZ/250 G) CREAM CHEESE	1
3/4 CUP	CELERY, FINELY CHOPPED	175 ML
1/2 CUP	SHREDDED CHEDDAR CHEESE	125 ML
2 TBSP	ONION, FINELY CHOPPED	30 ML
1/4 TSP	SALT	1 ML
1	LARGE DILL PICKLE	1
2	PACKAGES (EACH 4 OZ/125 G) HAM (8 SLICES)	2

CUT BREAD LENGTHWISE; HOLLOW OUT EACH HALF
WITH FORK, LEAVING 1/2-INCH (1 CM) THICK SHELL (SAVE
INSIDES FOR BREAD CRUMBS). SPREAD MAYONNAISE OVER
HOLLOWS; SPRINKLE PARSLEY OVER MAYONNAISE. BLEND
CREAM CHEESE, CELERY, CHEDDAR CHEESE, ONION AND
SALT AND SPOON INTO BREAD HALVES, PACKING DOWN
WELL WITH BACK OF SPOON. LEAVE A SMALL HOLLOW
DOWN THE CENTER. QUARTER PICKLE LENGTHWISE.
ROLL EACH QUARTER INSIDE A DOUBLE THICK SLICE OF
HAM. PLACE ROLLS, END TO END, IN CENTER OF HALF OF
BREAD AND TOP WITH OTHER HALF. WRAP LOAF TIGHTLY
IN PLASTIC WRAP. CHILL SEVERAL HOURS. TO SERVE, CUT
INTO 16 SLICES. SERVES 8.

DEVILED CORN

GOOD FOR BUFFETS AND GOES WITH PRACTICALLY EVERYTHING.

1/4 CUP	BUTTER	60 ML
2 TBSP	FLOUR	30 ML
1 TSP	DRY MUSTARD	5 ML
1 TBSP	LEMON JUICE	15 ML
1/2 TSP	SALT	2 ML
PINCH	BLACK PEPPER	PINCH
1/2 CUP	MILK	125 ML
3	SLICES BACON, COOKED AND CRUMBLED	3
2	HARD-COOKED EGGS, CHOPPED	2
1	CAN (14 OZ/398 ML) CORN KERNELS, DRAINED	1
1	CAN (14 OZ/398 ML) CREAMED CORN	1
1/2 CUP	GRATED PARMESAN CHEESE	125 ML
1/2 CUP	CRACKER CRUMBS	125 ML
1 TBSP	BUTTER, MELTED	15 ML
2	HARD-COOKED EGGS, SLICED	2
	SLICED RIPE OLIVES, PITTED	

IN LARGE SAUCEPAN, MELT BUTTER AND ADD FLOUR, MUSTARD, LEMON JUICE, SALT AND PEPPER. MIX WELL. ADD MILK AND STIR UNTIL THICK AND BUBBLY. REMOVE PAN FROM HEAT AND STIR IN BACON, CHOPPED EGGS AND BOTH CANS OF CORN. SPOON INTO 6-CUP (1.5 L) CASSEROLE AND SPRINKLE WITH PARMESAN CHEESE. COMBINE CRUMBS AND MELTED BUTTER AND SPRINKLE OVER CHEESE. BAKE AT 350°F (180°C) FOR 45 MINUTES. GARNISH WITH EGGS AND OLIVES. SERVES 6.

BAKED CRAB CASSEROLE

1/2 CUP	CURRANTS	125 ML
1 CUP	CELERY, CHOPPED FINE	250 ML
1/2 CUP	CHOPPED PEELED APPLE	125 ML
2 TBSP	FLOUR	30 ML
1/3 CUP	BUTTER	75 ML
	CURRY POWDER (ADD AS DESIRED)	
1 CUP	MILK	250 ML
	SALT AND BLACK PEPPER TO TASTE	
3 CUPS	HOT COOKED RICE	750 ML
1 LB	CRABMEAT	500 G
1/2 CUP	CRUSHED CANNED FRIED ONION RINGS	125 ML

COOK CURRANTS, CELERY AND APPLE IN SMALL AMOUNT OF WATER UNTIL SOFT. MAKE SAUCE WITH FLOUR, BUTTER AND CURRY POWDER, MELTING BUTTER AND ADDING FLOUR AND THE AMOUNT OF CURRY POWDER DESIRED. ADD MILK STIRRING CONSTANTLY. WHEN THICKENED ADD CURRANTS, CELERY AND APPLE. SALT AND PEPPER TO TASTE. PLACE COOKED RICE IN BUTTERED CASSEROLE. MIX CRABMEAT WITH SAUCE MIXTURE. POUR OVER RICE. TOP WITH CRUSHED ONIONS. PLACE IN 375°F (190°C) OVEN AND COOK 25 MINUTES. SERVES 6.

DON'T DO ANYTHING THAT YOU'RE NOT PREPARED TO EXPLAIN TO A PARAMEDIC.

TUNA NOODLE BAKE WITH CHEDDAR CRUMB TOPPING

THIS RECIPE TAKES AN OLD STANDBY TO NEW HEIGHTS. WHAT'S GREAT, TOO, IS THAT IT KEEPS WELL IN THE FRIDGE FOR UP TO 2 DAYS BEFORE BAKING.

I TBSP	BUTTER	15 ML
8 OZ	MUSHROOMS, SLICED	250 G
3/4 CUP	CHOPPED GREEN ONIONS	175 ML
2 TBSP	ALL-PURPOSE FLOUR	30 ML
I	CAN (10 OZ/284 ML) CHICKEN BROTH, UNDILUTED	I
I CUP	MILK	250 ML
4 OZ	CREAM CHEESE, SOFTENED	125 G
I	CAN (6 OZ/170 G) SOLID WHITE TUNA, DRAINED AND FLAKED	I
I CUP	FROZEN PEAS	250 ML
8 OZ	BROAD EGG NOODLES	250 G
1/2 CUP	DRY BREAD CRUMBS	125 ML
2 TBSP	MELTED BUTTER	30 ML
I CUP	SHREDDED CHEDDAR CHEESE	250 ML

PREHEAT OVEN TO 350°F (180°C) AND LIGHTLY GREASE A 13- BY 9-INCH (33 BY 23 CM) CASSEROLE DISH. IN A SAUCEPAN, MELT BUTTER OVER MEDIUM HEAT. ADD MUSHROOMS AND GREEN ONIONS; COOK, STIRRING, FOR 3 MINUTES OR UNTIL SOFTENED. BLEND IN FLOUR; POUR IN BROTH AND MILK. BRING TO A BOIL, STIRRING CONSTANTLY, UNTIL SLIGHTLY THICKENED. STIR IN CREAM CHEESE UNTIL MELTED. ADD TUNA AND PEAS; COOK 2 MINUTES MORE OR UNTIL HEATED THROUGH. REMOVE FROM HEAT. COOK NOODLES IN A LARGE POT

OF BOILING WATER UNTIL TENDER BUT STILL FIRM. DRAIN
WELL. STIR NOODLES INTO SAUCE. SPOON INTO PREPARED
CASSEROLE DISH.

IN A BOWL, TOSS BREAD CRUMBS WITH MELTED
BUTTER; ADD CHEDDAR CHEESE. JUST BEFORE BAKING,
SPRINKLE TOPPING OVER NOODLES. BAKE FOR ABOUT
30 MINUTES (10 MINUTES LONGER IF REFRIGERATED) OR
UNTIL TOP IS GOLDEN. SERVES 4 TO 6.

TIP: TO MAKE AHEAD, COOK NOODLES, RINSE UNDER COLD
WATER TO CHILL; DRAIN. COMBINE COLD NOODLES AND
COLD SAUCE; SPOON INTO CASSEROLE DISH, COVER AND
REFRIGERATE. ADD CRUMB TOPPING JUST BEFORE BAKING
TO PREVENT IT FROM GETTING SOGGY.

RELY ON THE RABBIT'S FOOT IF YOU MUST,
BUT REMEMBER IT DIDN'T WORK FOR THE RABBIT.

CAJUN CRAB CAKES
WITH HERB DIPPING SAUCE

ALWAYS A POPULAR HIT WHEN ENTERTAINING — WATCH THESE TASTY CRAB CAKES DISAPPEAR!

HERB DIPPING SAUCE

1/2 CUP	LIGHT MAYONNAISE	125 ML
1/2 CUP	SOUR CREAM	125 ML
2 TSP	WHOLE-SEED MUSTARD	10 ML
2 TSP	FRESH LEMON JUICE	10 ML
2 TBSP	FINELY CHOPPED FRESH FLAT-LEAF (ITALIAN) PARSLEY	30 ML
2 TBSP	FINELY CHOPPED FRESH CHIVES	30 ML
	HOT PEPPER SAUCE	

CRAB CAKES

1	EGG	1
1/4 CUP	LIGHT MAYONNAISE	60 ML
1 TBSP	DIJON MUSTARD	15 ML
2 TSP	CAJUN SPICE	10 ML
1 TSP	WORCESTERSHIRE SAUCE	5 ML
1 LB	CRABMEAT, SQUEEZED DRY	500 G
3	GREEN ONIONS, FINELY CHOPPED	3
1/2 CUP	MINCED RED BELL PEPPER	125 ML
1/2 CUP	MINCED CELERY	125 ML
1 1/2 CUPS	SOFT FRESH BREAD CRUMBS	375 ML
1 CUP	FINELY CRUSHED FLAVORED BAKED TORTILLA OR CORN CHIPS	250 ML
1/4 CUP	OLIVE OIL (APPROX.)	60 ML

HERB DIPPING SAUCE: IN A BOWL, COMBINE MAYONNAISE, SOUR CREAM, MUSTARD, LEMON JUICE, PARSLEY AND CHIVES. SEASON WITH HOT PEPPER SAUCE TO TASTE. SET ASIDE.

CRAB CAKES: IN A BOWL, BEAT EGG; ADD MAYONNAISE, MUSTARD, CAJUN SPICE AND WORCESTERSHIRE SAUCE. STIR IN CRABMEAT, GREEN ONIONS, RED PEPPER AND CELERY. STIR IN BREAD CRUMBS. SHAPE HEAPING TABLESPOONS (15 ML) INTO 2-INCH (5 CM) PATTIES. PLACE CRUSHED TORTILLA CHIPS IN SHALLOW BOWL AND COAT PATTIES ON BOTH SIDES WITH CRUMBS. PLACE ON A BAKING SHEET LINED WITH WAXED PAPER.

IN A LARGE NONSTICK SKILLET, HEAT HALF OF THE OIL OVER MEDIUM-HIGH HEAT. FRY CRAB CAKES IN BATCHES, ADDING MORE OIL IF NEEDED, FOR 2 MINUTES PER SIDE OR UNTIL GOLDEN. ACCOMPANY WITH HERB DIPPING SAUCE. MAKES ABOUT 30 APPETIZERS.

TIP: TO PREVENT SOGGY CRAB CAKES, MAKE SURE TO SQUEEZE CRABMEAT OF EXCESS MOISTURE.

TIP: TO MAKE AHEAD, PREPARE CRAB CAKES AS DIRECTED IN RECIPE. LET COOL, PLACE ON GREASED BAKING SHEET, COVER AND REFRIGERATE. TO REHEAT, PLACE IN PREHEATED 400°F (200°C) OVEN FOR 8 TO 10 MINUTES.

VARIATION: ANY FLAVORED CRISPY TORTILLA OR CHIP-STYLE CRACKER CAN BE USED. TRY BARBECUE, JALAPEÑO OR ANY OTHER SPICY-FLAVORED VARIETIES.

SEAFOOD SCALLOP SHELLS

A PERFECT MAKE-AHEAD. ALL INGREDIENTS CAN BE COMBINED, PLACED IN SHELLS AND FROZEN WITHOUT COOKING. JUST THAW AND BAKE TO SERVE.

1	CAN (10 OZ/284 ML) CREAM OF CELERY SOUP		1
1/4 CUP	MILK	60 ML	
1	BEATEN EGG		1
1/4 CUP	PARMESAN CHEESE	60 ML	
1	CAN (5 OZ/142 G) CRABMEAT, FLAKED		1
1	CAN (4 1/4 OZ/120 G) SHRIMP, RINSED AND DRAINED		1
1	CAN (10 OZ/284 ML) SLICED MUSHROOMS, DRAINED		1
1/4 CUP	FINE BREAD CRUMBS	60 ML	
1 TBSP	MELTED BUTTER	15 ML	

COMBINE SOUP, MILK, BEATEN EGG AND 2 TBSP (30 ML) CHEESE IN SAUCEPAN. STIR OVER LOW HEAT TILL HOT. ADD SEAFOOD AND MUSHROOMS. SPOON INTO ONE LARGE CASSEROLE OR FOUR LARGE SHELLS. MELT BUTTER. ADD LAST 2 TBSP (30 ML) CHEESE AND BREAD CRUMBS. SPRINKLE OVER SEAFOOD MIXTURE. BAKE AT 375°F (190°C) FOR 30 MINUTES. SERVES 4.

THIS RECIPE MAY BE DOUBLED.

NEVER BUY A DVD ON THE STREET FROM SOMEONE WHO IS OUT OF BREATH.

CREAMED SEAFOOD

*A TASTY DISH TO SERVE TO THE LADIES FOR
LUNCH OR BRIDGE THAT CAN BE REHEATED.*

1½ CUPS	SLICED FRESH MUSHROOMS	375 ML
6 TBSP	BUTTER, DIVIDED	90 ML
¼ CUP	FLOUR	60 ML
2 CUPS	MILK	500 ML
½ CUP	SHERRY	125 ML
1 LB	SMALL COOKED SHRIMP, KING CRAB OR LOBSTER	500 G
1 TBSP	CHOPPED FRESH PARSLEY	15 ML
	SALT AND BLACK PEPPER TO TASTE	
8	PATTY SHELLS (PEPPERIDGE FARM FROZEN PATTY SHELLS ARE SUPER — RIGHT THERE IN YOUR FREEZER AND THEY NEVER FAIL!)	8

BROWN MUSHROOMS IN 2 TBSP (30 ML) BUTTER. PREPARE
WHITE SAUCE: MELT REMAINING BUTTER OVER LOW HEAT.
ADD AND BLEND FLOUR; COOK AT LEAST 3 MINUTES.
STIR IN MILK SLOWLY. CONTINUE STIRRING TILL SAUCE
IS SMOOTH AND THICKENED. ADD SHERRY. ADD SEAFOOD,
COOKED MUSHROOMS AND PARSLEY. SEASON WITH
SALT AND PEPPER. HEAT THROUGH. SERVE OVER PATTY
SHELLS AND GARNISH WITH A SPRIG OF PARSLEY, RIPE
OLIVES, CARROT CURLS AND CELERY STICKS. TO REHEAT,
PLACE OVER DOUBLE BOILER. SERVES 8.

BEST SEAFOOD LASAGNA

A TASTY VARIATION OF AN OLD FAVORITE.

8	LASAGNA NOODLES	8
1 CUP	CHOPPED ONION	250 ML
2 TBSP	BUTTER	30 ML
1	PACKAGE (8 OZ/250 G) CREAM CHEESE, SOFTENED	1
1 1/2 CUPS	RICOTTA CHEESE	375 ML
1	EGG, BEATEN	1
2 TSP	BASIL	10 ML
1/2 TSP	SALT	2 ML
1/8 TSP	BLACK PEPPER	0.5 ML
2	CANS (EACH 10 OZ/284 ML) CREAM OF MUSHROOM SOUP	2
1/3 CUP	DRY WHITE WINE OR DRY VERMOUTH	75 ML
5 OZ	CRABMEAT	150 G
1 LB	SHRIMP, DEVEINED AND COOKED	500 G
1/4 CUP	GRATED PARMESAN CHEESE	50 ML
1/2 CUP	SHREDDED SHARP (OLD) CHEDDAR CHEESE	125 ML

COOK NOODLES. PLACE 4 NOODLES IN A 13- BY 9-INCH (33 BY 23 CM) BAKING DISH. COOK ONION IN BUTTER. ADD CHEESES, EGG, BASIL, SALT AND PEPPER. SPREAD HALF THE CHEESE MIXTURE OVER NOODLES. COMBINE SOUP AND WINE. STIR IN CRAB AND SHRIMP AND SPREAD HALF OVER CHEESE LAYER. REPEAT ALL LAYERS. SPRINKLE WITH PARMESAN AND CHEDDAR. BAKE, UNCOVERED, AT 350°F (180°C) FOR 45 MINUTES. LET STAND 15 MINUTES BEFORE SERVING. SERVES 8 TO 10. FREEZES WELL.

LASAGNA

EVERYONE HAS A LASAGNA RECIPE,
BUT THIS IS OUR FAVORITE.

$1\frac{1}{2}$ LBS	GROUND BEEF	750 G
1	CAN (28 OZ/796 ML) TOMATOES	1
1	CAN (14 OZ/398 ML) SEASONED TOMATO SAUCE	1
2	ENVELOPES SPAGHETTI SAUCE MIX	2
2	CLOVES GARLIC, MINCED	2
8 OZ	LASAGNA OR BREAD NOODLES	250 G
2	PACKAGES (EACH 6 OR 8 OZ/175 OR 250 G) THINLY SLICED MOZZARELLA CHEESE	2
1 CUP	CREAMED COTTAGE CHEESE	250 ML
$\frac{1}{2}$ CUP	GRATED PARMESAN CHEESE	125 ML

BROWN MEAT SLOWLY; DRAIN OFF EXCESS FAT. ADD NEXT
FOUR INGREDIENTS. COVER AND SIMMER 40 MINUTES,
STIRRING OCCASIONALLY. SALT TO TASTE. COOK NOODLES
IN BOILING SALTED WATER UNTIL TENDER, FOLLOWING
PACKAGE INSTRUCTIONS. DRAIN. RINSE IN COLD WATER.
PLACE HALF THE NOODLES IN 13- BY 9-INCH (33 BY 23 CM)
BAKING DISH. COVER WITH ONE-THIRD OF THE SAUCE,
THEN LAYER HALF THE MOZZARELLA AND HALF THE
COTTAGE CHEESE. REPEAT LAYERS, ENDING WITH SAUCE.
TOP WITH PARMESAN.

BAKE AT 350°F (180°C) FOR 25 TO 30 MINUTES. LET
STAND 15 MINUTES. CUT IN SQUARES. SERVE WITH
GREEN SALAD AND FRENCH BREAD. SERVES 6 TO 8.

CANNELLONI

PREPARE MINDLESS MEAT SAUCE (SEE PAGE 119)
AND CHICKEN FILLING AHEAD OF TIME AND THIS WILL
SEEM EFFORTLESS. REGARDLESS, THE RESULTS
ARE WORTH THE TIME INVOLVED.

CHICKEN FILLING

3	LARGE CHICKEN BREASTS, COOKED IN OVEN, RESERVE 1/2 CUP (125 ML) PAN JUICES FOR FILLING	3
2 TBSP	OIL	30 ML
1/4 CUP	MINCED ONION	60 ML
1/4 CUP	FINELY CHOPPED CELERY	60 ML
1/4 CUP	FINELY CHOPPED CARROT	60 ML
2 TBSP	MINCED PARSLEY	30 ML
2	EGG YOLKS	2
1/2 CUP	FRESHLY GROUND PARMESAN CHEESE	125 ML
1 CUP	RICOTTA OR CREAMED COTTAGE CHEESE	250 ML
3/4 TSP	SALT	3 ML
1/4 TSP	EACH DRIED OREGANO AND BASIL	1 ML
1/8 TSP	GROUND NUTMEG	0.5 ML
1/2 TSP	WHITE PEPPER	2 ML
1/2 CUP	CHICKEN BROTH	125 ML

CHEDDAR SAUCE

1/4 CUP	MELTED BUTTER	60 ML
5 TBSP	FLOUR	75 ML
1	CAN (10 OZ/284 ML) CHICKEN BROTH	1
	SALT AND BLACK PEPPER TO TASTE	
1 CUP	GRATED CHEDDAR CHEESE	250 ML
1 CUP	MINDLESS MEAT SAUCE (PAGE 119)	250 ML
1/2 CUP	LIGHT (5%) CREAM	125 ML

1	PACKAGE KNORR'S SWISS HOLLANDAISE SAUCE OR YOUR OWN RECIPE	1
3	PACKAGES (EACH 6 OZ/175 G) MONTEREY JACK CHEESE	3
20	CANNELLONI SHELLS, OR 20 CRÊPES (SEE PAGE 36)	20

CHICKEN FILLING: COOK CHICKEN AND FINELY CHOP OR GRIND MEAT. COMBINE OIL, ONION, CELERY, CARROTS AND PARSLEY IN SAUCEPAN AND COOK FOR 10 MINUTES. BEAT EGG YOLKS IN LARGE BOWL, ADD PARMESAN CHEESE AND RICOTTA OR COTTAGE CHEESE AND BEAT UNTIL SMOOTH. ADD SALT, OREGANO, BASIL, NUTMEG AND PEPPER. ADD CHICKEN, PAN JUICE AND CHICKEN BROTH. BEAT UNTIL WELL MIXED. THIS MAY BE COVERED AND REFRIGERATED OR FROZEN UNTIL READY TO USE.

CHEDDAR SAUCE: MELT BUTTER IN SAUCEPAN, ADD FLOUR UNTIL SMOOTH, THEN CAREFULLY ADD CHICKEN BROTH, STIRRING CONSTANTLY. ADD SALT AND PEPPER TO TASTE. STIR IN CHEDDAR CHEESE UNTIL WELL BLENDED AND THICK. NOW ADD PREPARED MEAT SAUCE AND CREAM. (SEE PAGE 119 FOR MINDLESS MEAT SAUCE.)

HOLLANDAISE SAUCE: PREPARE YOUR OWN OR COOK ACCORDING TO PACKAGE INSTRUCTIONS. ADD TO CHEDDAR SAUCE.

COOK CANNELLONI SHELLS IN BOILING SALTED WATER FOR 8 MINUTES, DRAIN AND RINSE IN COLD WATER, OR HAVE CRÊPES PREPARED. DON'T BE CONCERNED IF SHELLS SPLIT. IT MAKES THEM EASIER TO FILL.

CONTINUED ON NEXT PAGE...

SPOON THIN LAYER OF SAUCE IN TWO 13- BY 9-INCH (33 BY 23 CM) PANS. USING APPROXIMATELY 2 TBSP (30 ML) CHICKEN FILLING PER SHELL, SHAPE FILLING IN HANDS AND INSERT IN SHELL OR ROLL UP IN SHELL OR CRÊPE. PLACE IN PANS, SIDE BY SIDE, WITH 5 IN EACH ROW. CAREFULLY SPOON SAUCE AROUND CANNELLONI. COVER EACH CANNELLONI COMPLETELY WITH STRIPS OF MONTEREY JACK CHEESE. YOU REALLY CAN'T USE TOO MUCH. BAKE IN PREHEATED 425°F (220°C) OVEN FOR 10 MINUTES, UNTIL CHEESE IS BUBBLING. SERVE AT ONCE. MAKES 20 CANNELLONI, OR 10 SERVINGS.

NOTE: IF YOU'RE MAKING THE ENTIRE RECIPE IN ADVANCE, PREPARE TO THE BAKING STAGE AND FREEZE. AS THIS IS A RICH MEAL, SERVE WITH A GREEN SALAD AND ROLLS.

WHATEVER YOU DO, ALWAYS GIVE 100% — UNLESS YOU'RE DONATING BLOOD.

MINDLESS MEAT SAUCE

MINDLESS, BECAUSE OF ITS SIMPLICITY.

1 1/2 LBS	LEAN GROUND BEEF	750 G
1/4 TSP	DRIED SAGE	1 ML
1/4 TSP	DRIED OREGANO	1 ML
1 TBSP	SALT	15 ML
1/2 TSP	BLACK PEPPER	2 ML
1	MEDIUM ONION, FINELY CHOPPED	1
15	LARGE MUSHROOMS, FINELY CHOPPED	15
3	CLOVES GARLIC, MINCED	3
1	CAN (28 OZ/796 ML) TOMATOES, CHOPPED, WITH JUICE	1
1	CAN (10 OZ/284 ML) TOMATO SAUCE	1
1	CAN (5 1/2 OZ/156 ML) TOMATO PASTE	1

PREHEAT OVEN TO 350°F (180°C). IN LARGE ROASTING PAN, SPREAD GROUND BEEF. COOK FOR 30 MINUTES, STIRRING OCCASIONALLY TO SEPARATE. MEANWHILE, COMBINE SAGE, OREGANO, SALT, PEPPER, ONION, MUSHROOMS AND GARLIC IN SAUCEPAN AND COOK AT MEDIUM HEAT UNTIL ONIONS ARE TRANSPARENT. SPREAD OVER MEAT AND CONTINUE COOKING IN OVEN FOR 15 MINUTES MORE. REMOVE FROM OVEN AND ADD CANNED TOMATOES, TOMATO SAUCE AND PASTE. BRING TO BOIL, THEN SIMMER FOR 1 HOUR OR LONGER. ADD SALT TO TASTE. STORE IN CONTAINERS AND FREEZE. USE IT IN ANY RECIPE CALLING FOR MEAT SAUCE, SUCH AS SPAGHETTI, LASAGNA OR CANNELLONI. SERVES 6.

HONEY GARLIC CHICKEN WINGS

THESE SPICY WINGS ARE ALWAYS A PARTY HIT.

3 LBS	CHICKEN WINGS, SEPARATED AND TIPS REMOVED	1.5 KG
1/3 CUP	SOY SAUCE	75 ML
1/4 CUP	LIQUID HONEY	60 ML
2 TBSP	HOISIN SAUCE	30 ML
2 TBSP	RICE VINEGAR	30 ML
2	LARGE CLOVES GARLIC, FINELY CHOPPED	2
2 TSP	HOT PEPPER SAUCE (OR TO TASTE)	10 ML

PLACE CHICKEN WINGS IN A LARGE, HEAVY PLASTIC BAG AND SET IN A LARGE BOWL. IN A SMALL BOWL, COMBINE SOY SAUCE, HONEY, HOISIN SAUCE, VINEGAR, GARLIC AND HOT PEPPER SAUCE. POUR OVER WINGS, CLOSE TIGHTLY AND SEAL. LET MARINATE IN FRIDGE FOR SEVERAL HOURS OR OVERNIGHT.

PREHEAT OVEN TO 375°F (190°C). LINE A RIMMED BAKING SHEET WITH FOIL. PLACE A RACK ON THE BAKING SHEET AND BRUSH IT WITH OIL OR SPRAY IT WITH NONSTICK COOKING SPRAY. ARRANGE WINGS IN A SINGLE LAYER ON RACK. ROAST FOR 30 MINUTES. POUR OFF PAN JUICES AND TURN WINGS OVER.

MEANWHILE, PLACE MARINADE IN A SMALL SAUCEPAN. BRING TO A BOIL OVER MEDIUM HEAT; COOK 3 TO 5 MINUTES OR UNTIL SLIGHTLY THICKENED. BASTE WINGS LIBERALLY WITH MARINADE. ROAST FOR 25 TO 30 MINUTES OR UNTIL WINGS ARE TENDER AND NICELY GLAZED. MAKES 8 SERVINGS AS AN APPETIZER OR 4 AS A MAIN COURSE.

PARTY MEATBALLS WITH SWEET-AND-SOUR SAUCE

THIS VERSATILE DIPPING SAUCE IS ALSO
GOOD WITH CHICKEN OR PORK KEBABS, OR
WITH CHICKEN WINGS. FOR A SPICY VERSION,
ADD HOT PEPPER SAUCE TO TASTE.

1/2 CUP	ORANGE JUICE	125 ML
1/4 CUP	SOY SAUCE	60 ML
1/4 CUP	KETCHUP	60 ML
1/4 CUP	PACKED BROWN SUGAR	60 ML
2 TBSP	BALSAMIC VINEGAR	30 ML
1	CLOVE GARLIC, MINCED	1
1 1/2 TSP	CORNSTARCH	7 ML
36	APPETIZER BEEF MEATBALLS (SEE RECIPE, PAGE 122)	36

IN A MEDIUM SAUCEPAN, STIR TOGETHER ORANGE JUICE,
SOY SAUCE, KETCHUP, BROWN SUGAR, VINEGAR, GARLIC
AND CORNSTARCH UNTIL SMOOTH. BRING TO A BOIL OVER
MEDIUM HEAT, STIRRING CONSTANTLY, UNTIL SAUCE IS
THICK AND SMOOTH. STIR IN COOKED MEATBALLS; COVER
AND SIMMER FOR 5 MINUTES OR UNTIL HEATED THROUGH.
MAKES 36 APPETIZERS.

TIP: THE BROWN SUGAR YOU USE IN RECIPES IS
TOTALLY YOUR PREFERENCE. BROWN SUGAR COMES IN
BOTH LIGHT AND DARK BROWN. DARK BROWN SUGAR IS
NOTICEABLY DARKER IN COLOR AND HAS A STRONGER
MOLASSES TASTE.

APPETIZER BEEF MEATBALLS

WHO DOESN'T LOVE MEATBALLS? AS FAST AS YOU FILL
THE SERVING BOWLS, WATCH THEM DISAPPEAR.

1 TBSP	VEGETABLE OIL	15 ML
1	ONION, FINELY CHOPPED	1
2	CLOVES GARLIC, MINCED	2
3/4 TSP	SALT	3 ML
1/2 TSP	DRIED THYME	2 ML
1/2 TSP	FRESHLY GROUND BLACK PEPPER	2 ML
1/2 CUP	READY-TO-USE BEEF BROTH	125 ML
2 TSP	WORCESTERSHIRE SAUCE	10 ML
2 LBS	LEAN GROUND BEEF	1 KG
1 CUP	SOFT FRESH BREAD CRUMBS	250 ML
2 TBSP	FINELY CHOPPED FRESH PARSLEY	30 ML
1	EGG, LIGHTLY BEATEN	1

PREHEAT OVEN TO 400°F (200°C) AND GREASE A RIMMED
BAKING SHEET. IN A MEDIUM NONSTICK SKILLET, HEAT
OIL OVER MEDIUM HEAT. ADD ONION, GARLIC, SALT,
THYME AND PEPPER; COOK, STIRRING OFTEN, FOR
5 MINUTES OR UNTIL SOFTENED. STIR IN BEEF BROTH AND
WORCESTERSHIRE SAUCE; LET COOL SLIGHTLY. IN A BOWL,
COMBINE ONION MIXTURE, GROUND BEEF, BREAD CRUMBS,
PARSLEY AND EGG; MIX THOROUGHLY. FORM BEEF MIXTURE
INTO 1-INCH (2.5 CM) BALLS; ARRANGE ON PREPARED
BAKING SHEET SPACING 1 1/2 INCHES (4 CM) APART. BAKE
IN PREHEATED OVEN FOR 18 TO 20 MINUTES OR UNTIL
NICELY BROWNED. TRANSFER TO A PLATE LINED WITH
PAPER TOWELS TO DRAIN. MAKES ABOUT 72 MEATBALLS.

TIP: COOKED MEATBALLS CAN BE MADE UP TO 1 DAY AHEAD AND KEPT, COVERED, IN THE REFRIGERATOR, OR FROZEN FOR UP TO 1 MONTH. TO FREEZE, PLACE MEATBALLS IN A SINGLE LAYER ON BAKING SHEETS; WHEN FROZEN, TRANSFER TO AIRTIGHT CONTAINERS. TO DEFROST QUICKLY, PLACE MEATBALLS IN A CASSEROLE DISH AND MICROWAVE ON HIGH FOR 4 TO 5 MINUTES UNTIL JUST WARMED THROUGH, STIRRING ONCE.

WHY DO THEY SELL LUGGAGE IN SHOPS AT THE AIRPORT? WHO EVER FORGETS THEIR SUITCASE?

EUREKA! ENCHILADAS

2	CLOVES GARLIC (AS MUCH AS YOU CAN STAND), MINCED	2
1/2 CUP	OLIVE OIL	125 ML
1	CAN (14 OZ/398 ML) DARK PITTED OLIVES (RESERVE JUICE)	1
1	CAN (10 OZ/284 ML) TOMATO SAUCE	1
1	CAN (10 OZ/284 ML) WATER	1
2 TBSP	CHILI POWDER (ROUNDED TABLESPOONS)	30 ML
1 TSP	CUMIN	5 ML
2 TSP	SALT	10 ML
2	LARGE ONIONS, DICED	2
1 LB	MONTEREY JACK CHEESE	500 G
1 LB	LEAN GROUND BEEF	500 G
18	TORTILLAS (FROZEN ARE BEST)	18

SAUCE: SAUTÉ MINCED GARLIC IN OLIVE OIL. ADD OLIVE JUICE, TOMATO SAUCE, WATER, CHILI POWDER, CUMIN AND SALT. SIMMER 10 MINUTES.

FILLING: SAUTÉ DICED ONIONS, DICED OLIVES AND GROUND BEEF IN 1 TBSP (15 ML) OLIVE OIL UNTIL ONIONS ARE TRANSPARENT. ADD 3/4 LB (375 G) GRATED CHEESE, REMOVE FROM HEAT AND ALLOW CHEESE TO MELT THROUGH THE FILLING MIXTURE.

TORTILLAS: FRY TORTILLAS ONE AT A TIME IN 3 TBSP (45 ML) OLIVE OIL AT HIGH TEMPERATURE, TURNING ONCE. REMOVE FROM HEAT. DRY BETWEEN PAPER TOWELS. SPREAD WITH SMALL AMOUNT OF SAUCE. PLACE 1 HEAPING TBSP (15 ML) OF FILLING ON EACH TORTILLA. ROLL UP LIKE A CRÊPE AND LAY IN A RECTANGULAR OVEN DISH. ADD REMAINING SAUCE. SPRINKLE REMAINING FILLING

AND REMAINING 1/4 LB (125 G) GRATED CHEESE OVER THE ROLLED TORTILLAS.

BAKE AT 350°F (180°C) FOR 30 MINUTES. SERVES 8.

CHILI CON QUESO

THIS IS A DELICIOUS HOT DIP — A REAL HIT FOR MID-WINTER GET-TOGETHERS

1	SMALL ONION, FINELY CHOPPED	1
2 TBSP	BUTTER	30 ML
1 CUP	CANNED TOMATOES, CHOPPED AND DRAINED	250 ML
1	CAN PICKLED GREEN CHILES, CHOPPED	1
1 TSP	BASIL	5 ML
	SALT AND FRESHLY GROUND BLACK PEPPER, TO TASTE	
1/2 LB	MONTEREY JACK CHEESE, CUBED	250 G
1 CUP	TABLE (18%) CREAM	250 ML

SAUTÉ ONIONS IN BUTTER UNTIL TRANSPARENT. ADD TOMATOES, CHILES, BASIL, SALT AND PEPPER. SIMMER 15 MINUTES. ADD CUBED CHEESE AND, AS IT MELTS, STIR IN CREAM. COOK UNTIL BLENDED AND VERY SMOOTH.

SERVE HOT FROM CHAFING DISH OR AS A HOT DIP WITH STRIPS OF RAW VEGETABLES SUCH AS CARROTS, CELERY, GREEN PEPPER, ZUCCHINI OR CAULIFLOWER CHUNKS AND ARTICHOKE HEARTS, AS WELL AS TACO CHIPS. MAKES ABOUT 3 CUPS (750 ML).

TEXAS-STYLE CHILI CON CARNE

SERVE GARNISHED WITH SHREDDED CHEDDAR
OR MONTEREY JACK CHEESE, SOUR CREAM
AND FINELY CHOPPED GREEN ONIONS, WITH
HOT ONION BUNS ON THE SIDE. YUM!

4	SLICES BACON, FINELY CHOPPED	4
2 LBS	STEWING BEEF, CUT INTO 1-INCH (2.5 CM) CUBES AND PATTED DRY	1 KG
2	ONIONS, THINLY SLICED ON THE VERTICAL	2
4	CLOVES GARLIC, MINCED	4
1 TBSP	GROUND CUMIN	15 ML
1 TBSP	DRIED OREGANO	15 ML
1 TSP	SALT	5 ML
1 TSP	CRACKED BLACK PEPPERCORNS	5 ML
1	CAN (28 OZ/796 ML) TOMATOES, WITH JUICE, COARSELY CHOPPED	1
1 CUP	READY-TO-USE BEEF BROTH	250 ML
1 CUP	DRY RED WINE	250 ML
2 CUPS	COOKED RED KIDNEY BEANS (SEE TIP, PAGE 127)	500 ML
1	DRIED ANCHO, NEW MEXICO OR GUAJILLO CHILE PEPPER	1
1 CUP	BOILING WATER	250 ML
1 to 2	JALAPEÑO PEPPERS, QUARTERED	1 to 2

IN A SKILLET OVER MEDIUM-HIGH HEAT, COOK BACON
UNTIL CRISP. USING A SLOTTED SPOON, TRANSFER TO
PAPER TOWELS TO DRAIN. COVER AND REFRIGERATE UNTIL
READY TO USE. ADD BEEF TO PAN, IN BATCHES, AND
COOK, STIRRING, UNTIL BROWNED, ABOUT 4 MINUTES PER
BATCH. TRANSFER TO A LARGE (APPROX. 5-QUART) SLOW

CONTINUED ON PAGE 127...

René's Sandwich Loaf (page 104)

Best Seafood Lasagna (page 114)

Beer-Braised Chili with Black-Eyed Peas (page 128)

Classic French Onion Soup (page 134)

COOKER. ADD ONIONS TO PAN AND COOK, STIRRING, UNTIL SOFTENED, ABOUT 3 MINUTES. ADD CUMIN, OREGANO, SALT AND PEPPERCORNS AND COOK, STIRRING, FOR 1 MINUTE. STIR IN TOMATOES, BROTH AND WINE AND BRING TO A BOIL. TRANSFER TO SLOW COOKER. STIR IN BEANS. COVER AND COOK ON LOW FOR 6 TO 8 HOURS OR ON HIGH FOR 3 TO 4 HOURS, UNTIL BEEF IS VERY TENDER.

ABOUT AN HOUR BEFORE RECIPE HAS FINISHED COOKING, IN A HEATPROOF BOWL, SOAK DRIED CHILE IN BOILING WATER FOR 30 MINUTES, WEIGHING DOWN WITH A CUP TO ENSURE IT IS SUBMERGED. DRAIN AND DISCARD LIQUID. REMOVE STEM, PAT DRY AND COARSELY CHOP CHILE. IN A BLENDER, COMBINE REHYDRATED CHILE AND JALAPEÑO PEPPER TO TASTE WITH $1/2$ CUP (125 ML) OF LIQUID FROM THE CHILE. PURÉE. ADD TO SLOW COOKER ALONG WITH RESERVED BACON. COVER AND COOK ON HIGH FOR 20 MINUTES, UNTIL FLAVORS MELD. SERVES 6.

TIP: FOR THIS QUANTITY OF BEANS, COOK 1 CUP (250 ML) DRIED BEANS OR USE 1 CAN (14 TO 19 OZ/398 TO 540 ML) BEANS, DRAINED AND RINSED.

MY WIFE AND I HAD WORDS, BUT I DIDN'T GET TO USE MINE.

BEER-BRAISED CHILI WITH BLACK-EYED PEAS

IF YOU'RE TIRED OF BEEF-BASED CHILIS WITH
RED BEANS, TRY THIS EQUALLY DELICIOUS BUT LIGHTER
VERSION. IT MAKES A GREAT POTLUCK DISH OR THE
CENTERPIECE FOR A CASUAL EVENING WITH FRIENDS.
FOR A SIT-DOWN MEAL, SERVE WITH HOT CORNBREAD.

2 TBSP	OIL, DIVIDED	30 ML
4 OZ	CHUNK BACON, DICED	125 G
2 LBS	TRIMMED PORK SHOULDER OR BLADE (BUTT), CUT INTO 1-INCH (2.5 CM) CUBES AND PATTED DRY (SEE TIP, OPPOSITE)	1 KG
2	ONIONS, FINELY CHOPPED	2
2	STALKS CELERY, THINLY SLICED	2
4	CLOVES GARLIC, MINCED	4
2 TSP	GROUND CUMIN	10 ML
2 TSP	GROUND CORIANDER	10 ML
2 TSP	DRIED OREGANO, CRUMBLED	10 ML
1 TSP	SALT	5 ML
1 TSP	CRACKED BLACK PEPPERCORNS	5 ML
1	2-INCH (5 CM) CINNAMON STICK	1
1 CUP	FLAT BEER	250 ML
1	CAN (14 OZ/398 ML) CRUSHED TOMATOES	1
4 CUPS	COOKED BLACK-EYED PEAS (SEE TIP, OPPOSITE)	1 L
1	RED BELL PEPPER, FINELY CHOPPED	1
1	GREEN BELL PEPPER, FINELY CHOPPED	1
1 to 2	CHIPOTLE PEPPERS IN ADOBO SAUCE, MINCED	1 to 2
	SOUR CREAM, FINELY CHOPPED RED ONION AND/OR SHREDDED MONTEREY JACK CHEESE	

IN A SKILLET, HEAT 1 TBSP (15 ML) OF THE OIL OVER MEDIUM-HIGH HEAT. ADD BACON AND COOK, STIRRING, UNTIL BROWNED AND CRISP, ABOUT 4 MINUTES. USING A SLOTTED SPOON, TRANSFER TO A LARGE (MINIMUM 5-QUART) SLOW COOKER. ADD PORK, IN BATCHES, AND COOK, STIRRING, UNTIL BROWNED, ABOUT 4 MINUTES PER BATCH. TRANSFER TO SLOW COOKER AS COMPLETED. REDUCE HEAT TO MEDIUM. ADD REMAINING 1 TBSP (15 ML) OF OIL TO PAN. ADD ONIONS AND CELERY AND COOK, STIRRING, UNTIL SOFTENED, ABOUT 5 MINUTES. ADD GARLIC, CUMIN, CORIANDER, OREGANO, SALT, PEPPERCORNS AND CINNAMON STICK AND COOK, STIRRING, FOR 1 MINUTE. ADD BEER, BRING TO A BOIL AND BOIL FOR 1 MINUTE, SCRAPING UP BROWN BITS. STIR IN TOMATOES. TRANSFER TO SLOW COOKER. STIR IN PEAS. COVER AND COOK ON LOW FOR 6 HOURS OR ON HIGH FOR 3 HOURS. STIR IN RED AND GREEN BELL PEPPERS AND CHIPOTLES. COVER AND COOK ON HIGH ABOUT 20 MINUTES, UNTIL PEPPERS ARE TENDER. GARNISH WITH ANY COMBINATION OF SOUR CREAM, ONION AND/OR CHEESE. DISCARD CINNAMON STICK. SERVES 8.

TIP: USE 2 CANS (14 TO 19 OZ/398 TO 540 ML) DRAINED AND RINSED BLACK-EYED PEAS, OR SOAK AND COOK 2 CUPS (500 ML) DRIED PEAS YOURSELF.

TIP: MANY BUTCHERS SELL CUT-UP PORK STEWING MEAT, WHICH IS FINE TO USE IN THIS RECIPE.

CHILI WITH BLACK BEANS AND GRILLED CHICKEN

IF YOU ARE VERY FOND OF HEAT, ADD AN EXTRA JALAPEÑO PEPPER OR, BETTER STILL, A CHOPPED CHIPOTLE PEPPER IN ADOBO SAUCE, WHICH WILL INTENSIFY THE SMOKY FLAVOR AS WELL AS ADD HEAT.

I TBSP	VEGETABLE OIL	15 ML
2	ONIONS, FINELY CHOPPED	2
4	STALKS CELERY, DICED	4
4	CLOVES GARLIC	4
I TBSP	GROUND CUMIN	15 ML
2 TSP	DRIED OREGANO	10 ML
I TSP	SALT	5 ML
I TSP	CRACKED BLACK PEPPERCORNS	5 ML
2 TBSP	TOMATO PASTE	30 ML
I	CAN (14 OZ/ 398 ML) CRUSHED TOMATOES	I
2 CUPS	CHICKEN BROTH	500 ML
2 CUPS	COOKED BLACK BEANS (SEE TIP, PAGE 127)	500 ML
2 TSP	PURE CHILE POWDER (SEE TIP, OPPOSITE)	10 ML
$\frac{1}{2}$ TSP	CAYENNE PEPPER (OPTIONAL)	2 ML
2 CUPS	CUBED (I INCH/2.5 CM) GRILLED CHICKEN	500 ML
I	GREEN BELL OR POBLANO PEPPER, SEEDED AND FINELY CHOPPED	I
I	CAN (4$\frac{1}{2}$ OZ/127 ML) CHOPPED MILD GREEN CHILES	I
	AVOCADO TOPPING (SEE TIP, OPPOSITE), SHREDDED CHEDDAR OR JACK CHEESE OR SOUR CREAM	
	FINELY CHOPPED RED OR GREEN ONION	

IN A SKILLET, HEAT OIL OVER MEDIUM HEAT. ADD ONIONS
AND CELERY AND COOK, STIRRING, UNTIL SOFTENED,
ABOUT 5 MINUTES. ADD GARLIC, CUMIN, OREGANO, SALT
AND PEPPERCORNS AND COOK, STIRRING, FOR 1 MINUTE.
ADD TOMATO PASTE AND TOMATOES AND BRING TO
A BOIL. TRANSFER TO A MEDIUM TO LARGE ($3\frac{1}{2}$- TO
5-QUART) SLOW COOKER. ADD BROTH AND BEANS AND
STIR WELL. COVER AND COOK ON LOW FOR 6 HOURS
OR ON HIGH FOR 3 HOURS. STIR IN CHILE POWDER AND
CAYENNE, IF USING. ADD CHICKEN, BELL PEPPER AND GREEN
CHILES AND STIR WELL. COVER AND COOK ON HIGH FOR
20 MINUTES, UNTIL BELL PEPPER IS TENDER AND CHICKEN
IS HEATED THROUGH. SERVE WITH TOPPING(S) OF YOUR
CHOICE. SERVES 6.

TIP: USE CHILE POWDER MADE FROM A SINGLE GROUND
MILD CHILE, SUCH AS ANCHO OR ANAHEIM, OR A
COMBINATION THEREOF.

TIP: AVOCADO TOPPING: CHOP 1 WHOLE AVOCADO INTO
$\frac{1}{2}$-INCH (1 CM) CUBES AND TOSS WITH 1 TBSP (15 ML) LIME
JUICE, 2 TBSP (30 ML) FINELY CHOPPED RED ONION AND
2 TBSP (30 ML) FINELY CHOPPED CILANTRO. ADD SALT AND
PEPPER TO TASTE.

TIP: TO MAKE AHEAD, PREPARE THROUGH ADDING THE
TOMATOES AND BRINGING TO A BOIL. COVER AND
REFRIGERATE MIXTURE FOR UP TO 2 DAYS. WHEN YOU'RE
READY TO COOK, COMPLETE THE RECIPE.

SIT-DOWN DINNERS

THIS CHAPTER FOCUSES ON THE MAIN COURSE, ALONG WITH ACCOMPANIMENTS, THAT PROVIDES THE FOCAL POINT FOR AN AROUND-THE-TABLE HOLIDAY DINNER. APPETIZERS TO COMPLEMENT THE MEAL CAN BE SELECTED FROM CHAPTER 2 AND SERVED AS PRE-DINNER NIBBLES. BECAUSE YOU MAY WANT TO PROVIDE SMALL SERVINGS OF AN ELEGANT SOUP AFTER YOUR GUESTS ARE SEATED, WE'VE INCLUDED A FEW APPROPRIATE RECIPES.

SIDES

CLASSIC FRENCH ONION SOUP

ON A CHILLY DAY, THERE'S NOTHING MORE APPETIZING THAN A BOWL OF STEAMING HOT ONION SOUP BUBBLING AWAY UNDER A BLANKET OF BROWNED CHEESE.

6	ONIONS, THINLY SLICED	6
3 TBSP	MELTED BUTTER	45 ML
1 TBSP	GRANULATED SUGAR	15 ML
8 CUPS	GOOD-QUALITY READY-TO-USE BEEF BROTH (SEE TIP, OPPOSITE)	2 L
1 TSP	SALT	5 ML
1 TSP	CRACKED BLACK PEPPERCORNS	5 ML
2 TBSP	BRANDY OR COGNAC	30 ML
12	SLICES BAGUETTE (ABOUT $1/2$ INCH/1 CM THICK)	12
2 CUPS	SHREDDED SWISS OR GRUYÈRE CHEESE	500 ML

IN A MEDIUM TO LARGE (4- TO 5-QUART) SLOW COOKER, COMBINE ONIONS AND BUTTER. STIR WELL TO COAT ONIONS THOROUGHLY. COVER AND COOK ON HIGH FOR 30 MINUTES TO 1 HOUR, UNTIL ONIONS ARE SOFTENED. ADD SUGAR AND STIR WELL. PLACE TWO CLEAN TEA TOWELS, EACH FOLDED IN HALF (SO YOU WILL HAVE FOUR LAYERS), OVER TOP OF SLOW COOKER STONEWARE TO ABSORB MOISTURE. COVER AND COOK ON HIGH FOR 4 HOURS, STIRRING TWO OR THREE TIMES TO ENSURE THAT ONIONS ARE BROWNING EVENLY, REPLACING TOWELS EACH TIME. ADD BROTH, SALT, PEPPER AND BRANDY OR COGNAC. DO NOT REPLACE TOWELS, COVER AND COOK ON HIGH FOR 2 HOURS.

PREHEAT BROILER. LADLE SOUP INTO 6 OVENPROOF SOUP BOWLS. PLACE 2 SLICES BAGUETTE IN EACH BOWL. SPRINKLE LIBERALLY WITH CHEESE AND BROIL UNTIL TOP IS BUBBLY AND BROWN, 2 TO 3 MINUTES. SERVE IMMEDIATELY. SERVES 6.

TIP: SINCE IT'S IMPORTANT THAT THE BROTH FOR THIS SOUP BE TOP QUALITY, USE HOMEMADE BROTH OR ENHANCE STORE-BOUGHT BROTH. TO ENHANCE 8 CUPS (2 L) BEEF BROTH, COMBINE IT IN A LARGE SAUCEPAN WITH 2 CARROTS, PEELED AND COARSELY CHOPPED, 1 TSP (5 ML) CELERY SEED, 1 TSP (5 ML) CRACKED BLACK PEPPERCORNS, $1/2$ TSP (2 ML) DRIED THYME, 4 PARSLEY SPRIGS, 1 BAY LEAF AND 1 CUP (250 ML) WHITE WINE. BRING TO A BOIL, THEN REDUCE HEAT AND SIMMER, COVERED, FOR 30 MINUTES. STRAIN.

VARIATION: SUBSTITUTE VEGETABLE BROTH FOR THE BEEF BROTH AND FOLLOW THE INSTRUCTIONS FOR ENHANCING THE FLAVOR (SEE TIP, ABOVE).

NEVER ARGUE WITH A WOMAN WHO'S TIRED . . . OR RESTED.

MUSHROOM BARLEY SOUP

DRIED WILD MUSHROOMS GIVE THIS SOUP A DEEP, RICH FLAVOR. WITH THE ADDITION OF SALAD AND WHOLE-GRAIN BREAD, IT'S EVEN HEARTY ENOUGH TO SERVE FOR SUPPER AFTER A BUSY DAY.

I CUP	HOT WATER	250 ML
I	PACKAGE ($\frac{1}{2}$ OZ/14 G) DRIED WILD MUSHROOMS (SUCH AS PORCINI)	I
2 TBSP	BUTTER OR VEGETABLE OIL, DIVIDED	30 ML
3	ONIONS, FINELY CHOPPED	3
6	CLOVES GARLIC, MINCED	6
I	BAY LEAF	I
I TSP	SALT	5 ML
I TSP	CRACKED BLACK PEPPERCORNS	5 ML
$1\frac{1}{2}$ LBS	MUSHROOMS, TRIMMED AND SLICED (SEE TIP, OPPOSITE)	750 G
$\frac{2}{3}$ CUP	BARLEY (SEE TIP, OPPOSITE)	150 ML
6 CUPS	READY-TO-USE BEEF, VEGETABLE OR MUSHROOM BROTH	1.5 L
$\frac{1}{4}$ CUP	SOY SAUCE	60 ML
	FINELY CHOPPED GREEN ONIONS OR FRESH PARSLEY (OPTIONAL)	

IN A BOWL, COMBINE HOT WATER AND DRIED MUSHROOMS. LET STAND FOR 30 MINUTES, THEN STRAIN THROUGH A FINE SIEVE, RESERVING LIQUID. FINELY CHOP MUSHROOMS AND SET ASIDE. IN A SKILLET, MELT I TBSP (15 ML) OF THE BUTTER OVER MEDIUM HEAT. ADD ONIONS AND COOK, STIRRING, UNTIL SOFTENED, ABOUT 3 MINUTES. ADD GARLIC, BAY LEAF, SALT AND PEPPERCORNS AND COOK, STIRRING, FOR I MINUTE. TRANSFER TO A LARGE (APPROX. 5-QUART) SLOW COOKER.

IN SAME PAN, MELT REMAINING BUTTER AND COOK MUSHROOMS OVER MEDIUM-HIGH HEAT UNTIL THEY BEGIN TO LOSE THEIR LIQUID, ABOUT 6 MINUTES. ADD DRIED MUSHROOMS, TOSS TO COMBINE AND COOK FOR 1 MINUTE. ADD BARLEY AND RESERVED MUSHROOM SOAKING LIQUID AND BRING TO A BOIL. TRANSFER TO SLOW COOKER.

ADD BROTH TO SLOW COOKER. COVER AND COOK ON LOW FOR 8 HOURS OR ON HIGH FOR 4 HOURS, UNTIL BARLEY IS TENDER. STIR IN SOY SAUCE. DISCARD BAY LEAF. LADLE INTO INDIVIDUAL BOWLS AND GARNISH WITH CHOPPED GREEN ONIONS OR PARSLEY, IF USING. SERVES 6 TO 8.

TIP: I LIKE THE ROBUST FLAVOR OF CREMINI MUSHROOMS IN THIS SOUP, BUT WHITE MUSHROOMS WORK WELL, TOO.

TIP: USE THE KIND OF BARLEY YOU PREFER — WHOLE, POT OR PEARL — ALL WORK WELL IN THIS RECIPE. WHOLE (OR HULLED) BARLEY IS THE MOST NUTRITIOUS FORM OF THE GRAIN, AND PEARL BARLEY HAS THE FEWEST NUTRIENTS.

VARIATION: WHEN SERVING THIS SOUP TO GUESTS, SPIFF IT UP BY ADDING 1/2 CUP (125 ML) SHERRY OR MADEIRA JUST BEFORE SERVING.

DEFINITION OF A FANCY RESTAURANT:
ONE THAT SERVES COLD SOUP ON PURPOSE.

POTATO AND LEEK SOUP

SMOOTH AS A SWEET-TALKIN' MAN!

1½ CUPS	CHOPPED LEEKS (USE WHITE PART ONLY)	375 ML
½ CUP	CHOPPED ONIONS	125 ML
1	CLOVE GARLIC, MINCED	1
¼ CUP	MARGARINE	60 ML
4 CUPS	READY-TO-USE CHICKEN BROTH	1 L
1½ CUPS	PEELED, DICED RAW POTATO	375 ML
1 CUP	HEAVY OR WHIPPING (35%) CREAM	250 ML
1 TSP	SALT	5 ML
¼ TSP	BLACK PEPPER	1 ML
	FINELY CHOPPED GREEN ONIONS OR CHIVES	

SAUTÉ LEEKS, ONIONS AND GARLIC IN MARGARINE UNTIL TRANSLUCENT. ADD BROTH AND POTATOES; COOK UNTIL TENDER. PURÉE MIXTURE IN BLENDER OR FOOD PROCESSOR. ADD CREAM, SALT AND PEPPER. CHILL AT LEAST 24 HOURS. GARNISH WITH GREEN ONIONS OR CHIVES. HEAT GENTLY OR SERVE COLD. SERVES 4 TO 6.

ONE GOOD THING ABOUT AIRLINE FOOD: AT LEAST THEY'RE CONSIDERATE ENOUGH TO GIVE YOU ONLY SMALL PORTIONS.

PUMPKIN SOUP

SOMETIMES KNOWN AS MYSTERY SOUP!
WHAT IS THIS ORANGE STUFF ANYWAY?

1	SMALL ONION, CHOPPED	1
2 CUPS	SLICED MUSHROOMS	500 ML
1/4 CUP	BUTTER	60 ML
1/4 CUP	ALL-PURPOSE FLOUR	60 ML
4 CUPS	READY-TO-USE CHICKEN BROTH	1 L
1 CUP	CANNED PUMPKIN (NOT PIE FILLING)	250 ML
1 CUP	LIGHT (5%) CREAM	250 ML
2 TBSP	LIQUID HONEY	30 ML
1 TSP	GROUND NUTMEG	5 ML
	CROUTONS	

IN A LARGE POT, SAUTÉ ONION AND MUSHROOMS IN
BUTTER FOR 1 TO 2 MINUTES. REMOVE FROM HEAT. STIR
IN FLOUR. ADD CHICKEN BROTH AND PUMPKIN AND BRING
TO A BOIL. REDUCE HEAT AND SIMMER FOR 20 MINUTES.
STIR IN CREAM, HONEY AND NUTMEG. SERVE WITH
CROUTONS SPRINKLED ON TOP. SERVES 4.

CURRIED BUTTERNUT AND CHESTNUT SOUP

THIS SOUP IS DELICIOUS, BUT VERY RICH; A LITTLE GOES A LONG WAY. SERVE SMALL BOWLS AS THE FIRST COURSE OF A SPECIAL DINNER OR MAKE IT A COLD-WEATHER TREAT. LIKE CHESTNUTS ROASTING ON AN OPEN FIRE, IT'S AN IDEAL ANTIDOTE TO A WINTER FREEZE. LADLE HOT SOUP INTO MUGS AND HAND THEM TO BRAVE SOULS RETURNING FROM OUTDOOR EXCURSIONS.

1 TBSP	VEGETABLE OIL	15 ML
3	LEEKS, CLEANED AND CHOPPED (SEE TIP, OPPOSITE)	3
2	CLOVES GARLIC, CHOPPED	2
1 TBSP	MINCED GINGERROOT	15 ML
1/2 TSP	CRACKED BLACK PEPPERCORNS	2 ML
1	WHOLE STAR ANISE	1
5 CUPS	VEGETABLE OR CHICKEN STOCK	1.25 L
3 CUPS	CUBED PEELED BUTTERNUT SQUASH (ABOUT 1 LB/500 G, CUT INTO 1-INCH/2.5 CM CUBES)	750 ML
1 TBSP	CURRY POWDER (PREFERABLY MADRAS)	15 ML
1/2 CUP	HEAVY OR WHIPPING (35%) CREAM OR SOY CREAMER, DIVIDED	125 ML
1	CAN (15 OZ/435 ML) UNSWEETENED CHESTNUT PURÉE, REMOVED FROM CAN AND CUT INTO 1-INCH (2.5 CM) CUBES	1

IN A SKILLET, HEAT OIL OVER MEDIUM HEAT FOR 30 SECONDS. ADD LEEKS AND COOK, STIRRING, UNTIL SOFTENED, ABOUT 5 MINUTES. ADD GARLIC, GINGERROOT, PEPPERCORNS AND STAR ANISE AND COOK, STIRRING, FOR 1 MINUTE. ADD STOCK AND BRING TO A BOIL. TRANSFER

TO A LARGE (MINIMUM 5-QUART) SLOW COOKER. STIR IN SQUASH. COVER AND COOK ON LOW FOR 6 TO 8 HOURS OR ON HIGH FOR 3 TO 4 HOURS, UNTIL SQUASH IS VERY TENDER.

IN A SMALL BOWL, PLACE CURRY POWDER. GRADUALLY ADD $\frac{1}{4}$ CUP (60 ML) OF THE CREAM, BEATING UNTIL SMOOTH. SET ASIDE FOR 2 MINUTES TO ALLOW CURRY TO ABSORB THE CREAM. STIR INTO SLOW COOKER. ADD CHESTNUT PURÉE AND STIR WELL, MASHING PURÉE INTO SOUP AS BEST YOU CAN. COVER AND COOK ON HIGH FOR 30 MINUTES, UNTIL FLAVORS MELD. DISCARD STAR ANISE. WORKING IN BATCHES, PURÉE SOUP IN A FOOD PROCESSOR OR BLENDER. (YOU CAN ALSO DO THIS IN THE STONEWARE USING AN IMMERSION BLENDER.) LADLE INTO BOWLS AND DRIZZLE WITH REMAINING CREAM. SERVES 8 TO 10.

TIP: TO CLEAN LEEKS, FILL SINK FULL OF LUKEWARM WATER. SPLIT LEEKS IN HALF LENGTHWISE AND SUBMERGE IN WATER, SWISHING THEM AROUND TO REMOVE ALL TRACES OF DIRT. TRANSFER TO A COLANDER AND RINSE UNDER COLD WATER.

TIP: STRAIGHT FROM THE CAN, CHESTNUT PURÉE IS VERY CONGEALED. CUTTING IT INTO SMALL CUBES BEFORE ADDING IT TO THE SOUP HELPS IT TO INTEGRATE INTO THE STOCK. USE A WOODEN SPOON TO MASH IT UP A BIT AND BE AWARE THAT ONCE THE SOUP IS PURÉED, IF NOT BEFORE, IT WILL BE COMPLETELY INTEGRATED.

CHAMPAGNE SQUASH SOUP

WHEN YOU WANT TO FUSS . . .

4 LBS	SQUASH, ACORN OR BUTTERNUT	2 KG
2	MEDIUM ONIONS, HALVED AND THINLY SLICED	2
2 TBSP	BUTTER	30 ML
1/4 CUP	CHAMPAGNE (YOU'LL FIND SOME WAY TO USE THE REMAINDER OF THE BOTTLE)	60 ML
4 to 5 CUPS	CHICKEN BROTH	1 to 1.25 L
2 TBSP	BUTTER	30 ML
1/2 TSP	GROUND NUTMEG	2 ML
	SALT AND BLACK PEPPER TO TASTE	
1/4 CUP	SOUR CREAM	60 ML

PREHEAT OVEN TO 350°F (180°C). LINE A COOKIE SHEET WITH FOIL. QUARTER SQUASH. SCOOP OUT SEEDS. PLACE SKIN SIDE UP ON COOKIE SHEET AND BAKE 1 TO 1 1/2 HOURS, UNTIL SQUASH IS TENDER. (YOU MAY MICROWAVE, USING THE SAME METHOD, COVERED WITH PLASTIC WRAP, ON HIGH UNTIL A SKEWER CAN PENETRATE THE SKIN, ABOUT 10 MINUTES.) COOL. SCOOP OUT PULP AND PURÉE IN BATCHES IN FOOD PROCESSOR. SAUTÉ ONIONS IN 2 TBSP (30 ML) BUTTER. ADD CHAMPAGNE. COOK UNTIL LIQUID IS ABSORBED AND ONIONS ARE GOLDEN BROWN, STIRRING OFTEN. PURÉE ONIONS IN FOOD PROCESSOR WITH A LITTLE OF THE SQUASH PURÉE. IN LARGE SAUCEPAN, COMBINE ONION AND SQUASH PURÉES. WHISK IN BROTH TO DESIRED CONSISTENCY. COVER AND HEAT THROUGH

OVER MEDIUM HEAT, STIRRING OCCASIONALLY. WHISK IN 2 TBSP (30 ML) BUTTER.

SEASON WITH NUTMEG, SALT AND PEPPER. TO DECORATE, DROP A SMALL SPOONFUL OF SOUR CREAM IN EACH BOWL OF SOUP AND SWIRL WITH A KNIFE. SERVES 6 TO 8.

CRAB BISQUE

1/4 LB	CRABMEAT	125 G
3 TBSP	SHERRY	45 ML
1	CAN (10 OZ/284 ML) TOMATO SOUP	1
1 CUP	LIGHT (5%) CREAM	250 ML
	SALT AND WHITE PEPPER TO TASTE	

FLAKE CRAB AND SOAK IN SHERRY 10 MINUTES. SIMMER UNDILUTED SOUP UNTIL HOT. ADD CREAM AND BLEND THOROUGHLY. ADD CRABMEAT AND SEASONINGS. HEAT BUT DO NOT BOIL. SERVES 4.

DRIVE CAREFULLY. IT'S NOT ONLY CARS THAT CAN BE RECALLED BY THEIR MAKER.

CRAB AND CORN CHOWDER

WHAT COULD BE BETTER THAN CHOWDER, FRENCH BREAD AND WINE AFTER A DAY'S SKIING — OR A DAY OF ANYTHING!

4	SLICES BACON	4
1/4 CUP	BUTTER	60 ML
1	SMALL ONION, CHOPPED	1
1/3 CUP	FLOUR	75 ML
3 CUPS	MILK	750 ML
2	MEDIUM POTATOES, PEELED AND DICED AND SET IN COLD WATER	2
1	SMALL GREEN PEPPER, SEEDED AND CHOPPED	1
1	STALK CELERY, DICED	1
1	BAY LEAF	1
1 CUP	HALF-AND-HALF (10%) CREAM	250 ML
10 OZ	CRABMEAT	300 G
1	CAN (12 OZ/341 ML) WHOLE KERNEL CORN	1
	SALT AND BLACK PEPPER TO TASTE	
1 TBSP	CHOPPED PARSLEY	15 ML

FRY BACON UNTIL CRISP. COOL AND CRUMBLE. SET ASIDE. IN A LARGE SAUCEPAN, MELT BUTTER AND SAUTÉ ONION UNTIL SOFT. ADD FLOUR, STIR AND COOK GENTLY FOR 1 MINUTE. GRADUALLY ADD MILK, STIRRING CONSTANTLY UNTIL THICKENED. DRAIN POTATOES AND ADD TO SAUCE WITH PEPPER, CELERY, BAY LEAF AND CREAM. SIMMER 35 TO 40 MINUTES. ADD CRAB, CORN AND BACON; HEAT THROUGH. SEASON WITH SALT AND PEPPER. GARNISH EACH BOWL WITH PARSLEY. SERVES 6.

GRAMPA MAC'S OYSTER STEW

THIS VERY RICH SOUP RECIPE COMES FROM A
GRANDFATHER FROM P.E.I. SERVES FOUR HUNGRY
PEOPLE — A MEAL BY ITSELF SERVED WITH
TOAST AND CHEESE.

2	CANS (EACH 5 OZ/142 G) OYSTERS, WITH LIQUID	2
1/3 CUP	BUTTER	75 ML
3/4 TSP	SALT	3 ML
1/8 TSP	WORCESTERSHIRE SAUCE	0.5 ML
	PEPPER TO TASTE	
1	CAN (16 OZ/454 ML) EVAPORATED MILK	1
12	SINGLE SODA CRACKERS	12
2/3 CUP	REGULAR MILK	150 ML

HEAT EVERYTHING EXCEPT MILK AND CRACKERS OVER
MEDIUM HEAT TO A NEAR BOIL. ADD EVAPORATED MILK AND
CONTINUE STIRRING OVER HEAT. BREAK SODA CRACKERS
ON TOP AND STIR. ADD REMAINING MILK, BEING CAREFUL
NOT TO BOIL. SERVES 4.

HAVE YOU NOTICED, NO MATTER HOW LOUD CAR ALARMS ARE,
THEY NEVER SEEM TO WAKE UP?

HAMBURGER SOUP

*DON'T BE DECEIVED BY THE NAME; THIS IS A
FAMILY FAVORITE. FREEZES VERY WELL.*

1½ LBS	LEAN GROUND BEEF	750 G
1	MEDIUM ONION, FINELY CHOPPED	1
1	CAN (28 OZ/796 ML) TOMATOES	1
2 CUPS	WATER	500 ML
3	CANS (EACH 10 OZ/284 ML) CONSOMMÉ	3
1	CAN (10 OZ/284 ML) TOMATO SOUP	1
4	CARROTS, FINELY CHOPPED	4
1	BAY LEAF	1
3	CELERY STALKS, FINELY CHOPPED	3
	PARSLEY	
½ TSP	THYME	2 ML
	BLACK PEPPER TO TASTE	
½ CUP	BARLEY	125 ML

BROWN MEAT AND ONIONS. DRAIN WELL. COMBINE ALL
INGREDIENTS IN LARGE POT. SIMMER, COVERED, A
MINIMUM OF 2 HOURS. SERVES 10.

*I'VE FIGURED OUT HOW TO AVOID GETTING PARKING TICKETS:
I'VE TAKEN THE WINDSHIELD WIPERS OFF MY CAR.*

CARROT SOUP

A GREAT BEGINNING FOR AN ELEGANT ENTRÉE!

1/4 CUP	BUTTER	60 ML
2 CUPS	FINELY CHOPPED ONION	500 ML
12	LARGE CARROTS, PEELED AND SLICED	12
4 CUPS	READY-TO-USE CHICKEN BROTH	1 L
1 CUP	FRESH ORANGE JUICE	250 ML
	SALT AND BLACK PEPPER TO TASTE	
	GRATED ORANGE ZEST	

MELT BUTTER IN POT AND ADD ONIONS, COOKING OVER LOW HEAT UNTIL LIGHTLY BROWNED. ADD CARROTS AND BROTH AND BRING TO A BOIL. REDUCE HEAT. COVER AND COOK UNTIL CARROTS ARE VERY TENDER, ABOUT 30 MINUTES. POUR THROUGH A STRAINER, RESERVING BROTH. ADD STRAINED VEGETABLES IN BATCHES TO FOOD PROCESSOR OR BLENDER AND PURÉE UNTIL SMOOTH. RETURN PURÉE TO POT, ADD ORANGE JUICE AND RESERVED BROTH. SEASON TO TASTE. ADD ORANGE ZEST. SIMMER UNTIL HEATED THROUGH. SERVES 6 TO 8.

ROAST TURKEY WITH SAGE-BREAD STUFFING

TURKEY ALMOST ALWAYS HAS THE PLACE OF HONOR WHEN FAMILY AND FRIENDS GATHER FOR HOLIDAY MEALS. IT'S PERFECT WHEN SERVING A CROWD. IT'S ECONOMICAL, TOO, AND EVERYONE LOVES IT. BEST OF ALL ARE THE LEFTOVERS THAT GET WRAPPED AND PLACED IN THE FRIDGE FOR HEARTY SANDWICHES THE NEXT DAY — OR EVEN LATER THAT NIGHT.

STUFFING

1/3 CUP	BUTTER	75 ML
2 CUPS	CHOPPED ONIONS	500 ML
2 CUPS	CHOPPED CELERY	500 ML
8 OZ	MUSHROOMS, CHOPPED	250 G
4	CLOVES GARLIC, MINCED	4
1 TBSP	DRIED RUBBED SAGE	15 ML
1 TSP	DRIED THYME	5 ML
1 TSP	DRIED MARJORAM	5 ML
1 TSP	SALT	5 ML
1/2 TSP	FRESHLY GROUND BLACK PEPPER	2 ML
12 CUPS	WHITE OR WHOLE WHEAT BREAD CUBES, TOASTED ON BAKING SHEET IN 350°F (180°C) OVEN FOR 15 MINUTES	3 L
1/2 CUP	CHOPPED FRESH PARSLEY	125 ML
1 CUP	TURKEY GRAVY STOCK (SEE TIP, PAGE 150)	250 ML

TURKEY

1	TURKEY (ABOUT 12 TO 14 LBS/6 TO 7 KG)	1
2 TBSP	MELTED BUTTER	30 ML
6	CLOVES GARLIC, UNPEELED	6
1	LARGE ONION, CUT INTO 8 WEDGES	1

2	CARROTS, CUT INTO CHUNKS	2
1	LARGE STALK CELERY, CUT INTO CHUNKS	1
1 TSP	DRIED ROSEMARY, CRUMBLED	5 ML
1/2 TSP	DRIED THYME	2 ML
1/2 TSP	DRIED MARJORAM	2 ML
	SALT AND FRESHLY GROUND BLACK PEPPER	

GRAVY

1/4 CUP	ALL-PURPOSE FLOUR	60 ML
1/2 CUP	WHITE WINE OR ADDITIONAL STOCK	125 ML
3 CUPS	TURKEY GRAVY STOCK (SEE TIP, PAGE 150)	750 ML
	SALT AND FRESHLY GROUND BLACK PEPPER	

STUFFING: IN A LARGE SKILLET, MELT BUTTER OVER MEDIUM HEAT; COOK ONIONS, CELERY, MUSHROOMS, GARLIC, SAGE, THYME, MARJORAM, SALT AND PEPPER, STIRRING OFTEN, FOR 15 MINUTES OR UNTIL TENDER. IN A LARGE BOWL, COMBINE ONION MIXTURE, BREAD CUBES AND PARSLEY. SPOON INTO A GREASED 12-CUP (3 L) CASSEROLE DISH. TO BAKE, ADD ENOUGH TURKEY STOCK TO MOISTEN STUFFING AND TOSS. (IF YOU PLAN TO STUFF THE BIRD, OMIT STOCK.) COVER WITH LID OR FOIL AND PLACE IN OVEN FOR THE LAST HOUR OF ROASTING TURKEY, UNCOVERING FOR LAST 30 MINUTES TO BROWN AND CRISP THE TOP.

TURKEY: PREHEAT OVEN TO 325°F (160°C). REMOVE NECK AND GIBLETS FROM BIRD; RESERVE TO MAKE STOCK.

CONTINUED ON NEXT PAGE...

RINSE TURKEY WITH COLD WATER; PAT DRY. SECURE LEGS BY TYING WITH STRING OR TUCK UNDER SKIN AROUND THE TAIL; FOLD WINGS BACK AND SECURE NECK SKIN WITH SKEWER. PLACE TURKEY, BREAST SIDE UP, ON A GREASED RACK IN A LARGE ROASTING PAN OR BROILER PAN. BRUSH BIRD WITH MELTED BUTTER. LIGHTLY CRUSH GARLIC WITH SIDE OF KNIFE; SCATTER GARLIC, ONION, CARROTS AND CELERY IN PAN. SEASON TURKEY AND VEGETABLES WITH ROSEMARY, THYME, MARJORAM, SALT AND PEPPER. INSERT MEAT THERMOMETER INTO THICKEST PART OF INNER TURKEY THIGH, BEING CAREFUL NOT TO TOUCH BONE. ROAST TURKEY FOR $3\frac{1}{4}$ TO $3\frac{1}{2}$ HOURS; NO NEED TO BASTE. (IF TURKEY STARTS TO BROWN TOO QUICKLY, TENT BIRD LOOSELY WITH HEAVY-DUTY FOIL, SHINY SIDE DOWN.) TURKEY IS DONE WHEN MEAT THERMOMETER REGISTERS 165°F (74°C) FOR UNSTUFFED BIRD; 170°F (77°C) IF STUFFED. REMOVE FROM OVEN; COVER WITH FOIL AND LET STAND FOR 15 MINUTES FOR EASY CARVING.

GRAVY: SKIM FAT FROM ROASTING PAN; PLACE OVER MEDIUM HEAT. STIR IN FLOUR; COOK, STIRRING, FOR 1 MINUTE. ADD WINE; COOK, STIRRING, UNTIL REDUCED BY HALF. STIR IN STOCK; BRING TO BOIL, SCRAPING UP BROWN BITS FROM BOTTOM OF PAN, UNTIL GRAVY THICKENS. STRAIN THROUGH A FINE SIEVE INTO A SAUCEPAN, PRESSING DOWN ON VEGETABLES; DISCARD THE VEGETABLES. SEASON GRAVY WITH SALT AND PEPPER TO TASTE. SERVES 8 TO 10, PLUS LEFTOVERS.

TIP: TURKEY GRAVY STOCK: PAT NECK AND GIBLETS DRY. (DO NOT USE LIVER.) IN A LARGE SAUCEPAN, HEAT 1 TBSP

(15 ML) VEGETABLE OIL OVER MEDIUM-HIGH HEAT; COOK
NECK AND GIBLETS, STIRRING, FOR 8 MINUTES OR UNTIL
NICELY BROWNED. ADD 1 EACH CHOPPED ONION, CARROT
AND CELERY STALK INCLUDING LEAVES ALONG WITH 1 TSP
(5 ML) DRIED THYME; COOK, STIRRING, FOR 3 MINUTES
OR UNTIL VEGETABLES ARE LIGHTLY COLORED. ADD 1 CUP
(250 ML) WHITE WINE, IF DESIRED. STIR IN 6 CUPS (1.5 L)
WATER; SEASON LIGHTLY WITH SALT AND PEPPER. BRING
TO A BOIL, COVER AND SIMMER OVER MEDIUM-LOW HEAT
FOR 3 HOURS. STRAIN STOCK THROUGH CHEESECLOTH-
LINED OR FINE SIEVE; DISCARD SOLIDS. MAKES ABOUT
4 CUPS (1 L) STOCK.

VARIATION: **SAUSAGE-APPLE STUFFING: COOK 1 LB
(500 G) BULK SAUSAGE MEAT IN A LARGE SKILLET
OVER MEDIUM-HIGH HEAT, BREAKING UP WITH BACK OF
SPOON, UNTIL NO LONGER PINK; DRAIN OFF FAT. ADD
2 PEELED, FINELY CHOPPED APPLES; COMBINE WITH BREAD
STUFFING MIXTURE.**

*MY CAR HAS A GAS-SAVING FEATURE FOR WINTER DRIVING.
IT WON'T START.*

ROAST DUCK WITH
PAT'S ORANGE SAUCE

2	DUCKS, WILD OR DOMESTIC	2
1	LARGE ONION	1
1	CARROT	1
2	STALKS CELERY	2
1 CUP	DRY WHITE WINE	250 ML
1 CUP	WATER	250 ML
	BUTTER	
	SALT AND FRESHLY GROUND BLACK PEPPER	

SOAK CLEANED DUCKS FOR $1/2$ HOUR IN BAKING SODA WATER ($1/2$ CUP/125 ML BAKING SODA MIXED IN SINK OF COLD WATER). RINSE AND DRY CAVITIES AND OUTSIDES OF BIRDS WITH PAPER TOWELS. PLACE IN ROASTING PAN AND FILL CAVITIES AND SURROUND DUCKS WITH SLICES OF ONION, CARROT AND CELERY. (THESE WILL BE DISCARDED AFTER ROASTING.) COVER DUCKS WITH LAYER OF BUTTER. SPRINKLE GENEROUSLY WITH SALT AND PEPPER. POUR WHITE WINE AND 1 CUP (250 ML) WATER OVER DUCKS. COVER AND ROAST AT 350°F (180°C) FOR THE FIRST HOUR AND 300°F (150°C) FOR THE FINAL $3 1/2$ HOURS. (THIS IS THE SECRET FOR COOKING ANY WILD FOWL — SLOWLY AND FOR A LONG TIME.) MEAT WILL BE VERY TENDER AND LITERALLY FALL FROM THE CARCASS. YOU MAY WANT TO REMOVE THE MEAT FROM THE BONES AND SERVE IT IN THIS INFORMAL MANNER. SERVE WITH PAT'S SPECIAL ORANGE SAUCE, PAGE 153. SERVES 4.

PAT'S SPECIAL ORANGE SAUCE

ESPECIALLY FOR ROAST DUCK

1/4 CUP	BUTTER	60 ML
1/4 CUP	FLOUR	60 ML
2 TBSP	CHICKEN BOUILLON POWDER	30 ML
I CUP	HOT WATER	250 ML
I CUP	ORANGE JUICE (MADE FROM UNSWEETENED FROZEN CONCENTRATE)	250 ML
	SHREDDED ORANGE PEEL	
DASH	HOT PEPPER SAUCE	DASH
3/4 CUP	CREAMED HONEY	175 ML
I	CAN (10 OZ/284 ML) MANDARIN ORANGE SECTIONS, DRAINED	I

MELT BUTTER IN A SAUCEPAN, ADD FLOUR AND STIR UNTIL
BUBBLY. MIX BOUILLON POWDER, HOT WATER, ORANGE
JUICE AND SHREDDED ORANGE PEEL. (USING POTATO
PEELER, REMOVE PEEL FROM AN ORANGE AND CUT IN THIN
JULIENNE STRIPS.) ADD TO BUTTER MIXTURE. STIR UNTIL
THICKENED. ADD HOT PEPPER SAUCE AND HONEY. KEEP
STIRRING AND ADD ORANGE SECTIONS. BEAT UNTIL FAIRLY
SMOOTH AND SERVE HOT WITH DUCK. MAKES ABOUT
4 CUPS (I L).

Q: MY DOG CHASES EVERYONE ON A BICYCLE. WHAT CAN I DO?
A: TAKE HIS BIKE AWAY.

COMPANY PORK ROAST WITH FRUIT STUFFING

THE SWEETNESS OF DRIED FRUIT ACCENTS THE DELICATE TASTE OF PORK IN THIS RECIPE. AND WHEN YOU STUFF THE LOIN WITH A FRUIT AND SPICE MIXTURE, YOU ENSURE THAT THE MEAT WILL BE EXTRA MOIST AND FLAVORFUL.

STUFFING

I TBSP	BUTTER	15 ML
1/3 CUP	CHOPPED GREEN ONIONS	75 ML
I TSP	GROUND CUMIN	5 ML
I TSP	MILD CURRY PASTE (OR TO TASTE)	5 ML
I	EGG	I
I CUP	CHOPPED MIXED DRIED FRUITS (SUCH AS APRICOTS, PRUNES, APPLES, CRANBERRIES)	250 ML
1/2 CUP	SOFT FRESH BREAD CRUMBS	125 ML
I TSP	GRATED ORANGE ZEST	5 ML
	SALT AND FRESHLY GROUND BLACK PEPPER	

PORK ROAST

3 LB	BONELESS SINGLE PORK LOIN ROAST	1.5 KG
2 TSP	VEGETABLE OIL	10 ML
I	LARGE CLOVE GARLIC, FINELY CHOPPED	I
I TSP	DRIED SAGE	5 ML
1/2 TSP	DRIED THYME	2 ML
	SALT AND FRESHLY GROUND BLACK PEPPER	

GRAVY

1 TBSP	ALL-PURPOSE FLOUR	15 ML
1/2 CUP	WHITE WINE OR READY-TO-USE CHICKEN BROTH	125 ML
3/4 CUP	READY-TO-USE CHICKEN BROTH	175 ML
	SALT AND FRESHLY GROUND BLACK PEPPER	

TO MAKE STUFFING: IN A SMALL SKILLET, MELT BUTTER OVER MEDIUM HEAT. ADD GREEN ONIONS, CUMIN AND CURRY PASTE; COOK, STIRRING, FOR 2 MINUTES OR UNTIL SOFTENED. IN A BOWL, BEAT EGG. ADD ONION MIXTURE, DRIED FRUITS, BREAD CRUMBS AND ORANGE ZEST; SEASON WITH SALT AND PEPPER.

TO MAKE PORK ROAST: PREHEAT OVEN TO 350°F (180°C). PLACE ROAST ON A CUTTING BOARD, FAT SIDE UP, WITH THE SHORTER END FACING YOU. WITH YOUR KNIFE PARALLEL TO BOARD, CUT PORK LOIN IN HALF BUT DO NOT CUT ALL THE WAY THROUGH. OPEN LIKE A BOOK. COVER MEAT WITH PLASTIC WRAP AND, USING A MEAT MALLET OR ROLLING PIN, POUND TO ABOUT 1-INCH (2.5 CM) THICKNESS. SEASON WITH SALT AND PEPPER. SPREAD STUFFING DOWN CENTER OF MEAT AND FOLD MEAT OVER TO ENCLOSE. TIE SECURELY AT SIX INTERVALS WITH BUTCHER'S STRING. PLACE ROAST ON A RACK IN A ROASTING PAN. IN A SMALL BOWL, COMBINE OIL, GARLIC, SAGE AND THYME; SPREAD OVER PORK ROAST AND SEASON WITH SALT AND PEPPER.

CONTINUED ON NEXT PAGE...

ROAST IN PREHEATED OVEN FOR $1\frac{1}{2}$ TO $1\frac{3}{4}$ HOURS OR UNTIL AN INSTANT-READ THERMOMETER REGISTERS 160°F (70°C). TRANSFER ROAST TO CUTTING BOARD; TENT WITH FOIL AND LET STAND FOR 10 MINUTES BEFORE CARVING.

TO MAKE GRAVY: DRAIN FAT FROM PAN. PLACE OVER MEDIUM HEAT; SPRINKLE WITH FLOUR. COOK, STIRRING, FOR 1 MINUTE OR UNTIL LIGHTLY COLORED. ADD WINE; COOK UNTIL PARTIALLY REDUCED. ADD BROTH AND BRING TO A BOIL, SCRAPING ANY BROWN BITS FROM BOTTOM OF PAN. SEASON WITH SALT AND PEPPER TO TASTE. STRAIN SAUCE THROUGH A FINE SIEVE INTO A WARM SAUCEBOAT. CUT PORK INTO THICK SLICES AND SERVE ACCOMPANIED WITH GRAVY. SERVES 8.

TIP: STORE-BOUGHT CURRY PASTES VARY IN FLAVOR AND STRENGTH DEPENDING ON THE BRAND. SOME PASTES ARE LABELED AS MILD BUT HAVE MORE HEAT THAN EXPECTED. ADD A SMALLER AMOUNT OF CURRY PASTE TO THE RECIPE TO TEST THE STRENGTH AND ADD MORE TO GET THE DEPTH OF FLAVOR YOU PREFER.

TIP: TO MAKE FRESH BREAD CRUMBS, PROCESS 1 SLICE WHITE SANDWICH BREAD IN A FOOD PROCESSOR UNTIL FINELY CRUMBLED.

TIP: IT MAY APPEAR THAT YOU HAVE TOO MUCH STUFFING WHEN YOU FIRST TIE THE PORK. BUT ONCE ALL THE STRINGS ARE IN PLACE, IT'S EASY TO ENCLOSE THE MEAT COMPLETELY AROUND THE FRUIT MIXTURE.

CIDER HAM STEAK WITH APPLES AND CRANBERRIES

THIS TASTY SAUCE ALSO GOES WELL WITH BONELESS CHICKEN BREASTS OR TURKEY SCALLOPS. PAIR THIS DISH WITH SCALLOPED POTATOES OR RICE AND A GREEN VEGETABLE SUCH AS BROCCOLI.

2/3 CUP	APPLE CIDER OR JUICE	150 ML
1 TBSP	PACKED BROWN SUGAR	15 ML
2 TSP	FRESHLY SQUEEZED LEMON JUICE (OR TO TASTE)	10 ML
1 1/2 TSP	DIJON MUSTARD	7 ML
1 1/2 TSP	CORNSTARCH	7 ML
1 LB	CENTER-CUT HAM STEAK, TRIMMED AND CUT INTO 4 PORTIONS	500 G
1 TBSP	BUTTER	15 ML
2	GREEN ONIONS, SLICED	2
1	APPLE, PEELED, CORED AND DICED	1
1/4 CUP	DRIED CRANBERRIES OR RAISINS	60 ML

IN A GLASS MEASURE, COMBINE APPLE CIDER, BROWN SUGAR, LEMON JUICE, MUSTARD AND CORNSTARCH UNTIL SMOOTH; SET ASIDE. PAT HAM DRY WITH PAPER TOWELS. IN A LARGE NONSTICK SKILLET, HEAT BUTTER OVER MEDIUM-HIGH HEAT; BROWN HAM ON BOTH SIDES. TRANSFER TO A PLATE. REDUCE HEAT TO MEDIUM. ADD GREEN ONIONS, APPLE AND CRANBERRIES TO SKILLET; COOK, STIRRING, FOR 2 MINUTES OR UNTIL SOFTENED. ADD CIDER MIXTURE; COOK, STIRRING, UNTIL SAUCE IS THICKENED. RETURN HAM TO SKILLET; COOK FOR 2 MINUTES, TURNING ONCE, OR UNTIL HEATED THROUGH. PLACE HAM STEAKS ON SERVING PLATES AND SPOON SAUCE OVER TOP. SERVES 4.

BAKED HAM WITH CITRUS MUSTARD GLAZE

THE ORANGE AND LEMON ZEST ADD A WONDERFUL FLAVOR TO THE HAM, AS WELL AS A TERRIFIC GARNISH.

I	BONE-IN SMOKED HAM (ABOUT 8 LBS/4 KG)	I
2 TBSP	COARSELY GRATED ORANGE ZEST	30 ML
2 TBSP	COARSELY GRATED LEMON ZEST	30 ML
1/2 CUP	CITRUS MARMALADE	125 ML
1/4 CUP	PURE MAPLE SYRUP	60 ML
1/4 CUP	WHITE WINE VINEGAR	60 ML
2 TBSP	ORANGE JUICE	30 ML
2 TSP	DRY MUSTARD	10 ML
I CUP	READY-TO-USE CHICKEN BROTH (APPROX.)	250 ML
I TSP	CORNSTARCH	5 ML

PREHEAT OVEN TO 325°F (160°C). REMOVE SKIN AND TRIM FAT FROM HAM, LEAVING A 1/4-INCH (0.5 CM) THICK LAYER. SCORE THE FAT TO MAKE A DIAMOND PATTERN. PLACE HAM IN A SHALLOW ROASTING PAN AND BAKE, UNCOVERED, FOR 1 1/4 HOURS. DRAIN OFF ANY FAT IN PAN.

IN A SMALL SAUCEPAN OF BOILING WATER, BLANCH ORANGE AND LEMON ZEST FOR 1 MINUTE TO REMOVE BITTERNESS. DRAIN AND RESERVE. IN A FOOD PROCESSOR, PURÉE MARMALADE, MAPLE SYRUP, VINEGAR, ORANGE JUICE AND MUSTARD UNTIL SMOOTH. TRANSFER TO A BOWL. POUR GLAZE OVER HAM AND SPRINKLE WITH ZESTS. BAKE, BASTING EVERY 15 MINUTES, FOR ABOUT 45 MINUTES OR UNTIL NICELY GLAZED AND MEAT THERMOMETER REGISTERS 140°F (60°C). (ADD A SMALL

AMOUNT OF BROTH TO BOTTOM OF PAN IF GLAZE BEGINS TO BROWN.) TRANSFER HAM TO A WARM PLATTER, COVER LOOSELY WITH FOIL AND LET REST FOR 15 MINUTES BEFORE CARVING.

PLACE ROASTING PAN ON STOVETOP OVER MEDIUM HEAT. BLEND BROTH AND CORNSTARCH UNTIL SMOOTH; POUR INTO PAN; COOK, STIRRING, UNTIL SAUCE BOILS AND IS SLIGHTLY THICKENED. CUT HAM INTO SLICES AND SERVE ACCOMPANIED WITH SAUCE. SERVES 8 TO 10, PLUS LEFTOVERS.

TIP: YOU WILL NEED THE ZEST FROM ABOUT 2 ORANGES AND 2 LEMONS.

TIP: ONCE OPENED, MAKE SURE TO STORE MAPLE SYRUP IN THE REFRIGERATOR. IT ALSO CAN BE FROZEN.

I NEVER FORGET MY WIFE'S BIRTHDAY.
IT'S THE DAY AFTER SHE REMINDS ME ABOUT IT.

ROAST BEEF WITH MUSTARD-PEPPERCORN CRUST

SOMETIMES NOTHING WILL DO BUT ROAST BEEF,
WHICH HAS BECOME A SPECIAL OCCASION DISH,
PERFECT FOR A HOLIDAY DINNER.

1 TBSP	COARSE SEA SALT	15 ML
1 TBSP	BLACK PEPPERCORNS	15 ML
1 TBSP	WHITE PEPPERCORNS	15 ML
1/3 CUP	DIJON MUSTARD	75 ML
2 TSP	WHOLE MUSTARD SEEDS	10 ML
1	BONELESS BEEF ROAST, SUCH AS TOP SIRLOIN PRIME RIB OR EYE OF ROUND (ABOUT 3 LBS/1.5 KG), PATTED DRY	1

IN A SPICE GRINDER, COMBINE SALT AND BLACK AND WHITE PEPPERCORNS. GRIND COARSELY. (YOU CAN ALSO DO THIS IN A MORTAR, WITH A PESTLE OR BETWEEN 2 SHEETS OF WAXED PAPER, USING THE BOTTOM OF A WINE BOTTLE OR MEASURING CUP.) TRANSFER TO A SMALL BOWL. STIR IN MUSTARD AND MUSTARD SEEDS. RUB MUSTARD-PEPPER MIX INTO THE MEAT, COVERING ALL SURFACES. LET STAND AT ROOM TEMPERATURE FOR 30 MINUTES.

MEANWHILE, PREHEAT OVEN TO 400°F (200°C). PLACE ROAST ON A RACK IN A ROASTING PAN. ROAST UNTIL NICELY BROWNED, ABOUT 20 MINUTES. REDUCE OVEN TEMPERATURE TO 325°F (160°C) AND CONTINUE ROASTING UNTIL AN INSTANT-READ THERMOMETER INSERTED INTO THE THICKEST PART OF THE MEAT REGISTERS THE DESIRED DEGREE OF DONENESS (125°F/52°C FOR RARE, ABOUT 25 MINUTES). REMOVE FROM OVEN, PLACE ON

A WARM PLATTER, TENT WITH FOIL AND LET REST FOR 10 MINUTES. SLICE THINLY ACROSS THE GRAIN. SERVES 8.

TIP: GENERALLY, 120°F TO 130°F (49°C TO 54°C) IS RARE; MEDIUM RANGES BETWEEN 135°F AND 145°F (57°C TO 63°C) AND WELL DONE IS 155°F (68°C) OR MORE.

YORKSHIRE PUDDING

A FAVORITE WITH ROAST BEEF DINNER!

I CUP	FLOUR	250 ML
$\frac{1}{2}$ TSP	SALT	2 ML
$\frac{1}{2}$ CUP	MILK	125 ML
2	EGGS, BEATEN	2
$\frac{1}{2}$ CUP	WATER	125 ML
	MELTED BUTTER OR OIL	

IN A BLENDER, MIX FLOUR, SALT, MILK, EGGS AND WATER. BLEND WELL AND LEAVE AT ROOM TEMPERATURE FOR I HOUR. EVERY TIME YOU WALK BY — GIVE IT A WHIRL! WHEN ROAST IS DONE, REMOVE FROM OVEN AND COVER WITH FOIL TO KEEP WARM. PREHEAT OVEN TO 400°F (200°C). POUR I TBSP (15 ML) BEEF DRIPPINGS, MELTED BUTTER OR OIL INTO 8 MEDIUM MUFFIN TINS. PLACE IN OVEN UNTIL BUBBLING HOT. (WATCH CLOSELY BECAUSE YOU DON'T WANT THE BUTTER TO BURN.) REMOVE FROM OVEN AND POUR BATTER INTO HOT BUTTER. BAKE AT 400°F (200°C) FOR 20 MINUTES AND THEN AT 350°F (180°C). FOR 10 MINUTES LONGER. YORKSHIRE WILL PUFF UP AND BE HOLLOW INSIDE. SERVE IMMEDIATELY WITH GRAVY.

CHÂTEAUBRIAND WITH COGNAC SAUCE

IF YOU'RE GOING ALL OUT BUT WANT TO STAY IN . . .

2	BEEF TENDERLOINS (2½ LBS/1.25 KG EACH)	2
5	MEDIUM CLOVES GARLIC, FINELY SLIVERED	5
2½ TBSP	OLIVE OIL	37 ML

COGNAC MUSTARD SAUCE

1½ TBSP	BUTTER OR MARGARINE	22 ML
4	MEDIUM SHALLOTS, MINCED	4
2 CUPS	READY-TO-USE BEEF BROTH	500 ML
2 TBSP	COGNAC OR BRANDY	30 ML
2 TBSP	DIJON MUSTARD	30 ML
½ CUP	BUTTER, CUT INTO 8 PIECES	125 ML
3 TBSP	CHOPPED FRESH PARSLEY	45 ML
	SALT AND FRESHLY GROUND BLACK PEPPER TO TASTE	

CUT ¾-INCH (2 CM) DEEP SLITS IN MEAT. INSERT GARLIC SLIVERS INTO SLITS. PREHEAT OVEN TO 450°F (230°C). IN LARGE SKILLET, HEAT OIL AND BROWN MEAT ON ALL SIDES. PLACE MEAT ON A RACK IN ROASTING PAN. SET SKILLET ASIDE. ROAST MEAT TO DESIRED DONENESS, ABOUT 40 MINUTES FOR MEDIUM-RARE.

TO MAKE SAUCE: MELT 1½ TBSP (22 ML) BUTTER IN RESERVED SKILLET. ADD SHALLOTS AND SAUTÉ UNTIL SOFTENED. STIR IN STOCK, SCRAPING UP BROWN BITS. BRING TO BOIL AND COOK UNTIL REDUCED BY HALF. ADD COGNAC AND BOIL 1 MINUTE. REDUCE HEAT TO LOW.

WHISK IN MUSTARD, THEN BUTTER, ONE PIECE AT A TIME.
COOK JUST UNTIL BUTTER IS MELTED. STIR IN PARSLEY.
SEASON WITH SALT AND PEPPER.

CARVE MEAT IN $\frac{1}{2}$-INCH (1 CM) SLICES. SPOON SAUCE
OVER AND SERVE IMMEDIATELY WITH A VARIETY OF
FRESH GARDEN VEGETABLES AND YOUR BEST BEAUJOLAIS.
SERVES 12.

*IF GOD HAD MEANT US TO TOUCH OUR TOES,
HE WOULD HAVE PUT THEM FARTHER UP OUR BODY.*

ENGLISH SPICED BEEF

THIS IS TRADITIONAL CHRISTMAS FARE. PRODUCES A PINK AND HAM-LIKE TEXTURE THAT, SLICED THINLY, IS A GREAT FAVORITE FOR HOLIDAY FEASTING. WELL WORTH THE TROUBLE!

	PIECE OF LEAN BEEF, UP TO 25 LBS (12.5 KG) DEBONED AND ROLLED	
1½ OZ	SALTPETER	45 G
1½ CUPS	BROWN SUGAR	375 ML
1½ CUPS	SALT	375 ML
¼ CUP	BLACK PEPPER	60 ML
¼ CUP	GROUND ALLSPICE	60 ML
2 TBSP	GROUND MACE	30 ML
2 TBSP	GROUND NUTMEG	30 ML
2 TBSP	GROUND CLOVES	30 ML

MIX INGREDIENTS TOGETHER AND RUB ROUND OF BEEF. COVER LOOSELY WITH FOIL. SET IN A COOL PLACE (A CROCK POT IS IDEAL) AND TURN EVERY 2 OR 3 DAYS FOR 3 WEEKS. BEFORE BOILING, PUT IN A PIECE OF SUET WHERE BONE WAS TAKEN OUT. TIE FIRMLY WITH CORD UNTIL IT IS OF UNIFORM SHAPE. SIMMER GENTLY FOR 5 TO 7 HOURS, TURNING AT HALF TIME. DO NOT WASH OFF SPICES BEFORE BOILING. FOR SMALLER PIECE OF BEEF (10 TO 12 LBS/5 TO 6 KG), USE SAME AMOUNT OF SPICES BUT REDUCE PICKLING TIME TO 12 DAYS AND REDUCE BOILING TIME TO 3 TO 5 HOURS.

BEEF TENDERLOIN WITH PEPPERCORN SAUCE

LIGHT THE CANDLES, POUR THE WINE,
ISN'T ENTERTAINING JUST DIVINE?

PEPPERCORN SAUCE

2 TBSP	BUTTER	30 ML
1/4 CUP	CHOPPED SHALLOTS	60 ML
2 TBSP	GREEN PEPPERCORNS (CANNED)	30 ML
1/4 CUP	BRANDY	60 ML
1 1/2 CUPS	HEAVY OR WHIPPING (35%) CREAM	375 ML
1 TBSP	STEAK SAUCE OR BARBECUE SAUCE	15 ML
2 TBSP	CHOPPED FRESH PARSLEY	30 ML
1	BEEF TENDERLOIN (ABOUT 2 1/2 LBS/1.25 KG)	1
	VEGETABLE OIL	
	SALT AND COARSELY GROUND BLACK PEPPER	

FOR THE SAUCE: MELT BUTTER IN SAUCEPAN, ADD SHALLOTS AND PEPPERCORNS AND SAUTÉ UNTIL SOFT. ADD BRANDY AND BRING TO BOIL. ADD CREAM AND STEAK SAUCE AND SIMMER UNTIL SLIGHTLY THICKENED — ABOUT 5 MINUTES. ADD PARSLEY AND SET ASIDE.

TO PREPARE MEAT: BRUSH TENDERLOIN WITH OIL AND SEASON WITH SALT AND PEPPER. BAKE AT 450°F (230°C) FOR 30 MINUTES FOR MEDIUM. SLICE AND SERVE WITH WARMED PEPPERCORN SAUCE.

BEEF BOURGUIGNON

AN ELEGANT FRENCH STEW FOR 8 GOOD FRIENDS.
SERVE WITH BEAUCOUP BAGUETTES . . . C'EST SI BON!

1/2 LB	THICK-SLICED BACON	250 G
12 to 15	SMALL WHOLE ONIONS, PEELED, OR 4 HANDFULS PEARL ONIONS, SKINS REMOVED	12 to 15
3 LBS	LEAN BEEF CHUCK, CUT INTO 1-INCH (2.5 CM) PIECES	1.5 KG
	OLIVE OIL	
2	CLOVES GARLIC, MINCED	2
3 TBSP	FLOUR	45 ML
	SALT AND BLACK PEPPER TO TASTE	
3 CUPS	DRY RED WINE	750 ML
2 CUPS	BEEF BROTH	500 ML
	BAY LEAF	
1/2 TSP	DRIED THYME	2 ML
2 CUPS	SLICED MUSHROOMS	500 ML
4 to 6	LARGE CARROTS, PEELED AND CUT IN BITE-SIZE PIECES	4 to 6
2 TBSP	BUTTER	30 ML
	CHOPPED FRESH PARSLEY FOR GARNISH	

PREHEAT OVEN TO 300°F (150°C). IN A DUTCH OVEN, SAUTÉ
BACON UNTIL CRISP. REMOVE, COOL AND COARSELY CHOP.
RESERVE 1 TO 2 TBSP (15 TO 30 ML) BACON DRIPPINGS.
ADD ONIONS AND SAUTÉ LIGHTLY; REMOVE TO ANOTHER
DISH. ADD BEEF TO POT (AND SOME OIL IF NECESSARY)
AND BROWN OVER MEDIUM-HIGH HEAT FOR 5 MINUTES;
ADD GARLIC FOR THE LAST MINUTE (BE CAREFUL NOT TO
BURN). SPRINKLE WITH FLOUR, SALT AND PEPPER; STIR
UNTIL FLOUR BEGINS TO BROWN. ADD WINE, BEEF BROTH,

BAY LEAF AND THYME. STIR TO LOOSEN BROWNED BITS ON BOTTOM OF POT, ADD ONIONS, COVER AND PLACE IN OVEN FOR AT LEAST 2 HOURS.

MEANWHILE, LIGHTLY SAUTÉ MUSHROOMS AND CARROTS IN BUTTER AND SET ASIDE. REMOVE POT FROM OVEN, ADD SAUTÉED VEGGIES AND RETURN TO OVEN FOR ANOTHER $1/2$ HOUR. IF MORE LIQUID IS NEEDED, ADD BEEF BROTH. GARNISH WITH PARSLEY. SERVES 8.

A BUS IS A VEHICLE THAT TRAVELS TWICE AS FAST WHEN YOU ARE RUNNING AFTER IT AS IT DOES WHEN YOU ARE ON IT.

TOURTIÈRE WITH RHUBARB RELISH

THIS IS A VERY OLD FRENCH CANADIAN RECIPE FOR MEAT PIES. IT IS PARTICULARLY GOOD BECAUSE THE MEAT IS CHOPPED, NOT GROUND. THIS RECIPE USUALLY MAKES ABOUT SIX PIES, BUT THIS CAN VARY WITH THE AMOUNT OF MEAT USED. ALWAYS USE A COMBINATION OF PORK (OR HAM) AND BEEF. THE ADDITION OF BREAST OF CHICKEN LENDS A FULLER FLAVOR. SEVERAL PIES CAN BE PREPARED AND FROZEN UNCOOKED IN DEEP ALUMINUM PIE PLATES (9- BY 1½-INCH/23 BY 4 CM). ALWAYS SERVE WITH RHUBARB RELISH. A TOURTIÈRE AND A JAR OF RELISH IS A SPECIAL GIFT AT CHRISTMAS TIME. THIS TAKES LOTS OF TIME, SO PROCEED AT A LEISURELY PACE AND ENJOY YOURSELF.

6 LBS	MEAT (THIS SHOULD BE A TOTAL WEIGHT AFTER REMOVAL OF BONE AND FAT. START WITH APPROXIMATELY 12 LBS/6 KG)	3 KG
	PORK (BOSTON BUTT) OR FRESH HAM, OR MIXTURE OF BOTH	
	BEEF: POT ROAST	
	CHICKEN: BREAST OF SMALL CHICKEN	
	BUTTER (ENOUGH TO BROWN ALL MEAT)	
2	MEDIUM ONIONS	2
2	CLOVES GARLIC, MINCED	2
1 TBSP	GROUND ALLSPICE	15 ML
1 TBSP	DRIED SAVORY	15 ML
	SALT, PEPPER, CHILI POWDER, POULTRY SEASONING TO TASTE	
1 CUP	BREAD OR CRACKER CRUMBS	250 ML
	RHUBARB RELISH (PAGE 169)	

CUT MEAT INTO BITE-SIZE CUBES, REMOVING ALL EXCESS FAT. BROWN MEAT IN BUTTER, SAUTE ONIONS AND GARLIC,

ADD SEASONING. COVER WITH HOT WATER AND SIMMER, UNCOVERED, FOR 3 HOURS. ALLOW TO COOL. SKIM OFF ANY EXCESS FAT. DRAIN OFF WATER, CORRECT SEASONING, ADD CRUMBS IN LAST HALF HOUR TO THICKEN, AND PLACE IN UNBAKED PIE SHELLS. COVER WITH TOP CRUST. BAKE AT 350°F (180°C) UNTIL CRUST IS GOLDEN. SERVE WITH RHUBARB RELISH. MAKES ABOUT 6 PIES.

RHUBARB RELISH

8 CUPS	CHOPPED RHUBARB	2 L
1 CUP	CHOPPED COOKING ONION	250 ML
$1/2$ TSP	GROUND CINNAMON	2 ML
$1/2$ TSP	GROUND ALLSPICE	2 ML
$1/2$ TSP	GROUND CLOVES	2 ML
1 CUP	WHITE VINEGAR	250 ML
2 CUPS	GRANULATED SUGAR	500 ML
1 TBSP	SALT	15 ML

SIMMER, UNCOVERED, APPROXIMATELY 4 HOURS (SOMETIMES MORE), UNTIL QUITE THICK. WATCH CLOSELY AS IT BURNS EASILY. LADLE INTO HOT, STERILIZED JARS, LEAVING $1/2$ INCH (1 CM) HEADSPACE. WIPE RIMS AND SEAL WITH TWO-PIECE CANNING LIDS. PROCESS IN A BOILING WATER CANNER FOR 10 MINUTES. CHECK SEALS AND REFRIGERATE ANY JARS THAT ARE NOT SEALED. MAKES ABOUT NINE 8-OZ (250 ML) JARS.

OSSO BUCO MILANESE

*CLASSIC ITALIAN FARE — A FLAVORFUL STEW
MADE WITH VEAL SHANKS.*

1/4 CUP	ALL-PURPOSE FLOUR	60 ML
	SALT AND FRESHLY GROUND BLACK PEPPER	
6	PIECES VEAL SHANK (8 OZ/250 G EACH)	6
1/3 CUP	OLIVE OIL	75 ML
3 TBSP	BUTTER	45 ML
2	LARGE CARROTS, PEELED AND SLICED	2
1	LARGE ONION, DICED	1
2	CELERY STALKS, SLICED	2
1 TBSP	CHOPPED GARLIC	15 ML
2	BAY LEAVES, CRUSHED	2
3 TBSP	CHOPPED FRESH MARJORAM OR 1 TBSP (15 ML) DRIED	45 ML
3 TBSP	CHOPPED FRESH BASIL OR 1 TBSP (15 ML) DRIED	45 ML
1 CUP	CHOPPED FRESH PARSLEY	250 ML
	GRATED ZEST OF 1 LEMON	
1 1/2 CUPS	DRY WHITE WINE	375 ML
1	CAN (19-OZ/540 ML) ITALIAN PLUM TOMATOES, DRAINED AND COARSELY CHOPPED	1
1 1/2 CUPS	READY-TO-USE CHICKEN BROTH	375 ML

GREMOLATA FOR GARNISH

4 TSP	CHOPPED FRESH PARSLEY	20 ML
2 TSP	LEMON ZEST	10 ML
1	CLOVE GARLIC, FINELY CHOPPED	1

COMBINE FLOUR, SALT AND PEPPER IN A PLASTIC BAG. ADD VEAL SHANKS AND COAT WITH FLOUR MIXTURE. HEAT OIL IN A LARGE SKILLET AND BROWN VEAL ON BOTH SIDES. REMOVE VEAL FROM SKILLET, REDUCE HEAT AND ADD BUTTER, CARROTS, ONION, CELERY, GARLIC, BAY LEAVES, MARJORAM, BASIL, PARSLEY AND LEMON ZEST. SAUTÉ FOR 5 MINUTES. ADD WINE AND CONTINUE COOKING FOR 5 MINUTES MORE. STIR IN TOMATOES AND BROTH. PLACE VEAL IN A CASSEROLE WITH THE SAUCE AND BAKE, COVERED, AT 325°F (160°C) FOR 2 HOURS. GARNISH WITH GREMOLATA. SERVES 6.

A STONE IN A HIKING BOOT ALWAYS MIGRATES TO THE POINT OF MAXIMUM PRESSURE.

ROSEMARY ROAST LAMB WITH NEW POTATOES

LAMB IS ALWAYS A CROWD PLEASER. THE HEAVENLY AROMA OF GARLIC AND ROSEMARY IN THIS RECIPE FILLS THE HOUSE AND MAKES AN ESPECIALLY WARM WELCOME FOR FRIENDS AS THEY COME THROUGH THE DOOR.

8	CLOVES GARLIC	8
1	LEG OF LAMB (ABOUT 5 TO 6 LBS/ 2.5 TO 3 KG)	1
	GRATED ZEST AND JUICE OF 1 LEMON	
2 TBSP	OLIVE OIL	30 ML
2 TBSP	CHOPPED FRESH ROSEMARY (OR 2 TSP/10 ML DRIED ROSEMARY, CRUMBLED)	30 ML
1/2 TSP	SALT	2 ML
1/2 TSP	FRESHLY GROUND BLACK PEPPER	2 ML
12	WHOLE NEW POTATOES (ABOUT 3 LBS/1.5 KG), SCRUBBED	12
1 TBSP	ALL-PURPOSE FLOUR	15 ML
1/2 CUP	WHITE WINE	125 ML
1 CUP	READY-TO-USE CHICKEN BROTH	250 ML

PREHEAT OVEN TO 350°F (180°C) AND GREASE A LARGE SHALLOW ROASTING PAN. CUT 6 CLOVES GARLIC INTO 8 TO 10 SLIVERS EACH. USING THE TIP OF A KNIFE, CUT SHALLOW SLITS ALL OVER LAMB AND INSERT A GARLIC SLIVER INTO EACH. FINELY CHOP REMAINING 2 GARLIC CLOVES. IN A BOWL, COMBINE GARLIC, LEMON ZEST AND JUICE, OIL, ROSEMARY, SALT AND PEPPER. PLACE LAMB IN

PREPARED ROASTING PAN; SURROUND WITH POTATOES.
BRUSH LAMB AND POTATOES GENEROUSLY WITH LEMON-
GARLIC MIXTURE. ROAST FOR ABOUT 1½ HOURS, TURNING
POTATOES OVER HALFWAY THROUGH ROASTING, UNTIL AN
INSTANT-READ THERMOMETER REGISTERS 135°F (57°C) FOR
MEDIUM-RARE. (FOR MEDIUM, REMOVE THE POTATOES AND
CONTINUE TO ROAST LAMB FOR 15 TO 20 MINUTES MORE
OR TO YOUR LIKING.) REMOVE LAMB TO A PLATTER; TENT
WITH FOIL AND LET REST 10 MINUTES BEFORE CARVING.
TRANSFER POTATOES TO A DISH; KEEP WARM.

SKIM FAT IN PAN; PLACE OVER MEDIUM HEAT. STIR IN
FLOUR AND COOK, STIRRING, UNTIL LIGHTLY COLORED.
POUR IN WINE; COOK, SCRAPING UP ANY BROWN BITS,
UNTIL WINE IS REDUCED BY HALF. STIR IN BROTH; BRING
TO A BOIL, STIRRING, UNTIL THICKENED. STRAIN THROUGH
A FINE SIEVE INTO A WARM SAUCEBOAT. CARVE THE LAMB.
ARRANGE SLICES ON A SERVING PLATE AND MOISTEN
WITH SOME OF THE SAUCE; SURROUND WITH ROASTED
POTATOES. SERVE WITH REMAINING SAUCE. SERVES 8.

TIP: TAKE THE LAMB OUT OF THE FRIDGE ABOUT
30 MINUTES BEFORE ROASTING.

TIP: CHOOSE POTATOES THAT ARE THE SAME SIZE SO
THEY ROAST EVENLY.

GARLIC AND HERB-CRUSTED RACK OF LAMB

HERE'S A CLASSIC LAMB DISH, OFTEN FEATURED ON
RESTAURANT MENUS, THAT CAN BE EASILY PREPARED IN
YOUR HOME KITCHEN FOR A SPECIAL DINNER. MUCH OF
IT CAN BE PREPARED AHEAD, SO YOU NEED ONLY
TO PLACE THE MEAT IN THE OVEN WHEN GUESTS
ARRIVE. SERVE IT WITH SMALL OVEN-ROASTED
POTATOES AND TENDER GREEN BEANS.

2	RACKS OF LAMB, EACH WITH 7 RIBS	2
	SALT AND FRESHLY GROUND BLACK PEPPER	
2 TBSP	OLIVE OIL	30 ML

GARLIC AND HERB CRUST

1½ CUPS	SOFT FRESH BREAD CRUMBS (ABOUT 3 SLICES BREAD)	375 ML
¾ CUP	FINELY CHOPPED FLAT-LEAF (ITALIAN) PARSLEY	175 ML
2 TSP	CHOPPED FRESH ROSEMARY LEAVES	10 ML
2 TSP	CHOPPED FRESH THYME LEAVES	10 ML
5 to 6	CLOVES GARLIC, FINELY CHOPPED	5 to 6
½ TSP	SALT	2 ML
½ TSP	FRESHLY GROUND BLACK PEPPER	2 ML
3 TBSP	BUTTER, SOFTENED	45 ML
2 TBSP	DIJON MUSTARD	30 ML

PREHEAT OVEN TO 425°F (220°C). SEASON LAMB WITH
SALT AND PEPPER. IN A LARGE NONSTICK SKILLET, HEAT
OIL OVER MEDIUM-HIGH HEAT; SEAR LAMB ON ALL SIDES
UNTIL LIGHTLY BROWNED. TRANSFER TO A HEAVY RIMMED
BAKING SHEET OR SHALLOW ROASTING PAN AND LET
COOL SLIGHTLY.

TO MAKE GARLIC AND HERB CRUST: IN A BOWL, COMBINE BREAD CRUMBS, PARSLEY, ROSEMARY, THYME, GARLIC, SALT AND PEPPER; BLEND IN BUTTER TO MAKE A PASTE-LIKE MIXTURE. SPREAD MUSTARD OVER FAT SIDE OF LAMB. SPREAD WITH BREAD CRUMB MIXTURE, PATTING DOWN SLIGHTLY. DISCARD ANY EXCESS BREAD CRUMB MIXTURE.

PLACE RACKS CRUMB SIDE UP ON BAKING SHEET. ROAST IN PREHEATED OVEN FOR 15 TO 20 MINUTES OR UNTIL MEDIUM-RARE. (INSTANT-READ THERMOMETER SHOULD READ 130°F/55°C.) REMOVE FROM OVEN. TRANSFER TO CUTTING BOARD AND CUT INTO CHOPS. SERVES 4.

TIP: HAVE THE BUTCHER REMOVE CHINE BONE, EXCESS FAT AND MEAT BETWEEN THE BONES.

WE KNOW CATS ARE SMARTER THAN DOGS BECAUSE YOU CAN'T GET EIGHT CATS TO PULL A SLED THROUGH SNOW.

POACHED SALMON

WHEN IT COMES TO SALMON, POACHING PRODUCES THE MOISTEST RESULT. A LARGE OVAL SLOW COOKER PRODUCES GREAT RESULTS, WITH LITTLE FUSS.

POACHING LIQUID

6 CUPS	WATER	1.5 L
1	ONION, CHOPPED	1
2	STALKS CELERY, CHOPPED (OR $1/2$ TSP/2 ML CELERY SEEDS)	2
4	SPRIGS FRESH PARSLEY	4
$1/2$ CUP	WHITE WINE OR LEMON JUICE	125 ML
8	PEPPERCORNS	8
1	BAY LEAF	1

SALMON

1	FILLET OF SALMON (ABOUT 3 LBS/1.5 KG)	1
	LEMON SLICES	
	SPRIGS FRESH PARSLEY OR DILL	

SORREL SAUCE (OPTIONAL)

1 LB	SORREL LEAVES, WASHED THOROUGHLY AND STEMS REMOVED	500 G
$1/4$ CUP	WATER	60 ML
$1/2$ TSP	DRIED TARRAGON	2 ML
1 TSP	DIJON MUSTARD	5 ML
$1/4$ CUP	HEAVY OR WHIPPING (35%) CREAM	60 ML
	SALT AND FRESHLY GROUND BLACK PEPPER	

TO MAKE POACHING LIQUID: IN A SAUCEPAN, COMBINE INGREDIENTS OVER MEDIUM HEAT. BRING TO A BOIL AND SIMMER FOR 30 MINUTES. STRAIN AND DISCARD SOLIDS.

TO MAKE SALMON: PREHEAT A LARGE (MINIMUM 5-QUART) OVAL SLOW COOKER ON HIGH FOR 15 MINUTES. FOLD A 2-FOOT (60 CM) PIECE OF FOIL IN HALF LENGTHWISE. PLACE ON BOTTOM AND UP SIDES OF STONEWARE. LAY SALMON OVER FOIL STRIP. RETURN POACHING LIQUID TO A BOIL AND POUR OVER SALMON. COVER AND COOK ON HIGH FOR 1 HOUR. REMOVE STONEWARE FROM SLOW COOKER. ALLOW SALMON TO COOL IN STONEWARE FOR 20 MINUTES. IF SERVING COLD, PLACE STONEWARE IN REFRIGERATOR AND ALLOW SALMON TO CHILL IN LIQUID. WHEN COLD, LIFT OUT AND TRANSFER TO A PLATTER. IF SERVING HOT, LIFT OUT AND TRANSFER TO A PLATTER. GARNISH AND SERVE.

TO MAKE SORREL SAUCE: IN A HEAVY SAUCEPAN WITH A TIGHT-FITTING LID, COMBINE SORREL, WATER AND TARRAGON. COVER AND COOK OVER LOW HEAT UNTIL SORREL IS WILTED. TRANSFER SORREL AND COOKING LIQUID TO A FOOD PROCESSOR. ADD DIJON MUSTARD AND WHIPPING CREAM AND PROCESS UNTIL SMOOTH. SEASON WITH SALT AND FRESHLY GROUND BLACK PEPPER TO TASTE. SPOON OVER SALMON, OR PASS SEPARATELY IN A SAUCEBOAT. SERVES 6 TO 8 AS A MAIN COURSE OR 12 TO 15 AS A BUFFET DISH.

TIP: MAKE SURE THAT THE SALMON IS COMPLETELY COVERED WITH THE POACHING LIQUID. IF YOU DO NOT HAVE SUFFICIENT LIQUID, ADD WATER TO COVER.

TIP: WHEN THE SALMON IS COOKED, IT SHOULD FEEL FIRM TO THE TOUCH AND THE SKIN SHOULD PEEL OFF EASILY.

SALMON WITH LEMON GINGER SAUCE

FRESH GINGER GIVES SUCH A SPARKLING FLAVOR TO SALMON — OR ANY FISH, FOR THAT MATTER. SUBSTITUTING DRIED GROUND GINGER JUST DOESN'T COME CLOSE TO IMPARTING THE SAME CRISP TASTE AS GINGERROOT.

4	SALMON FILLETS, EACH 5 OZ (150 G)	4
2	GREEN ONIONS	2
1½ TSP	MINCED GINGERROOT	7 ML
1	CLOVE GARLIC, MINCED	1
2 TBSP	SOY SAUCE	30 ML
1 TBSP	FRESHLY SQUEEZED LEMON JUICE	15 ML
1 TSP	GRATED LEMON ZEST	5 ML
1 TSP	GRANULATED SUGAR	5 ML
1 TSP	SESAME OIL	5 ML

PREHEAT OVEN TO 425°F (220°C) AND GREASE AN 11- BY 7-INCH (28 BY 18 CM) BAKING DISH. PLACE SALMON FILLETS IN A SINGLE LAYER IN BAKING DISH. CHOP GREEN ONIONS; SET ASIDE CHOPPED GREEN TOPS FOR GARNISH. IN A BOWL, COMBINE WHITE PART OF GREEN ONIONS, GINGER, GARLIC, SOY SAUCE, LEMON JUICE AND ZEST, SUGAR AND SESAME OIL. POUR MARINADE OVER SALMON; LET STAND AT ROOM TEMPERATURE FOR 15 MINUTES OR IN THE REFRIGERATOR FOR UP TO 1 HOUR. BAKE, UNCOVERED, FOR 13 TO 15 MINUTES OR UNTIL SALMON TURNS OPAQUE. ARRANGE ON SERVING PLATES, SPOON SAUCE OVER AND SPRINKLE WITH RESERVED GREEN ONION TOPS. SERVES 4.

TIP: ONE OF THE BEST USES FOR THE MICROWAVE IS FOR QUICKLY COOKING FISH. ARRANGE FISH AND SAUCE IN

A SHALLOW BAKING DISH AND COVER WITH MICROWAVE-SAFE PLASTIC WRAP; TURN BACK ONE CORNER TO VENT. MICROWAVE ON MEDIUM (50%) FOR 4 MINUTES. TURN FISH OVER AND RECOVER; MICROWAVE ON MEDIUM (50%) FOR 3 TO 5 MINUTES OR UNTIL SALMON TURNS OPAQUE.

TIP: THIS FISH DISH IS ALSO GREAT TO COOK ON THE BARBECUE.

PRIDE IS WHAT YOU FEEL WHEN YOUR KIDS
NET $180 FROM A GARAGE SALE.
PANIC IS WHEN YOU REALIZE YOUR CAR IS MISSING.

STUFFED ARCTIC CHAR

I	WHOLE ARCTIC CHAR, DEBONED AS MUCH AS POSSIBLE (5 LBS/2.5 KG)	I
I CUP	SOFTENED BUTTER	250 ML
I	LARGE ONION, CHOPPED	I
4	STALKS CELERY, CHOPPED	4
I	LARGE GREEN PEPPER, CHOPPED	I
	PIMENTO (JUST TO ADD SOME COLOR), SLICED	
	SALT AND BLACK PEPPER TO TASTE	

MIX BUTTER, ONION, CELERY, GREEN PEPPER, PIMENTO, SALT AND PEPPER. FILL THE FISH CAVITY WITH MIXTURE. SECURE THE FISH BY TYING IN SEVERAL PLACES WITH STRING. RUB GENEROUSLY WITH BUTTER. WRAP IN FOIL. PLACE IN ROASTING PAN ON TRIVET AND ADD ENOUGH WATER TO COVER THE BOTTOM (ADD MORE WATER AS NEEDED THROUGHOUT COOKING TIME). BAKE FOR 50 MINUTES AT 350°F (180°C). SERVES 6.

NEVER PUT A CHILD WEARING SUPERMAN PAJAMAS ON THE TOP BUNK.

Roasted Winter Vegetable and Orange Soup (page 140)

Roast Turkey with Sage-Bread Stuffing (page 148)

Beef Bourguignon (page 166)

Red Cabbage (page 190)

COQUILLE DAVID

OUR FRIEND DAVID IS A GREAT COOK.
THIS FRENCH CLASSIC IS HIS SIGNATURE DISH.

1 LB	SCALLOPS	500 G
1/2 LB	FRESH MUSHROOMS, SLICED	250 G
1 CUP	DRY WHITE WINE OR 3/4 CUP (175 ML) DRY VERMOUTH	250 ML
1/2 TSP	SALT	2 ML
4	PEPPERCORNS	4
2	SLICES OF ONION	2
1	BAY LEAF	1
1/4 TSP	THYME	1 ML

SAUCE

3 TBSP	BUTTER	45 ML
1/4 CUP	FLOUR	60 ML
3/4 CUP	MILK	175 ML
2	EGG YOLKS	2
1/2 CUP	HEAVY OR WHIPPING (35%) CREAM	125 ML
PINCH	CAYENNE	PINCH
	SALT TO TASTE	
2 TBSP	DRY SHERRY OR BRANDY	30 ML
1/2 CUP	SWISS CHEESE, GRATED	125 ML

RINSE SCALLOPS IN COLD WATER. COMBINE SCALLOPS AND MUSHROOMS IN A SAUCEPAN WITH NEXT SIX INGREDIENTS AND ENOUGH WATER TO BARELY COVER. BRING TO BOIL, COVER AND SIMMER GENTLY FOR 5 MINUTES. REMOVE SCALLOPS AND MUSHROOMS. STRAIN LIQUID AND BOIL RAPIDLY UNTIL REDUCED TO 1 CUP (250 ML). REMOVE SCALLOPS AND CUT INTO SMALL PIECES.

SEARED SCALLOPS WITH ORZO RISOTTO

ORZO RISOTTO

1²/₃ CUPS	ORZO PASTA	400 ML
1 TBSP	OLIVE OIL	15 ML
1 CUP	DICED MUSHROOMS	250 ML
¹/₃ CUP	DICED ONION	75 ML
¹/₃ CUP	DICED SUN-DRIED TOMATOES	75 ML
¹/₃ CUP	DICED RED PEPPER	75 ML
2 CUPS	CHICKEN STOCK	500 ML
¹/₂ CUP	FRESHLY GRATED PARMESAN CHEESE	125 ML
2 TBSP	CHOPPED PARSLEY	30 ML
¹/₂ CUP	HEAVY OR WHIPPING (35%) CREAM	125 ML

SCALLOPS

2 TBSP	OLIVE OIL	30 ML
16 LARGE (³/₄ LB)	NOVA SCOTIA SCALLOPS (LARGE SHRIMP ARE AN EXCELLENT SUBSTITUTE)	16 LARGE (340 G)
	SALT AND FRESHLY GROUND PEPPER TO TASTE	
	FRESHLY GRATED PARMESAN CHEESE	

COOK ORZO ACCORDING TO PACKAGE DIRECTIONS AND SET ASIDE. IN LARGE HEAVY POT, HEAT OIL AND SAUTÉ MUSHROOMS, ONION, SUN-DRIED TOMATOES AND RED PEPPER UNTIL SOFT. ADD STOCK AND BRING TO A BOIL. STIR IN ORZO, PARMESAN AND PARSLEY. ADD CREAM AND SIMMER GENTLY, STIRRING FREQUENTLY, UNTIL MIXTURE IS CREAMY BUT NOT RUNNY, ABOUT 20 MINUTES.

HEAT OIL IN VERY HOT PAN. SEASON SCALLOPS WITH SALT AND PEPPER AND SEAR UNTIL BROWN ON OUTSIDE

BUT JUST OPAQUE IN THE MIDDLE. SPRINKLE PARMESAN OVER RISOTTO AND TOP WITH SCALLOPS. AWESOME WITH ASPARAGUS! AN ELEGANT DINNER FOR 4.

TIP: SCALLOPS TEND TO PLUMP UP WITH WATER, SO BEFORE COOKING SET THEM ON PAPER TOWELS TO DRAW OUT SOME OF THE MOISTURE. SCALLOPS HAVE A TOUGH LITTLE MUSCLE ON THE SIDE. PEEL IT OFF BEFORE USING.

HAVING ONE CHILD MAKES YOU A PARENT;
HAVING TWO MAKES YOU A REFEREE.

LOBSTER NEWBURG

THIS IS A SPECIAL DISH AND REQUIRES SPECIAL CARE. IT MUST BE COOKED SLOWLY AT LOW HEAT OR IT WILL SEPARATE. IT ALSO SUFFERS WITH REHEATING, SO SERVE IMMEDIATELY.

1/3 CUP	BUTTER	75 ML
2 TBSP	FLOUR	30 ML
2 CUPS	TABLE (18%) CREAM	500 ML
4	SLIGHTLY BEATEN EGG YOLKS	4
2	CANS (EACH 5 OZ/142 G) LOBSTER	2
1/4 CUP	SHERRY	60 ML
2 TSP	LEMON JUICE	10 ML
1/4 TSP	SALT	1 ML
1 CUP	SLICED SAUTÉED FRESH MUSHROOMS	250 ML
6	PATTY SHELLS (FROZEN OR FRESH)	6

IN DOUBLE BOILER, MELT BUTTER AND BLEND IN FLOUR. GRADUALLY STIR IN CREAM. COOK SLOWLY, STIRRING CONSTANTLY UNTIL THICKENED. STIR SMALL AMOUNT OF SAUCE INTO EGG YOLKS. RETURN TO HOT MIXTURE AND COOK, STIRRING CONSTANTLY FOR 1 MINUTE. ADD LOBSTER, SHERRY, LEMON JUICE, SALT AND MUSHROOMS. HEAT THROUGH AND STIR. DO NOT BOIL! SERVE OVER PATTY SHELLS. SPRINKLE WITH PAPRIKA AND GARNISH WITH CELERY AND BLACK OLIVES.

SERVES 6.

TERRIFIC TURKEY STUFFING

FINALLY SOMETHING THAT'S GOOD FOR YOUR CAVITIES!

3 CUPS	COOKED WILD RICE	750 ML
2 CUPS	FRESH BREAD CRUMBS	500 ML
I LB	BULK PORK SAUSAGE	500 G
2	STALKS CELERY, FINELY CHOPPED	2
I	MEDIUM ONION, FINELY CHOPPED	I
	SALT AND BLACK PEPPER TO TASTE	
I to 2 TSP	DRIED SAGE	5 to IO ML
1/2 CUP	DRIED CRANBERRIES	125 ML

PLACE COOKED RICE AND BREAD CRUMBS IN A LARGE
BOWL. FRY SAUSAGE, CELERY AND ONION UNTIL SAUSAGE
IS BROWN. DRAIN AND ADD TO RICE MIXTURE. ADD
SEASONINGS AND DRIED CRANBERRIES AND TOSS. MIXTURE
SHOULD BE MOIST BUT NOT STICKY. ADD MORE BREAD
CRUMBS IF NECESSARY. SPOON, BUT DON'T PACK, INTO
NECK CAVITY AND BREAST CAVITY OF TURKEY. BE SURE
TO REMOVE STUFFING FROM BIRD IMMEDIATELY AFTER
REMOVING TURKEY FROM OVEN. KEEP WARM IN A SMALL
CASSEROLE. SERVES IO TO I2.

PEOPLE USUALLY GET WHAT'S COMING TO THEM —
UNLESS IT WAS MAILED.

CRANBERRY STUFFING

GREAT IN THE CENTER OF A CROWN ROAST
OF PORK — OR IN THE MIDDLE OF YOUR TURKEY!

1/4 CUP	BUTTER	60 ML
1	MEDIUM ONION, CHOPPED	1
1/2 CUP	CHOPPED CELERY	125 ML
4 CUPS	FRESH BREAD CRUMBS	1 L
1 TSP	SALT	5 ML
1/2 TSP	POULTRY SEASONING	2 ML
1/8 TSP	BLACK PEPPER	0.5 ML
1 CUP	CRANBERRIES, FRESH OR FROZEN AND THAWED	250 ML
2 CUPS	APPLES, PEELED, SLICED AND SPRINKLED WITH LEMON	500 ML

MELT BUTTER IN FRYING PAN; ADD ONIONS AND CELERY AND SAUTÉ. COMBINE NEXT FOUR INGREDIENTS. ADD TO ONION MIXTURE. STIR IN CRANBERRIES AND APPLES. STUFF!

SERVES 8.

WHY IS IT THAT WHENEVER YOU CALL A WRONG NUMBER, SOMEONE ALWAYS ANSWERS?

VIVA! VEGGIES

YUMMY FARE FOR COMPANY.

I	BUNCH BROCCOLI	I
8 OZ	MUSHROOMS, SLICED	250 G
2 TBSP	BUTTER	30 ML
1/2 CUP	MAYONNAISE	125 ML
1/2 CUP	SOUR CREAM	125 ML
1/2 CUP	GRATED PARMESAN CHEESE	125 ML
I	CAN (14 OZ/398 ML) ARTICHOKES, DRAINED AND CUT INTO BITE-SIZE PIECES	I
3	TOMATOES, SLICED	3
	SALT AND BLACK PEPPER TO TASTE	
1/4 CUP	BUTTER, MELTED	60 ML
1/2 CUP	DRY BREAD CRUMBS	125 ML

PRECOOK BROCCOLI UNTIL TENDER-CRISP. SAUTÉ MUSHROOMS IN 2 TBSP (30 ML) BUTTER. GREASE A 13- BY 9-INCH (33 BY 23 CM) DISH. BLEND MAYONNAISE, SOUR CREAM AND PARMESAN. MIX VEGETABLES IN SAUCE AND PLACE IN DISH. COVER WITH TOMATO SLICES. SEASON WITH SALT AND PEPPER. MIX MELTED BUTTER WITH BREAD CRUMBS AND SPRINKLE OVER TOMATOES. BAKE AT 325°F (160°C) FOR 20 MINUTES. SERVES 10 TO 12.

TISDALE ANNIE'S ASPARAGUS PUFF

10 OZ	GOUDA OR EDAM CHEESE	300 G
1 LB	ASPARAGUS (CANNED OR FROZEN MAY BE USED)	500 G
4	EGGS	4
1/2 TSP	SALT	2 ML
1/4 TSP	BLACK PEPPER	1 ML
1 CUP	CRACKER CRUMBS	250 ML
1	PIMENTO (OPTIONAL)	1
1 CUP	MILK	250 ML
1/4 CUP	MELTED BUTTER	60 ML

CUT CHEESE IN 1/2-INCH (1 CM) CUBES AND ASPARAGUS IN 1/2-INCH (1 CM) PIECES. BEAT EGGS WELL. ADD SALT, PEPPER, CRUMBS, PIMENTO (IF USING), MILK, ASPARAGUS AND CHEESE. POUR INTO 6-CUP (1.5 L) CASSEROLE DISH. POUR MELTED BUTTER OVER TOP. BAKE AT 350°F (180°C) FOR 40 MINUTES. MAY BE PREPARED AHEAD OF SERVING TIME, BUT DO NOT POUR BUTTER OVER UNTIL READY TO BAKE. SERVE IMMEDIATELY OR YOUR "PUFF" WILL LOSE ITS "POOF." SERVES 6.

SAUCY BRUSSELS SPROUTS

CHEEKY LITTLE DEVILS!

2 to 3 CUPS	BRUSSELS SPROUTS	500 to 750 ML
1/4 CUP	BUTTER	60 ML
1/4 CUP	FINELY CHOPPED ONION	60 ML
PINCH	GRANULATED SUGAR	PINCH
1 TBSP	RED WINE OR BURGUNDY COOKING WINE	15 ML
2 TBSP	CHOPPED FRESH PARSLEY	30 ML
2 TBSP	DIJON MUSTARD	30 ML
	SALT AND BLACK PEPPER TO TASTE	

SIMMER SPROUTS, UNCOVERED, ABOUT 10 MINUTES. WHILE SPROUTS ARE COOKING, PREPARE SAUCE BY MELTING BUTTER AND SAUTÉ ONIONS UNTIL SOFT. ADD REMAINING INGREDIENTS AND STIR TO BLEND. POUR OVER COOKED SPROUTS AND PLACE IN SERVING DISH. YUM! SERVES 4.

A CLEAN HOUSE IS A SIGN OF A BROKEN COMPUTER.

RED CABBAGE

EXCELLENT WITH FOWL AND A MUST WITH WILD GAME!

3 LBS	RED CABBAGE	1.5 KG
2	GREEN APPLES, PEELED AND CHOPPED	2
1	ONION, FINELY CHOPPED	1
1/4 CUP	GRANULATED SUGAR	60 ML
1/4 CUP	VINEGAR	60 ML
2 TBSP	BACON FAT	30 ML
1 TSP	SALT	5 ML
	FRESHLY GROUND BLACK PEPPER	
1/2 CUP	BOILING WATER	125 ML

SHRED CABBAGE AND PLACE IN A LARGE SAUCEPAN WITH
REMAINING INGREDIENTS. BRING TO A BOIL; REDUCE HEAT;
COVER AND SIMMER FOR 1 HOUR. STIR OCCASIONALLY.
SERVES 6 TO 8.

WITH GREAT POWER COMES A HUGE ELECTRICITY BILL.

GINGERED CARROT PURÉE

SPICY YET SWEET!

3 LBS	CARROTS, CUT INTO 1-INCH (2.5 CM) PIECES	1.5 KG
3 TBSP	BUTTER	45 ML
1 TBSP	GRATED GINGERROOT OR $1/2$ TSP (2 ML) GROUND GINGER	15 ML
1/4 TSP	SALT	1 ML
1/4 TSP	BLACK PEPPER	1 ML
1/4 CUP	HALF-AND-HALF (10%) CREAM	60 ML

BOIL CARROTS UNTIL VERY TENDER, 25 TO 30 MINUTES. DRAIN AND TRANSFER TO A FOOD PROCESSOR. ADD REMAINING INGREDIENTS. WHIRL, SCRAPING SIDES OCCASIONALLY, UNTIL FAIRLY SMOOTH. PLACE "SIDE-BY-SIDE" IN SERVING DISH WITH HOLIDAY PARSNIPS (PAGE 197).

CORN SOUFFLÉ

A LOVELY CHANGE FOR THE CORN — ALWAYS GOOD
WHEN SERVED WITH HAM. MUST BE PREPARED AND
SERVED JUST BEFORE DINNER OR SOUFFLÉ WILL
FALL. DON'T FORGET THE SALT!

4	EGGS	4
I TBSP	GRANULATED SUGAR	15 ML
I	CAN (IO OZ/284 ML) CREAMED CORN	I
2 TBSP	BUTTER	30 ML
2 TBSP	FLOUR	30 ML
1/4 TSP	SALT	I ML

SEPARATE EGGS INTO TWO MEDIUM BOWLS. BEAT
TOGETHER YOLKS, SUGAR, SALT AND CORN. MELT BUTTER
AND FLOUR; BEAT INTO CORN MIXTURE. BEAT EGG WHITES
UNTIL STIFF AND FOLD INTO CORN. POUR INTO SOUFFLÉ
DISH OR CASSEROLE. BAKE AT 350°F (180°C) FOR 45
MINUTES. SERVE AT ONCE. SERVES 4 TO 6.

PEOPLE WHO DRIVE LIKE HELL ARE BOUND TO GET THERE.

GREEN BEAN CASSEROLE

THIS RECIPE YOU CAN MAKE AHEAD, SET IN THE
REFRIGERATOR AND HEAT JUST BEFORE DINNER.
TRY WITH HAM OR CORNED BEEF.

1 LB	FRESH MUSHROOMS, SLICED	500 G
1/2 CUP	BUTTER	125 ML
1/4 CUP	FLOUR	60 ML
2 CUPS	MILK	500 ML
1 CUP	TABLE (18%) CREAM	250 ML
1 1/2 CUPS	GRATED SHARP (OLD) CHEDDAR CHEESE	375 ML
1/8 TSP	HOT PEPPER SAUCE	0.5 ML
2 TSP	SOY SAUCE	10 ML
1 TSP	SALT	5 ML
1/2 TSP	BLACK PEPPER	2 ML
2	PACKAGES (EACH 12 OZ/375 G) FROZEN FRENCH-CUT BEANS, COOKED AND DRAINED	2
1	CAN (5 OZ/142 ML) WATER CHESTNUTS, DRAINED, SLICED	1
1/2 CUP	TOASTED SLIVERED ALMONDS	125 ML

SAUTÉ MUSHROOMS IN BUTTER. ADD FLOUR AND MIX. ADD
MILK AND CREAM; STIR UNTIL THICKENED. ADD CHEESE,
HOT PEPPER SAUCE, SOY SAUCE, SALT AND PEPPER;
SIMMER UNTIL CHEESE MELTS. ADD COOKED BEANS AND
WATER CHESTNUTS; MIX WELL. POUR INTO GREASED
SHALLOW CASSEROLE. SPRINKLE WITH TOASTED SLIVERED
ALMONDS. BAKE AT 350°F (180°C) FOR 35 TO 45 MINUTES.

SERVES 8.

FESTIVE MUSHROOMS

A VERY RICH DISH FOR SPECIAL OCCASIONS. SERVE SMALL HELPINGS! GOOD WITH ROAST BEEF.

2 LBS	FRESH MUSHROOMS, CUT INTO T'S	1 KG
3 TBSP	BUTTER	45 ML
1	CAN (14 OZ/398 ML) PITTED RIPE OLIVES, SLICED	1
1 CUP	GRATED SHARP (OLD) CHEDDAR CHEESE	250 ML
2 TBSP	FLOUR	30 ML
2 TBSP	BUTTER	30 ML
1/2 CUP	FRESH BREAD CRUMBS	125 ML
1 TBSP	MELTED BUTTER	15 ML

SAUTÉ MUSHROOMS IN 3 TBSP (45 ML) BUTTER UNTIL JUICY. IN A MEDIUM CASSEROLE, ADD A LAYER OF MUSHROOMS AND SLICED OLIVES. SPRINKLE WITH CHEDDAR CHEESE AND FLOUR; DOT WITH BUTTER. CONTINUE LAYERS IN THIS ORDER, AND TOP LAST LAYER WITH BUTTERED CRUMBS. BAKE AT 350°F (180°C) FOR 30 MINUTES. SERVES 8 TO 10.

PARMESAN PORTOBELLOS

1 LB	PORTOBELLO MUSHROOMS, SLICED	500 G
2 TBSP	SLICED SHALLOTS	30 ML
2	CLOVES GARLIC, CHOPPED	2
2 TBSP	OLIVE OIL	30 ML
1/4 CUP	BUTTER	60 ML
1/4 CUP	BALSAMIC VINEGAR	60 ML
1/3 CUP	GRATED PARMESAN CHEESE	75 ML
	PEPPER TO TASTE	

CLEAN TOPS OF MUSHROOMS WITH BRUSH OR MOIST PAPER TOWEL. DON'T PEEL THEM — YOU'LL LOSE THE FLAVOR! SAUTÉ SHALLOTS AND GARLIC IN OIL AND BUTTER FOR 2 TO 3 MINUTES. ADD MUSHROOMS, STIRRING UNTIL GOLDEN. ADD VINEGAR AND STIR WELL TO DEGLAZE PAN. ADD THE CHEESE AND STIR UNTIL MELTED. SEASON WITH PEPPER AND SERVE IMMEDIATELY. SERVES 4.

"I MISS MY WIFE'S COOKING — AS OFTEN AS I CAN."
— HENNY YOUNGMAN

CREAMED ONIONS

THE WAY YOUR GRANDMOTHER MADE THEM.

12	BOILING ONIONS (SMALL)	12

CREAM SAUCE

3 TBSP	BUTTER	45 ML
3 TBSP	FLOUR	45 ML
2 CUPS	MILK	500 ML
1/2 TSP	SALT	2 ML
	BLACK PEPPER TO TASTE	
1/4 TSP	GROUND NUTMEG	1 ML
1/2 CUP	CRACKER CRUMBS OR DRY BREAD CRUMBS	125 ML
2 TBSP	BUTTER	30 ML
	PARMESAN CHEESE	

PEEL ONIONS AND PLACE IN A POT WITH A LARGE AMOUNT OF BOILING SALTED WATER. BOIL, UNCOVERED, FOR 20 TO 30 MINUTES, UNTIL TENDER BUT NOT FALLING APART. DRAIN AND TRANSFER ONIONS TO A BUTTERED CASSEROLE.

TO PREPARE CREAM SAUCE: MELT BUTTER IN A MEDIUM SAUCEPAN AND STIR IN FLOUR. WHEN BLENDED, ADD MILK SLOWLY WHILE STIRRING. COOK ON LOW HEAT UNTIL SAUCE THICKENS. ADD SALT, PEPPER AND NUTMEG. POUR SAUCE OVER ONIONS. COMBINE CRACKER CRUMBS AND BUTTER AND SPRINKLE OVER ONIONS. TOP WITH PARMESAN CHEESE. BEFORE SERVING, PREHEAT OVEN TO 350°F (180°C) AND BAKE FOR 15 TO 20 MINUTES, UNTIL LIGHTLY BROWNED. SERVES 4.

HOLIDAY PARSNIPS

ENHANCED BY A LITTLE TASTE OF NUTMEG.

3 LBS	PARSNIPS, PEELED AND SLICED	1.5 KG
3 TBSP	BUTTER	45 ML
1/4 TSP	GROUND NUTMEG	1 ML
1/4 TSP	SALT	1 ML
1/4 TSP	WHITE PEPPER	1 ML
1/4 CUP	HALF-AND-HALF (10%) CREAM	60 ML

BOIL PARSNIPS UNTIL VERY TENDER (15 TO 20 MINUTES). DRAIN. IN A FOOD PROCESSOR, WHIRL UNTIL FAIRLY SMOOTH. ADD BUTTER, NUTMEG, SALT AND PEPPER. GIVE IT A WHIRL. ADD CREAM AND WHIRL AGAIN. THIS MAY BE MADE A DAY AHEAD. ARE YOU DIZZY YET? SERVE WITH GINGERED CARROT PURÉE (PAGE 191).

DO BAKERS WITH A SENSE OF HUMOR MAKE WRY BREAD?

TURNIPS AND APPLES

*EVERYBODY WHO TRIES THIS
WANTS THE RECIPE — YOU'VE GOT IT!*

I	LARGE TURNIP	I
I TBSP	BUTTER	15 ML
2	APPLES	2
1/4 CUP	BROWN SUGAR	60 ML
PINCH	CINNAMON	PINCH

CRUST

1/3 CUP	FLOUR	75 ML
1/3 CUP	BROWN SUGAR	75 ML
2 TBSP	BUTTER	25 ML

PEEL, DICE, COOK, DRAIN AND MASH THE TURNIP WITH
BUTTER. PEEL AND SLICE APPLES. TOSS WITH BROWN
SUGAR AND CINNAMON. ARRANGE IN GREASED CASSEROLE,
TURNIPS AND APPLES IN ALTERNATE LAYERS, BEGINNING
AND ENDING WITH TURNIPS. COMBINE CRUST INGREDIENTS
TO A CRUMBLY TEXTURE AND PAT ON TOP OF CASSEROLE.
BAKE AT 350°F (180°C) FOR I HOUR. SERVES 6 TO 8.

RICH FOODS ARE LIKE DESTINY. THEY, TOO, SHAPE OUR ENDS.

CHEESY ACORN SQUASH

SCORE ONE FOR SQUASH! SERVE WITH CORNISH HENS OR ROAST CHICKEN, RICE AND A GREEN SALAD.

3	MEDIUM ACORN SQUASH	3
1 CUP	DICED CELERY	250 ML
1 CUP	FINELY CHOPPED ONION	250 ML
1/4 CUP	BUTTER	60 ML
1 CUP	SLICED MUSHROOMS	250 ML
1/2 TSP	SALT	2 ML
PINCH	BLACK PEPPER	PINCH
2 TBSP	CHOPPED FRESH PARSLEY	30 ML
1 CUP	SHREDDED CHEDDAR CHEESE	250 ML

CUT SQUASH IN HALF, REMOVE SEEDS AND PLACE, CUT SIDE DOWN, IN ROASTING PAN. BAKE SQUASH AT 350°F (180°C) FOR 1 HOUR OR UNTIL ALMOST TENDER. SAUTÉ CELERY AND ONION IN BUTTER UNTIL TRANSPARENT; ADD MUSHROOMS AND COOK FOR 2 TO 3 MINUTES LONGER. ADD SALT, PEPPER AND PARSLEY. TURN SQUASH CUT SIDE UP AND DISTRIBUTE CELERY MIXTURE EVENLY IN SQUASH. COVER ROASTING PAN AND CONTINUE TO BAKE FOR 15 MINUTES. UNCOVER AND SPRINKLE CHEESE OVER MIXTURE. COOK FOR ABOUT 5 MINUTES OR UNTIL CHEESE MELTS AND IS BUBBLY. SERVES 6.

SWEET POTATO SUPREME

GREAT WITH HAM OR TURKEY.

4 CUPS	COOKED MASHED SWEET POTATOES	1 L
2 TBSP	TABLE (18%) CREAM OR MILK	30 ML
1 TSP	SALT	5 ML
1/4 TSP	PAPRIKA	1 ML
1/2 CUP	PACKED BROWN SUGAR	125 ML
1/3 CUP	BUTTER	75 ML
1 CUP	PECAN HALVES, TO COVER CASSEROLE	250 ML

THOROUGHLY MIX POTATOES, CREAM, SALT AND PAPRIKA. SPREAD IN GREASED CASSEROLE. MAKE THE TOPPING BY HEATING BROWN SUGAR AND BUTTER OVER LOW HEAT, STIRRING CONSTANTLY, UNTIL BUTTER IS BARELY MELTED. (IT IS IMPORTANT NOT TO COOK AFTER BUTTER IS MELTED, OR THE TOPPING WILL HARDEN WHEN CASSEROLE IS HEATED.) SPREAD TOPPING OVER POTATOES AND COVER WITH PECAN HALVES. REFRIGERATE UNTIL READY TO HEAT. THIS CASSEROLE MAY BE WARMED IN AN OVEN OF ANY TEMPERATURE. SHOULD BE BUBBLING HOT BEFORE SERVING. SERVES 6 TO 8.

YAMMY APPLES

THIS IS A HIT WITH CHILDREN.
IF THEY LIKE IT, EVERYONE WILL!

2	CANS (EACH 19 OZ/540 ML) YAMS, SLICED INTO THIN CHUNKS	2
4	JUICY RED APPLES, PEELED AND SLICED	4
3 TBSP	LEMON JUICE	45 ML
3 TBSP	BROWN SUGAR	45 ML
1½ TSP	GROUND CINNAMON	7 ML
3 TBSP	BUTTER	45 ML
	MINIATURE MARSHMALLOWS (OPTIONAL)	

THIS RECIPE IS MADE IN LAYERS; START WITH A BUTTERED 10-CUP (2.5 L) CASSEROLE DISH AND MAKE A 1-INCH (2.5 CM) LAYER OF SLICED YAMS. COVER COMPLETELY WITH 2 OF THE SLICED APPLES. SPRINKLE WITH HALF THE LEMON JUICE, HALF THE BROWN SUGAR AND HALF THE CINNAMON, THEN DAB WITH HALF THE BUTTER. REPEAT THE LAYERS. BAKE AT 350°F (180°C) FOR 30 MINUTES. IF DESIRED, 10 MINUTES BEFORE COOKING TIME HAS EXPIRED, COVER WITH A LAYER OF MINIATURE MARSHMALLOWS AND BAKE UNTIL THEY TURN GOLDEN BROWN. SERVES 8.

CHEESY SCALLOPED POTATOES

THIS RECIPE CAN ALL BE MIXED IN A
BLENDER OR FOOD PROCESSOR.

6	MEDIUM POTATOES, PEELED AND SLICED	6
1/4 CUP	DICED ONION	60 ML
1/4 CUP	CELERY LEAVES	60 ML
2	SPRIGS PARSLEY	2
3 TBSP	FLOUR	45 ML
1/4 CUP	BUTTER	60 ML
1 1/2 TSP	SALT	7 ML
1/4 TSP	PEPPER	1 ML
1 1/2 CUPS	MILK	375 ML
1 to 2 CUPS	GRATED SHARP (OLD) CHEDDAR CHEESE	250 to 500 ML
PINCH	PAPRIKA	PINCH

BLEND ONION, CELERY LEAVES, PARSLEY, FLOUR, BUTTER, SALT, PEPPER AND MILK IN A BLENDER, MIXING THOROUGHLY. ARRANGE POTATO SLICES IN BUTTERED 8-CUP (2 L) BAKING DISH. POUR MIXTURE OVER POTATOES; SPRINKLE WITH GRATED CHEESE AND PAPRIKA. BAKE IN 350°F (180°C) OVEN FOR APPROXIMATELY 50 MINUTES. THIS CAN BE FROZEN AND REHEATED. SERVES 8.

CREAMY WHIPPED POTATOES

THIS IS A DIFFERENT TWIST TO STANDARD POTATOES.
SERVE WITH STEAK, CHICKEN OR HAM. YUMMY!

8	MEDIUM POTATOES	8
I TSP	SALT	5 ML
2 CUPS	HEAVY OR WHIPPING (35%) CREAM	500 ML
	SALT AND BLACK PEPPER	
1/2 LB	GRATED SHARP (OLD) CHEDDAR CHEESE	250 G

BOIL POTATOES WITH THE SALT. MASH AND MIX WITH
I CUP (250 ML) OF WHIPPING CREAM UNTIL THICK AND
CREAMY. ADD SALT AND PEPPER TO TASTE AND A SPRINKLE
OF THE GRATED CHEESE. PUT IN A 13- BY 9-INCH (33 BY
23 CM) CASSEROLE. LAYER TOP WITH I CUP (250 ML)
CREAM, WHIPPED; SPRINKLE GRATED CHEESE ON TOP AND
BAKE AT 300°F (150°C) FOR I 1/2 HOURS. SERVES 6 TO 8.

I READ SOME RECIPES THE WAY I READ SCIENCE FICTION.
I GET TO THE END AND I THINK,
"WELL, THAT'S NOT GOING TO HAPPEN."

ELSIE'S POTATOES

*A MUST WITH TURKEY DINNER . . . CAN BE
MADE AHEAD AND FROZEN.*

5 LBS	POTATOES (ABOUT 9 LARGE)	2.5 KG
8 OZ	LOW-FAT CREAM CHEESE	250 G
I CUP	FAT-FREE SOUR CREAM	250 ML
2 TSP	ONION SALT	10 ML
I TSP	SALT	5 ML
PINCH	BLACK PEPPER	PINCH
2 TBSP	BUTTER	30 ML

COOK AND MASH POTATOES. ADD ALL INGREDIENTS,
EXCEPT BUTTER, AND COMBINE. PUT INTO LARGE GREASED
CASSEROLE. DOT WITH BUTTER. BAKE, COVERED, AT 350°F
(180°C). FOR 30 MINUTES. IF MAKING AHEAD, COVER
AND REFRIGERATE OR FREEZE. THAW BEFORE BAKING.

SERVES 10 TO 12.

ROASTED NEW POTATOES WITH HERBS

HERB AND ROSEMARY MAKE A NICE COUPLE!

8	MEDIUM NEW POTATOES	8
1/4 CUP	OLIVE OIL	60 ML
2 to 3	CLOVES GARLIC, CRUSHED	2 to 3
2 TBSP	DRIED HERBS (ROSEMARY OR MINT)	30 ML

WASH POTATOES AND CUT INTO QUARTERS. ARRANGE IN SHALLOW BAKING DISH AND TOSS WITH OIL, GARLIC AND HERBS. BAKE AT 375°F (190°C) FOR 1 HOUR, TURNING OCCASIONALLY. SERVES 4 TO 6.

WHEN YOU'RE ON YOUR THIRD MARGARITA, STAY AWAY FROM THE PHONE. NEVER MIND HOW I KNOW THIS.

SPANISH VEGETABLE PAELLA

TRADITIONAL PAELLA IS MADE IN A WIDE SHALLOW PAN, BUT TODAY'S NONSTICK SKILLET MAKES A VERY GOOD SUBSTITUTE AND REDUCES THE AMOUNT OF OIL NEEDED FOR THIS DISH.

4 CUPS	ASSORTED PREPARED VEGETABLES (SEE TIP, OPPOSITE)	1 L
3 1/2 CUPS	READY-TO-USE CHICKEN OR VEGETABLE BROTH	875 ML
1/4 TSP	SAFFRON THREADS, CRUSHED	1 ML
PINCH	HOT PEPPER FLAKES	PINCH
	SALT	
2 TBSP	OLIVE OIL	30 ML
4	GREEN ONIONS, CHOPPED	4
3	LARGE CLOVES GARLIC, FINELY CHOPPED	3
1 1/2 CUPS	SHORT-GRAIN WHITE RICE (SUCH AS ARBORIO)	375 ML

PREHEAT OVEN TO 375°F (190°C). MEANWHILE, COOK VEGETABLES (EXCEPT PEPPERS AND ZUCCHINI) IN A SAUCEPAN OF BOILING, LIGHTLY SALTED WATER FOR 1 MINUTE. RINSE UNDER COLD WATER TO CHILL; DRAIN WELL. IN THE SAME SAUCEPAN, BRING BROTH TO A BOIL. ADD SAFFRON AND HOT PEPPER FLAKES; SEASON WITH SALT TO TASTE. KEEP WARM.

IN A LARGE NONSTICK SKILLET, HEAT OIL OVER MEDIUM-HIGH HEAT. ADD GREEN ONIONS AND GARLIC; COOK, STIRRING, FOR 1 MINUTE. ADD VEGETABLES TO SKILLET; COOK, STIRRING OFTEN, FOR 4 MINUTES OR UNTIL LIGHTLY COLORED. STIR IN RICE AND HOT STOCK MIXTURE. REDUCE HEAT SO RICE COOKS AT A GENTLE BOIL:

COOK, UNCOVERED, WITHOUT STIRRING, FOR 10 MINUTES OR UNTIL MOST OF THE LIQUID IS ABSORBED. COVER SKILLET WITH LID OR FOIL. (IF SKILLET HANDLE IS NOT OVENPROOF, WRAP IN DOUBLE LAYER OF FOIL.) BAKE FOR 15 MINUTES OR UNTIL ALL LIQUID IS ABSORBED AND RICE IS TENDER. REMOVE; LET STAND, COVERED, FOR 5 MINUTES BEFORE SERVING. MAKES 4 SERVINGS AS A MAIN COURSE OR 6 AS A SIDE DISH.

TIP: TRY A VARIETY OF DIFFERENT VEGETABLES, INCLUDING BITE-SIZE PIECES OF BROCCOLI, CAULIFLOWER, ASPARAGUS, GREEN BEANS, BELL PEPPERS AND ZUCCHINI.

WILD RICE BROCCOLI CASSEROLE

THIS COMPLEMENTS ANY MEAT OR FOWL.

1	PACKAGE (6 OZ/170 G) WILD RICE MIXTURE	1
2	HEADS BROCCOLI, CUT INTO FLORETS	2
2	CANS (EACH 10 OZ/284 ML) MUSHROOM SOUP	2
2 CUPS	GRATED CHEDDAR CHEESE	500 ML

COOK RICE MIXTURE AS DIRECTED. COOK BROCCOLI UNTIL CRUNCHY. MIX SOUP AND $1\frac{1}{2}$ CUPS (375 ML) CHEESE. BUTTER A CASSEROLE. ALTERNATE SOUP MIXTURE, BROCCOLI AND RICE IN LAYERS. SPRINKLE WITH REMAINING $\frac{1}{2}$ CUP (125 ML) CHEESE. COOK AT 350°F (180°C) FOR 1 HOUR. SERVES 6.

LEMON RISOTTO

WHEN YOU'RE WILLING TO FUSS . . .

I TBSP	OLIVE OIL	15 ML
1 1/2 CUPS	SLICED SHIITAKE MUSHROOMS	375 ML
2	SHALLOTS OR GREEN ONIONS, THINLY SLICED	2
2	CLOVES GARLIC, MINCED	2
PINCH	BLACK PEPPER	PINCH
I CUP	ARBORIO OR SHORT-GRAIN RICE	250 ML
2 CUPS	CHICKEN BROTH	500 ML
1/2 CUP	DRY WHITE WINE OR WATER	125 ML
I	LARGE CARROT, CUT INTO I-INCH (2.5 CM) MATCHSTICKS	I
I	SMALL BUNCH ASPARAGUS SPEARS, CUT INTO I-INCH (2.5 CM) PIECES	I
1/4 CUP	PARMESAN CHEESE	60 ML
2 TSP	GRATED LEMON ZEST	10 ML
	FRESH BASIL OR PARSLEY (OPTIONAL)	

IN A LARGE SAUCEPAN, HEAT OIL AND COOK MUSHROOMS, SHALLOTS, GARLIC AND PEPPER UNTIL VEGETABLES ARE TENDER BUT NOT BROWN. ADD RICE AND COOK AND STIR 2 MINUTES MORE. STIR BROTH AND WINE INTO RICE MIXTURE AND BRING TO A BOIL. REDUCE HEAT; COVER AND SIMMER FOR 30 MINUTES (DO NOT LIFT COVER). REMOVE FROM HEAT. STIR IN CARROTS, ASPARAGUS, PARMESAN AND LEMON ZEST. COVER AND LET STAND FOR 5 MINUTES. ADD ADDITIONAL WATER, IF NECESSARY FOR THE DESIRED CONSISTENCY. GARNISH WITH BASIL OR PARSLEY.

SERVES 8.

WILD RICE AND ARTICHOKE HEARTS

1 CUP	UNCOOKED WILD RICE	250 ML
1	CAN (10 OZ/284 ML) CONSOMMÉ	1
1 3/4 CUPS	WATER	425 ML
1/2 TSP	SALT	2 ML
3 TBSP	BUTTER	45 ML
1/3 CUP	CHOPPED ONION	75 ML
2	CLOVES GARLIC, MINCED	2
2	JARS (EACH 6 OZ/170 ML) MARINATED ARTICHOKE HEARTS	2
1 TBSP	CHOPPED FRESH PARSLEY	15 ML
1/4 TSP	DRIED OREGANO	1 ML

WASH AND DRAIN WILD RICE. PLACE RICE, CONSOMMÉ, WATER AND SALT IN SAUCEPAN. HEAT TO BOILING; REDUCE HEAT AND SIMMER, COVERED, UNTIL TENDER, ABOUT 45 MINUTES.

IN A LARGE FRYING PAN, MELT BUTTER AND SAUTÉ ONION AND GARLIC UNTIL SOFT. DRAIN AND CUT ARTICHOKES INTO QUARTERS. ADD TO FRYING PAN WITH COOKED RICE, PARSLEY AND OREGANO. STIR UNTIL HEATED THROUGH. SERVES 4 TO 6.

I NEVER THOUGHT I'D BE THE TYPE TO GET UP EARLY IN THE MORNING TO EXERCISE. AND I WAS RIGHT.

WILD RICE, ORZO AND MUSHROOM CASSEROLE

A GREAT MAKE-AHEAD.

1 CUP	ORZO PASTA	250 ML
1 CUP	WILD RICE	250 ML
2 1/2 CUPS	BEEF BROTH	625 ML
8 CUPS	SLICED MUSHROOMS	2 L
1 TBSP	OIL	15 ML
2 TBSP	BUTTER	30 ML
1/4 CUP	FRESH PARSLEY	60 ML

COOK ORZO ACCORDING TO PACKAGE DIRECTIONS. COOK THE WILD RICE IN THE BROTH ACCORDING TO PACKAGE DIRECTIONS. SAUTÉ MUSHROOMS IN OIL AND BUTTER AND COOK UNTIL LIQUID HAS ALMOST EVAPORATED. ADD MUSHROOMS AND PARSLEY TO RICE AND ORZO. MIX WELL. THIS MAY BE PREPARED AHEAD AND REFRIGERATED. BRING TO ROOM TEMPERATURE AND BAKE AT 350°F (180°C) FOR 30 MINUTES, UNTIL HEATED THROUGH. SERVES 6 TO 8.

GOURMET CRANBERRY SAUCE

3 CUPS	FRESH OR FROZEN CRANBERRIES	750 ML
1	ORANGE, CUT IN QUARTERS	1
1 CUP	BERRY SUGAR	250 ML
1/4 CUP	GRAND MARNIER	60 ML

CHOP CRANBERRIES AND ORANGE IN BLENDER OR FOOD PROCESSOR. ADD BERRY SUGAR AND GRAND MARNIER. *FINI!* SERVES 12.

LEFTOVERS

THE ONLY PROBLEM WITH SUMPTUOUS HOLIDAY REPASTS IS THAT YOU ARE LIKELY TO HAVE LEFTOVERS — OR IS THAT A BENEFIT? IN THIS CHAPTER, WE'VE INCLUDED SOME OF OUR FAVORITE RECIPES FOR TRANSFORMING UNUSED FOOD INTO A SECOND DELICIOUS MEAL.

SOUTHWESTERN TURKEY CHOWDER

THIS SOUP IS SO GOOD YOU WON'T WANT TO WAIT TO FINISH THE CELEBRATORY TURKEY AND GET IT STARTED. IF YOU'RE PLANNING TO EAT LIGHT AFTER THE HOLIDAY, IT MAKES A PERFECT DINNER WITH THE ADDITION OF SALAD.

10 CUPS	TURKEY STOCK (SEE TIP, OPPOSITE)	2.5 L
1 TBSP	OLIVE OIL	15 ML
3	ONIONS, DICED	3
4	STALKS CELERY, DICED	4
1 TBSP	GROUND CUMIN	15 ML
2 TSP	DRIED OREGANO	10 ML
4	CLOVES GARLIC, MINCED	4
1/2 TSP	CRACKED BLACK PEPPERCORNS	2 ML
1 1/2 CUPS	LONG-COOKING WHOLE GRAINS, SOAKED, RINSED AND DRAINED (SEE TIP, OPPOSITE)	375 ML
1	CAN (28 OZ/796 ML) NO-SALT-ADDED DICED TOMATOES, WITH JUICE	1
2 to 3	ANCHO, GUAJILLO OR MILD NEW MEXICO DRIED CHILES	2 to 3
1 CUP	LOOSELY PACKED FRESH CILANTRO LEAVES	250 ML
2 CUPS	DICED COOKED TURKEY	500 ML
2 CUPS	CORN KERNELS	500 ML

IN A STOCKPOT, HEAT OIL OVER MEDIUM HEAT FOR 30 SECONDS. ADD ONIONS AND CELERY AND COOK, STIRRING, UNTIL VEGETABLES ARE SOFTENED, ABOUT 5 MINUTES. ADD CUMIN, OREGANO, GARLIC AND PEPPERCORNS AND COOK, STIRRING, FOR 1 MINUTE. ADD

WHOLE GRAINS AND TOSS UNTIL COATED. ADD TOMATOES
WITH JUICE AND STOCK AND BRING TO A BOIL. REDUCE
HEAT TO LOW. COVER AND SIMMER UNTIL GRAINS ARE
TENDER, ABOUT 1 HOUR.

IN A HEATPROOF BOWL, 30 MINUTES BEFORE GRAINS
HAVE FINISHED COOKING, COMBINE DRIED CHILES
AND 2 CUPS (500 ML) BOILING WATER. SET ASIDE FOR
30 MINUTES, WEIGHING CHILES DOWN WITH A CUP TO
ENSURE THEY REMAIN SUBMERGED. DRAIN, DISCARDING
SOAKING LIQUID AND STEMS, AND CHOP COARSELY.
TRANSFER TO A BLENDER. ADD CILANTRO AND $1/2$ CUP
(125 ML) OF STOCK FROM THE CHOWDER. PURÉE. ADD TO
STOCKPOT ALONG WITH THE TURKEY AND CORN. COVER
AND COOK UNTIL CORN IS TENDER AND FLAVORS MELD,
ABOUT 20 MINUTES. SERVES 8.

TIP: USE ANY COMBINATION OF LONG-COOKING WHOLE
GRAINS IN THIS SOUP, SUCH AS JOB'S TEARS, HOMINY OR
BROWN, RED OR WILD RICE. ALL WILL BE DELICIOUS.

TIP: TURKEY STOCK: TO MAKE TURKEY STOCK, BREAK
THE CARCASS INTO MANAGEABLE PIECES AND PLACE IN
A STOCKPOT. ADD 2 CARROTS, 2 CELERY STALKS AND
2 ONIONS, QUARTERED, PLUS 8 WHOLE PEPPERCORNS.
ADD WATER TO COVER. BRING TO A BOIL OVER MEDIUM-
HIGH HEAT. REDUCE HEAT TO LOW. COVER AND
SIMMER FOR 3 HOURS. STRAIN, RESERVING LIQUID AND
DISCARDING SOLIDS.

TURKEY SOUP

AHHH — THE AROMA OF SOUP BUBBLING ON
THE BACK BURNER — LIFE IS GOOD!

	LEFTOVER TURKEY CARCASS (BONES, SKIN, EVERYTHING!)	
8 CUPS	WATER	2 L
3	CHICKEN BOUILLON CUBES	3
1 TSP	SALT	5 ML
1/4 TSP	POULTRY SEASONING OR SAGE	1 ML
1	BAY LEAF	1
1/2 CUP	BARLEY	125 ML
2 CUPS	CHOPPED CARROTS	500 ML
1 CUP	CHOPPED ONION	250 ML
1 CUP	CHOPPED CELERY	250 ML
1	CAN (28 OZ/796 ML) TOMATOES	1
3 CUPS	CHOPPED TURKEY	750 ML
1 CUP	MACARONI OR NOODLES, UNCOOKED (OPTIONAL)	250 ML
1/4 CUP	CHOPPED FRESH PARSLEY	50 ML

IN A LARGE DUTCH OVEN, COMBINE TURKEY CARCASS, WATER, BOUILLON CUBES, SALT, POULTRY SEASONING AND BAY LEAF. BRING TO A BOIL. REDUCE HEAT, COVER AND SIMMER FOR 2 HOURS. STRAIN AND DISCARD BONES. PLACE BROTH IN REFRIGERATOR OVERNIGHT. SKIM FAT OFF SOLIDIFIED BROTH. SIMMER IN DUTCH OVEN WITH REMAINING INGREDIENTS FOR 2 TO 3 HOURS. SERVE WITH FRESH BREAD AND A GREEN SALAD. SERVES 6 TO 8.

MULLIGATAWNY SOUP

A BRITISH-INDIAN SOUP POPULAR WITH
THE RANKS — GUNGA DIN LOVED IT!

2 TBSP	BUTTER	30 ML
3	STALKS CELERY, SLICED	3
1	LARGE POTATO, PEELED AND DICED	1
2	LARGE ONIONS, FINELY CHOPPED	2
4	CLOVES GARLIC, FINELY CHOPPED	4
2	CARROTS, DICED	2
4 TSP	CURRY POWDER	20 ML
1/4 TSP	GROUND CLOVES	1 ML
1/2 TSP	GROUND GINGER	2 ML
2 TSP	CAYENNE PEPPER	10 ML
1 to 2 TSP	SALT	5 to 10 ML
2 TSP	BLACK PEPPER	10 ML
8 CUPS	CHICKEN OR TURKEY BROTH	2 L
3 CUPS	DICED COOKED CHICKEN OR TURKEY	750 ML
3 CUPS	COOKED RICE	750 ML
2	GRANNY SMITH APPLES, PEELED AND GRATED	2
2 TBSP	LEMON JUICE	30 ML
1 CUP	PLAIN YOGURT	250 ML

IN A LARGE POT, MELT BUTTER AND SAUTÉ CELERY,
POTATO, ONION, GARLIC, CARROT AND SEASONINGS FOR
5 MINUTES. ADD BROTH AND SIMMER FOR 20 MINUTES.
ADD CHICKEN/TURKEY, RICE, APPLES AND LEMON JUICE.
BEFORE SERVING, ADD YOGURT AND HEAT TO NEAR
BOILING. SERVES 8 TO 10.

TURKEY TETRAZZINI

THIS CLASSIC DISH, OFTEN MADE WITH CHICKEN,
IS NOT ITALIAN IN ORIGIN, AS THE NAME SUGGESTS.
IT WAS INVENTED IN SAN FRANCISCO, AROUND
THE TURN OF THE 20TH CENTURY, TO HONOR THE
GREAT OPERA SINGER LUISA TETRAZZINI.

8 OZ	SMALL TUBULAR PASTA, SUCH AS PENNE OR MACARONI	250 G
2 TBSP	BUTTER	30 ML
8 OZ	SLICED MUSHROOMS (ABOUT 3 CUPS/750 ML)	250 G
1 TBSP	VEGETABLE OIL	15 ML
1	ONION, MINCED	1
4	CLOVES GARLIC, MINCED	4
1/2 TSP	DRIED THYME	2 ML
2 TBSP	ALL-PURPOSE FLOUR	30 ML
2 CUPS	TURKEY STOCK (SEE TIP, PAGE 213) OR READY-TO-USE CHICKEN BROTH	500 ML
1/4 CUP	SWEET SHERRY, DRY WHITE WINE OR ADDITIONAL STOCK	60 ML
1/4 CUP	HEAVY OR WHIPPING (35%) CREAM	60 ML
1/2 CUP	GRATED PARMESAN CHEESE	125 ML
	SALT AND FRESHLY GROUND BLACK PEPPER	
1 CUP	FROZEN PEAS, THAWED	250 ML
2 CUPS	CUBED COOKED TURKEY, SKIN REMOVED (ABOUT 1-INCH/ 2.5 CM CUBES)	500 ML

TOPPING

1 CUP	DRY BREAD CRUMBS, SUCH AS PANKO	250 ML
1/4 CUP	GRATED PARMESAN CHEESE	60 ML
2 TBSP	MELTED BUTTER	30 ML

CONTINUED ON PAGE 217...

Mulligatawny Soup (page 215)

Fruit and Nut Shortbread (page 230)

Snowballs (page 235), Nanny's Real Scottish Shortbread (page 231), Ginger Cookies (page 237) and Chocolate Raspberry Truffle Squares (page 246)

Chocolate Raspberry Torte (page 262)

PREHEAT OVEN TO 350°F (180°C) AND GREASE A 10-CUP (2.5 L) BAKING DISH. COOK PASTA IN A POT OF BOILING SALTED WATER UNTIL TENDER TO THE BITE, ABOUT 8 MINUTES. DRAIN AND SET ASIDE. MEANWHILE, IN A SKILLET OVER MEDIUM HEAT, MELT BUTTER. ADD MUSHROOMS AND COOK, STIRRING, UNTIL THEY LOSE THEIR LIQUID AND PAN IS RELATIVELY DRY, ABOUT 8 MINUTES. TRANSFER TO PREPARED BAKING DISH AND SET ASIDE. RETURN SKILLET TO HEAT AND ADD VEGETABLE OIL. ADD ONION AND COOK, STIRRING, UNTIL SOFTENED, ABOUT 3 MINUTES. ADD GARLIC AND THYME AND COOK, STIRRING, FOR 1 MINUTE. ADD FLOUR AND COOK, STIRRING, FOR 1 MINUTE. ADD TURKEY STOCK AND BRING TO A BOIL. COOK, STIRRING, UNTIL MIXTURE THICKENS, ABOUT 3 MINUTES. STIR IN SHERRY, CREAM AND PARMESAN. SEASON WITH SALT AND PEPPER TO TASTE. ADD PEAS AND TURKEY AND STIR UNTIL HEATED THROUGH. POUR OVER MUSHROOMS. ADD PASTA AND STIR WELL.

TO MAKE TOPPING: IN A BOWL, COMBINE BREAD CRUMBS AND PARMESAN CHEESE. SPRINKLE EVENLY OVER TURKEY MIXTURE AND DRIZZLE WITH MELTED BUTTER. BAKE UNTIL TOP IS BROWNED AND MIXTURE IS HEATED THROUGH, ABOUT 20 MINUTES. SERVES 4.

SOUTHWEST TURKEY 'N' RICE

HERE'S A NUTRITIOUS AND FLAVORFUL SOLUTION TO USING UP LEFTOVER TURKEY. SERVE WITH A BIG TOSSED SALAD AND CRUSTY WHOLE-GRAIN ROLLS, AND EXPECT REQUESTS FOR SECONDS.

2	DRIED ANCHO OR NEW MEXICO CHILE PEPPERS (SEE TIP, OPPOSITE)	2
2 CUPS	BOILING WATER	500 ML
1 TBSP	VEGETABLE OIL	15 ML
1	ONION, FINELY CHOPPED	1
4	CLOVES GARLIC, MINCED	4
1 TBSP	CUMIN SEEDS, TOASTED AND GROUND	15 ML
1/4 TSP	GROUND CINNAMON	1 ML
1 CUP	BROWN RICE	250 ML
2 to 3 CUPS	CUBED COOKED TURKEY, SKIN REMOVED (1-INCH/2.5 CM CUBES)	500 to 750 ML
1 CUP	TURKEY STOCK (SEE TIP, PAGE 213) OR READY-TO-USE CHICKEN BROTH	250 ML
1 TBSP	FRESHLY SQUEEZED LEMON OR LIME JUICE	15 ML
1	CAN (28 OZ/796 ML) TOMATOES, WITH JUICE, COARSELY CHOPPED	1
	SALT AND FRESHLY GROUND BLACK PEPPER	
	FINELY CHOPPED FRESH CILANTRO OR PARSLEY (OPTIONAL)	

IN A HEATPROOF BOWL, SOAK DRIED CHILE PEPPERS IN BOILING WATER FOR 30 MINUTES. DRAIN AND DISCARD LIQUID. REMOVE STEMS, PAT DRY, CHOP FINELY AND SET ASIDE. IN A HEAVY POT OR DUTCH OVEN WITH A TIGHT-FITTING LID, HEAT VEGETABLE OIL OVER MEDIUM HEAT. ADD ONIONS AND COOK, STIRRING, UNTIL SOFTENED,

ABOUT 3 MINUTES. ADD GARLIC, CUMIN, CINNAMON, RESERVED CHILES AND RICE AND COOK, STIRRING, UNTIL RICE IS COATED, ABOUT 1 MINUTE. STIR IN TURKEY, STOCK, LEMON JUICE AND TOMATOES WITH JUICE. SEASON WITH SALT AND PEPPER TO TASTE. REDUCE HEAT TO LOW. COVER AND COOK UNTIL RICE IS TENDER, ABOUT 45 MINUTES. GARNISH WITH CILANTRO, IF USING, AND SERVE. SERVES 4 TO 6.

TIP: ANCHO AND NEW MEXICO CHILES ARE MILD TO MEDIUM-HOT CHILES WIDELY AVAILABLE IN DRIED FORM. GUAJILLO CHILES, WHICH HAVE A SIMILAR POSITION ON THE HEAT SCALE, WOULD ALSO WORK WELL IN THIS RECIPE.

YOU DON'T HAVE TO SWIM FASTER THAN THE SHARK, JUST FASTER THAN THE GUY NEXT TO YOU.

TURKEY CASSEROLE
WITH BROCCOLI

2 CUPS	NOODLES	500 ML
I	PACKAGE (IO OZ/300 G) FROZEN BROCCOLI	I
2 CUPS	COOKED TURKEY	500 ML
1/3 CUP	SLIVERED ALMONDS	75 ML

WHITE SAUCE

2 TBSP	BUTTER	30 ML
2 TBSP	FLOUR	30 ML
I TSP	SALT	5 ML
1/4 TSP	PREPARED MUSTARD	I ML
1/4 TSP	BLACK PEPPER	I ML
2 CUPS	MILK	500 ML
I CUP	GRATED CHEDDAR CHEESE	250 ML

HEAT OVEN TO 350°F (180°C). COOK NOODLES, THEN BROCCOLI. MAKE WHITE SAUCE; WHEN THICK STIR IN CHEESE. DICE BROCCOLI STEMS, LEAVING FLORETS FOR TOP. PUT NOODLES, BROCCOLI STEMS, TURKEY AND ALMONDS IN CASSEROLE. COVER WITH SAUCE. ARRANGE BROCCOLI FLORETS ON TOP AND BAKE FOR 15 TO 20 MINUTES. SERVES 4.

QUICK TURKEY CURRY

THIS RECIPE WILL MAKE YOU WANT TO ROAST
A TURKEY JUST SO YOU HAVE SOME LEFTOVERS
ON HAND. SERVE OVER BASMATI RICE AND SPRINKLE
WITH CHOPPED CILANTRO, IF DESIRED.

2 TSP	VEGETABLE OIL	10 ML
1	SMALL ONION, CHOPPED	1
1	LARGE CLOVE GARLIC, FINELY CHOPPED	1
2 TSP	MINCED GINGERROOT	10 ML
1	APPLE, PEELED AND CHOPPED	1
1/2 CUP	FINELY DICED CELERY	125 ML
2 TSP	MILD CURRY PASTE (OR TO TASTE)	10 ML
1 TBSP	ALL-PURPOSE FLOUR	15 ML
1 1/3 CUPS	READY-TO-USE CHICKEN BROTH	325 ML
3 TBSP	MANGO CHUTNEY	45 ML
2 CUPS	DICED COOKED TURKEY	500 ML
1/4 CUP	RAISINS	60 ML
	SALT AND BLACK PEPPER	

IN A LARGE NONSTICK SKILLET, HEAT OIL OVER MEDIUM
HEAT. ADD ONION, GARLIC, GINGER, APPLE, CELERY AND
CURRY PASTE; COOK, STIRRING, FOR 5 MINUTES OR UNTIL
SOFTENED. BLEND IN FLOUR; ADD CHICKEN BROTH AND
CHUTNEY. COOK, STIRRING, UNTIL SAUCE COMES TO A BOIL
AND THICKENS. STIR IN TURKEY AND RAISINS; SEASON
WITH SALT AND PEPPER TO TASTE. COOK FOR 3 MINUTES
OR UNTIL HEATED THROUGH. SERVES 4.

TIP: IF YOU WANT TO MAKE THIS RECIPE WHEN YOU
DON'T HAVE ANY LEFTOVER TURKEY ON HAND, BUY A
ROASTED CHICKEN FROM THE DELI SECTION OF THE
SUPERMARKET AND USE THE DICED MEAT.

THAI-STYLE BEEF SALAD

LEFTOVER ROAST BEEF OR STEAK
TRANSFORMS INTO A DELICIOUS SECOND MEAL.

1/4 CUP	FRESHLY SQUEEZED LIME OR LEMON JUICE	60 ML
3 TBSP	FISH SAUCE (NAM PLA)	45 ML
2 TSP	MINCED GINGERROOT	10 ML
2 TSP	ASIAN CHILI SAUCE	10 ML
3/4 CUP	THINLY SLICED COOKED ROAST BEEF OR STEAK, CHOPPED	175 ML
2 CUPS	DICED PEELED CUCUMBER	500 ML
1 CUP	THINLY SLICED RED OR GREEN ONIONS (WHITE PART ONLY)	250 ML
4 TBSP	FINELY CHOPPED CILANTRO, DIVIDED	60 ML
1 TBSP	THINLY SLICED LEMONGRASS OR BOTTLED PRESERVED LEMONGRASS (OR 1 TSP/5 ML GRATED LEMON ZEST)	15 ML
4 CUPS	MIXED SALAD GREENS OR ARUGULA, WASHED AND DRIED	1 L
12	CHERRY TOMATOES, HALVED	12

IN A BOWL, COMBINE LIME JUICE, FISH SAUCE, GINGERROOT AND CHILI SAUCE. MIX WELL. ADD BEEF, CUCUMBER, ONIONS, 2 TBSP (30 ML) CILANTRO AND LEMONGRASS. TOSS TO COMBINE. SPREAD SALAD GREENS OVER A DEEP PLATTER OR SERVING PLATE. ARRANGE MEAT MIXTURE ON TOP. SURROUND WITH CHERRY TOMATOES AND GARNISH WITH REMAINING 2 TBSP (30 ML) CILANTRO. SERVE IMMEDIATELY. SERVES 4.

TIP: FISH SAUCE (NAM PLA) IS MADE FROM BRINE-COVERED AND FERMENTED FISH, MOST OFTEN ANCHOVIES. IT'S

VERY PUNGENT BUT LENDS A DISTINCTIVE AND APPEALING NOTE TO MANY DISHES. IT IS AVAILABLE IN THE ASIAN FOOD SECTION OF MANY SUPERMARKETS.

TIP: IF USING FRESH LEMONGRASS, SMASH IT FIRST, DISCARD THE OUTER CORE AND SLICE IT VERY THINLY AS IT IS QUITE FIBROUS.

YOU KNOW YOU'RE DRINKING TOO MUCH COFFEE WHEN YOU WALK 18 MILES ON YOUR TREADMILL BEFORE YOU REALIZE IT'S NOT PLUGGED IN.

BROCCOLI, BEEF AND CABBAGE SALAD

THIS RECIPE IS A GREAT WAY TO USE UP LEFTOVER BEEF, AND IS A DELICIOUS AND NUTRITIOUS MEAL IN ITSELF.

VINAIGRETTE

1/4 CUP	RICE VINEGAR	60 ML
2 TBSP	SOY SAUCE	30 ML
1	CLOVE GARLIC, FINELY MINCED	1
2 TSP	PURÉED GINGERROOT	10 ML
1/4 CUP	EXTRA VIRGIN OLIVE OIL	60 ML
4 CUPS	BROCCOLI FLORETS	1 L
1 1/2 CUPS	COOKED BEEF, SUCH AS ROAST BEEF OR FLANK STEAK, CUT INTO THIN STRIPS	375 ML
2 CUPS	THINLY SLICED RED CABBAGE	500 ML
2 TBSP	TOASTED SESAME SEEDS	30 ML

TO MAKE VINAIGRETTE: IN A BOWL, COMBINE VINEGAR, SOY SAUCE, GARLIC AND GINGERROOT. GRADUALLY WHISK IN OLIVE OIL. SET ASIDE.

IN A LARGE POT OF BOILING SALTED WATER, BLANCH BROCCOLI FOR 1 1/2 MINUTES. DRAIN AND IMMEDIATELY PLUNGE INTO ICE WATER. (THE BROCCOLI SHOULD BE BRIGHT GREEN AND STILL CRUNCHY.) DRAIN AGAIN AND TRANSFER TO A PAPER TOWEL TO DRY. IN A SERVING BOWL, COMBINE BROCCOLI, BEEF AND RED CABBAGE. ADD DRESSING AND TOSS WELL. SPRINKLE WITH SESAME SEEDS. SERVES 4.

HAM CASSEROLE

THAT'S IT FOR THE LEFTOVER HAM!

2 TBSP	BUTTER	25 ML
1/2 CUP	CHOPPED ONION	125 ML
3 TBSP	FLOUR	45 ML
	SALT AND BLACK PEPPER TO TASTE	
1 1/4 CUPS	MILK	300 ML
1/2 CUP	SHREDDED SWISS CHEESE	125 ML
2 CUPS	CUBED COOKED HAM (OR MORE)	500 ML
1 CUP	CUBED COOKED POTATOES	250 ML
1 1/2 CUPS	FRESH BREAD CRUMBS	375 ML
2 TBSP	BUTTER	30 ML

IN A FRYING PAN, MELT BUTTER AND SAUTÉ ONION. BLEND IN FLOUR, SALT AND PEPPER. SLOWLY ADD MILK; STIR CONSTANTLY AND COOK UNTIL THICKENED. ADD CHEESE AND STIR UNTIL MELTED. ADD HAM AND POTATOES AND MIX GENTLY. POUR INTO A CASSEROLE. SPRINKLE WITH BREADCRUMBS AND DOT WITH BUTTER. PREHEAT OVEN TO 400°F (200°C) AND BAKE FOR 30 MINUTES. SERVES 6.

GARDENS NEED A LOT OF WATER — MOSTLY SWEAT.

SALMON BURGERS

NOTHING SAYS LUNCH OR A QUICK DINNER
BETTER THAN A GOOD BURGER. HERE'S A YUMMY
FISH-BASED VERSION THAT CAN BE EASILY VARIED
BY CHANGING THE TOPPINGS. TO SERVE MORE,
SIMPLY DOUBLE OR TRIPLE THE RECIPE.

1 CUP	FLAKED COOKED SALMON	250 ML
1	EGG, BEATEN	1
1 TSP	DRIED ITALIAN SEASONING	5 ML
1/2 CUP	FINE DRY BREAD CRUMBS, DIVIDED	125 ML
1/4 TSP	SALT	1 ML
	FRESHLY GROUND BLACK PEPPER	
1/4 CUP	FINELY CHOPPED RED OR GREEN ONION (OPTIONAL)	60 ML
2 TBSP	FINELY CHOPPED BELL PEPPER (OPTIONAL)	30 ML
2 TBSP	VEGETABLE OIL	30 ML
2	ONION OR WHOLE WHEAT BUNS, SPLIT AND TOASTED	2
	EASY TARTAR SAUCE (SEE TIP, OPPOSITE)	
	LETTUCE, SLICED TOMATO, SLICED RED ONION AND SLICED RED OR YELLOW BELL PEPPER	

IN A BOWL, COMBINE SALMON, EGG, ITALIAN SEASONING,
1/4 CUP (60 ML) BREAD CRUMBS, SALT, BLACK PEPPER TO
TASTE, AND ONION AND BELL PEPPER, IF USING. MIX WELL.
FORM MIXTURE INTO 2 PATTIES, EACH 1/2 INCH (1 CM)
THICK. SPREAD REMAINING BREAD CRUMBS ON A PLATE.
DIP EACH PATTY INTO CRUMBS, COVERING BOTH SIDES.
DISCARD ANY EXCESS CRUMBS. IN A NONSTICK SKILLET,
HEAT VEGETABLE OIL OVER MEDIUM HEAT. ADD PATTIES

AND COOK, TURNING ONCE, UNTIL HOT AND GOLDEN, ABOUT 3 MINUTES PER SIDE. SERVE ON WARM BUNS SLATHERED WITH TARTAR SAUCE AND LETTUCE, TOMATO, ONION AND/OR BELL PEPPER. SERVES 2.

TIP: EASY TARTAR SAUCE: IN A BOWL, COMBINE $1/2$ CUP (125 ML) MAYONNAISE WITH 2 TBSP (30 ML) SWEET GREEN PICKLE RELISH. STIR TO BLEND.

A KEY RING IS A HANDY LITTLE GADGET THAT ALLOWS YOU TO LOSE ALL YOUR KEYS AT ONCE.

LAMB AND PITA SALAD

THIS "SANDWICH IN A BOWL" SALAD IS LIKE A TASTY PITA POCKET THAT YOU CAN EAT WITH A FORK.

2 TBSP	FRESHLY SQUEEZED LEMON JUICE	30 ML
1/2 TSP	SALT	2 ML
PINCH	DRIED OREGANO	PINCH
1/4 CUP	EXTRA VIRGIN OLIVE OIL	60 ML
	FRESHLY GROUND BLACK PEPPER	
1 CUP	THINLY SLICED ROAST LAMB	250 ML
2	PITA BREADS, TOASTED, EACH CUT INTO 8 TRIANGLES	2
4	GREEN ONIONS (WHITE PART ONLY), THINLY SLICED	4
1/2 CUP	FINELY CHOPPED PARSLEY	125 ML
4 CUPS	MIXED SALAD GREENS	1 L

IN A SMALL BOWL, COMBINE LEMON JUICE, SALT AND OREGANO. MIX WELL UNTIL SALT IS DISSOLVED. GRADUALLY WHISK IN OLIVE OIL. SEASON WITH PEPPER TO TASTE AND ADDITIONAL SALT, IF DESIRED. IN A BOWL, COMBINE LAMB, PITA, ONIONS, PARSLEY AND SALAD GREENS. ADD DRESSING AND TOSS WELL. SERVES 4 TO 6.

VARIATION: SUBSTITUTE AN EQUAL QUANTITY OF BEEF FOR THE LAMB.

HOLIDAY COOKIES AND SQUARES

MANY COOKIES, SUCH AS SHORTBREAD, ARE TRADITIONALLY ASSOCIATED WITH THE HOLIDAY SEASON. THE RECIPES IN THIS CHAPTER CAN BE USED TO WELCOME GUESTS OR TO COMPLETE A FESTIVE MEAL. ARTFULLY ARRANGED ON A PRETTY TRAY, THEY ALSO ADD A DECORATIVE ELEMENT TO A BUFFET TABLE.

SHORTBREAD

1 LB	BUTTER	500 G
1 CUP	GRANULATED SUGAR	250 ML
4 to 5 CUPS	FLOUR	1 to 1.25 L

CREAM BUTTER WITH SUGAR. ADD FLOUR, BEATING FOR
5 MINUTES. CUT OUT COOKIES USING A 2-INCH (5 CM)
COOKIE CUTTER. BAKE AT 300°F (150°C) FOR 10 TO
15 MINUTES OR UNTIL LIGHTLY GOLDEN. *MAKES ABOUT
4 DOZEN COOKIES.*

FRUIT AND NUT SHORTBREAD

A COLORFUL ADDITION TO YOUR CHRISTMAS BAKING.

1/2 LB	BUTTER	250 G
1 CUP	BROWN SUGAR	250 ML
1	EGG YOLK	1
2 CUPS	FLOUR	500 ML
2/3 CUP	GLACÉ CHERRIES, HALVED	150 ML
1/2 CUP	WALNUTS, CHOPPED	125 ML

CREAM BUTTER AND SUGAR. ADD YOLK AND FLOUR. CUT IN
FRUIT AND NUTS. SHAPE DOUGH INTO TWO ROLLS 2 INCHES
(5 CM) IN DIAMETER AND ROLL IN WAXED PAPER. CHILL
OVERNIGHT. WHILE STILL COLD AND WAXED PAPER STILL ON,
TAKE A SHARP KNIFE AND CUT THIN SLICES (1/8 INCH/3 MM).
SET ON GREASED COOKIE SHEETS, REMOVE WAXED PAPER
AND BAKE AT 375°F (190°C) FOR 10 MINUTES. (SLIGHTLY
BROWN EDGES). *MAKES ABOUT 4 DOZEN COOKIES.*

NOTE: TWIST COOKIES OFF SHEET.

CHEESE SHORTBREAD

½ LB	SOFT EXTRA-SHARP CHEDDAR CHEESE	250 G
½ LB	BUTTER	250 G
2 CUPS	FLOUR	500 ML
2 TBSP	LIGHT BROWN SUGAR	25 ML

MIX INGREDIENTS TOGETHER AND KNEAD. FORM INTO A ROLL. SLICE THIN AND BAKE AT 250°F (120°C) TO 275°F (140°C) FOR 1 HOUR. MAKES ABOUT 4 DOZEN COOKIES.

THESE ARE PARTICULARLY GOOD TO SERVE WITH DRINKS.

NANNY'S REAL SCOTTISH SHORTBREAD

HOOT MON, I WANT TO MEET NANNY!

1 LB	BUTTER	500 G
1 CUP	BERRY SUGAR	250 ML
3 CUPS	ALL-PURPOSE FLOUR	750 ML
1 CUP	RICE FLOUR	250 ML
2 TSP	BAKING POWDER	10 ML
	GLACÉ CHERRIES, HALVED	

PREHEAT OVEN TO 300°F (150°C). USING ELECTRIC MIXER, CREAM BUTTER AND SUGAR UNTIL SMOOTH. GRADUALLY ADD FLOURS AND BAKING POWDER AND CONTINUE BEATING FOR SEVERAL MINUTES UNTIL WELL MIXED. KNEAD DOUGH UNTIL SHINY. ROLL DOUGH ¼ INCH (0.5 CM) THICK AND CUT WITH COOKIE CUTTER. DECORATE WITH HALVED GLACÉ CHERRIES. BAKE FOR 15 TO 20 MINUTES OR UNTIL EDGES ARE LIGHTLY GOLDEN. MAKES A TINFUL.

JEWISH SHORTBREAD

1 CUP	BUTTER, ROOM TEMPERATURE (NEVER USE MARGARINE)	250 ML
1/3 CUP	GRANULATED SUGAR	75 ML
1 TSP	VANILLA	5 ML
1/2 CUP	FINELY GROUND WALNUTS OR PECANS	125 ML
1²/3 CUPS	FLOUR	400 ML
PINCH	SALT	PINCH
1/2 CUP	GRANULATED SUGAR	125 ML
4 TSP	CINNAMON	20 ML

CREAM TOGETHER BUTTER AND SUGAR. ADD VANILLA, NUTS, FLOUR AND SALT AND BEAT WELL. SHAPE INTO CRESCENTS AND PLACE 1 INCH (2.5 CM) APART ON AN UNGREASED COOKIE SHEET. BAKE AT 325°F (160°C) FOR 15 TO 20 MINUTES. WHILE STILL WARM, COAT WITH SUGAR AND CINNAMON OR FOR VARIETY COAT WITH CONFECTIONERS' (ICING) SUGAR. MAKES 2 TO 3 DOZEN COOKIES.

IF YOU MAKE SOMETHING IDIOT-PROOF,
SOMEONE WILL MAKE A BETTER IDIOT.

PEPPERNUTS

FOR THE HOLIDAY SEASON!

1/3 CUP	LIGHT (FANCY) MOLASSES	75 ML
1/3 CUP	BUTTER	75 ML
1	EGG, BEATEN	1
2 CUPS	ALL-PURPOSE FLOUR	500 ML
1/3 CUP	GRANULATED SUGAR	75 ML
1/2 TSP	BAKING SODA	2 ML
1 TSP	GROUND CINNAMON	5 ML
1 TSP	GROUND GINGER	5 ML
1/4 TSP	GROUND NUTMEG	1 ML
1/4 TSP	GROUND CLOVES	1 ML
PINCH	SALT	PINCH
PINCH	BLACK PEPPER	PINCH
	BERRY SUGAR, TO COAT	

HEAT MOLASSES WITH BUTTER, STIRRING UNTIL BUTTER MELTS. COOL TO ROOM TEMPERATURE. STIR IN BEATEN EGG. THOROUGHLY MIX DRY INGREDIENTS. ADD DRY MIXTURE TO MOLASSES AND BUTTER GRADUALLY. BLEND THOROUGHLY. SHAPE INTO SMALL BALLS. BAKE AT 375°F (190°C) FOR 10 TO 12 MINUTES. ROLL IN FRUIT SUGAR WHILE WARM. STORE IN A TIGHTLY COVERED TIN TO KEEP THEM SEMISOFT. MAKES ABOUT 3 DOZEN COOKIES.

PECAN MACAROONS

THIS IS A PRETTY CHRISTMAS COOKIE AND IS GOOD TOO!

1/2 CUP	GRANULATED SUGAR	125 ML
1/4 CUP	BOILING WATER	50 ML
2	EGG WHITES	2
1/2 CUP	BROWN SUGAR	125 ML
1 1/2 CUPS	COCONUT	375 ML
2 TBSP	CARAMEL SYRUP (SEE BELOW)	30 ML
1/2 CUP	GLACÉ CHERRIES, WHOLE	125 ML
1 CUP	WHOLE PECANS	250 ML

TO MAKE CARAMEL SYRUP: MELT 1/2 CUP (125 ML) OF GRANULATED SUGAR IN POT OVER MEDIUM HEAT. CAREFULLY ADD 1/4 CUP (50 ML) BOILING WATER. (MIXTURE OF HOT SUGAR AND WATER CAN "EXPLODE" IF NOT ADDED AWAY FROM HEAT AND WITH CAUTION!) SUGAR WILL HARDEN, BUT THE LIQUID WILL MAKE AT LEAST 2 TBSP (25 ML) SYRUP. COOL COMPLETELY.

COOKIES: BEAT EGG WHITES, ADDING PINCH OF SALT. ADD ADDITIONAL INGREDIENTS AND 2 TBSP (25 ML) COOLED SYRUP. BAKE AT 300°F (150°C) FOR 20 MINUTES OR UNTIL LIGHTLY BROWNED. COOKIES WILL SLIGHTLY RUN TOGETHER ON SHEET; THEREFORE, WHILE STILL HOT, PUSH COOKIE BACK TOGETHER WITH A SPOON. COOL ON COOKIE SHEET. MAKES ABOUT 3 DOZEN COOKIES.

SNOWBALLS

1/2 CUP	BUTTER (NOT MARGARINE)	125 ML
I TBSP	SUGAR	15 ML
I CUP	FINELY GROUND PECANS (BE SURE THEY ARE FRESH)	250 ML
7/8 CUP	FLOUR	210 ML
I TSP	VANILLA	5 ML
PINCH	SALT	PINCH
I CUP	CONFECTIONERS' (ICING) SUGAR	250 ML

CREAM BUTTER AND SUGAR. ADD NUTS, FLOUR, VANILLA AND SALT. MIX, BUT DO NOT OVERBEAT. FORM SMALL BALLS AND BAKE ON UNGREASED SHEET AT 325°F (160°C) FOR 12 TO 15 MINUTES, UNTIL BARELY BROWN. COOL. COAT THOROUGHLY IN CONFECTIONERS' SUGAR. MAKES ABOUT 4 DOZEN.

TOFFEE KRISPS

HOORAY — RICE KRISPIE SQUARES FOR THE '90S!

2	2-OZ (56 G) MACKINTOSH'S TOFFEE BARS, BROKEN	2
2 TBSP	TABLE (18%) CREAM	30 ML
2 1/2 CUPS	RICE KRISPIES	625 ML

MELT TOFFEE PIECES WITH CREAM IN DOUBLE BOILER, STIRRING CONSTANTLY UNTIL MIXTURE IS WELL BLENDED. ADD RICE KRISPIES AND MIX UNTIL COATED. PRESS INTO GREASED 8-INCH (20 CM) SQUARE PAN. COOL AND CUT INTO SQUARES.

GINGER SNAPS

ALSO PERFECT FOR GINGERBREAD MEN.

3/4 CUP	BUTTER OR MARGARINE	175 ML
1 CUP	GRANULATED SUGAR	250 ML
1/4 CUP	LIGHT (FANCY) MOLASSES	60 ML
1	EGG, BEATEN	1
2 CUPS	ALL-PURPOSE FLOUR	500 ML
1/4 TSP	SALT	1 ML
2 TSP	BAKING SODA	10 ML
1 to 2 TSP	GROUND CINNAMON	5 to 10 ML
1 to 2 TSP	GROUND CLOVES	5 to 10 ML
1 to 2 TSP	GROUND GINGER	5 to 10 ML
	GRANULATED SUGAR	

CREAM TOGETHER BUTTER AND SUGAR. ADD MOLASSES AND EGG. BEAT TOGETHER. COMBINE FLOUR, SALT, BAKING SODA AND SPICES. ADD TO CREAMED MIXTURE AND MIX WELL. ROLL INTO BALLS, THEN IN SUGAR. PRESS FLAT WITH A FORK. BAKE AT 375°F (190°C) FOR 15 MINUTES. MAKES ABOUT 4 DOZEN COOKIES.

IF ONLY I COULD GROW GREEN STUFF IN MY GARDEN LIKE I CAN IN MY REFRIGERATOR.

GINGER COOKIES

1 1/2 CUPS	SHORTENING	375 ML
2 CUPS	GRANULATED SUGAR	500 ML
2	EGGS, BEATEN	2
1/4 CUP	MOLASSES	60 ML
4 CUPS	FLOUR	1 L
4 TSP	BAKING SODA	20 ML
1/2 TSP	SALT	2 ML
4 TSP	GROUND GINGER	20 ML
2 TSP	GROUND CINNAMON	10 ML
2 TSP	GROUND CLOVES	10 ML
1/4 TSP	GROUND WHITE PEPPER (OPTIONAL)	1 ML
	GRANULATED SUGAR	

IN LARGE BOWL, CREAM SHORTENING AND SUGAR TOGETHER. BEAT EGGS AND MOLASSES TOGETHER AND BLEND WITH CREAMED SUGAR MIXTURE. COMBINE FLOUR, BAKING SODA, SALT, GINGER, CINNAMON, CLOVES AND WHITE PEPPER. ADD DRY INGREDIENTS TO CREAMED MIXTURE AND BLEND WELL. CHILL FOR 1 HOUR. SHAPE DOUGH INTO 1-INCH (1.5 CM) BALLS AND ROLL IN SUGAR. PREHEAT OVEN TO 350°F (180°C). PLACE BALLS ON COOKIE SHEETS 2 INCHES (5 CM) APART AND BAKE FOR 8 TO 9 MINUTES. MAKES ABOUT 6 DOZEN SPICY COOKIES!

CHOCOLATE RUM COOKIES

NO SUGAR IN THESE COOKIES! CHOCOLATEY AND
SLIGHTLY BITTER — VERY ADDICTIVE!

1¼ CUPS	FLOUR	300 ML
1½ TSP	BAKING POWDER	7 ML
½ TSP	SALT	2 ML
½ CUP	GROUND HAZELNUTS	125 ML
12 OZ	BITTERSWEET CHOCOLATE	340 G
¼ CUP	BUTTER	60 ML
¼ CUP	DARK RUM	60 ML
2	LARGE EGGS	2
¼ CUP	CONFECTIONERS' (ICING) SUGAR (FOR SPRINKLING)	60 ML

IN A BOWL, MIX FLOUR, BAKING POWDER, SALT AND
HAZELNUTS TOGETHER. IN A DOUBLE-BOILER WITH BARELY
SIMMERING WATER, MELT CHOCOLATE AND BUTTER,
STIRRING OCCASIONALLY. STIR IN RUM AND COOL. WHISK
IN EGGS AND STIR IN FLOUR MIXTURE. COVER AND CHILL
DOUGH ABOUT 1 HOUR, OR UNTIL FIRM ENOUGH TO HANDLE.

HALVE DOUGH AND FORM INTO TWO 10-INCH (25 CM) LOGS
ON WAXED PAPER. WRAP IN PAPER AND CHILL 4 HOURS, OR
UNTIL FIRM. PREHEAT OVEN TO 350°F (180°C). SPRAY TWO
BAKING SHEETS. CUT LOGS INTO ½-INCH (1 CM) ROUNDS
AND ARRANGE ABOUT 1 INCH (2.5 CM) APART ON BAKING
SHEETS. BAKE COOKIES IN BATCHES FOR 8 MINUTES AND
TRANSFER TO RACK. COOKIES SHOULD BE THICK AND
CAKE-LIKE. COOL COOKIES COMPLETELY AND SPRINKLE
WITH CONFECTIONERS' SUGAR. MAKES ABOUT 3 DOZEN
COOKIES.

BUTTER TART SLICE

A SLICE OF LIFE — ALL TARTS SHOULD TASTE SO GOOD!

CRUST

I CUP	BUTTER	250 ML
2 CUPS	ALL-PURPOSE FLOUR	500 ML
1/4 CUP	GRANULATED SUGAR	60 ML
PINCH	SALT	PINCH

BUTTER TART FILLING

1/4 CUP	BUTTER	60 ML
3	EGGS, BEATEN	3
2 CUPS	BROWN SUGAR	500 ML
I TBSP	BAKING POWDER	15 ML
PINCH	SALT	PINCH
3/4 CUP	SHREDDED COCONUT	175 ML
I TSP	VANILLA EXTRACT	5 ML
I CUP	RAISINS	250 ML
I TBSP	ALL-PURPOSE FLOUR	15 ML
I CUP	CHOPPED PECANS (OPTIONAL)	250 ML

CRUST: CUT BUTTER INTO DRY INGREDIENTS WITH PASTRY BLENDER UNTIL CRUMBLY. PRESS INTO AN UNGREASED 13- BY 9-INCH (33 BY 23 CM) PAN.

FILLING: MELT BUTTER; ADD EGGS AND REMAINING INGREDIENTS. MIX AND POUR OVER CRUST. BAKE AT 350°F (180°C) FOR 35 MINUTES. CUT WHEN COOL.

MAKES 3 DOZEN SQUARES.

DREAM SLICES

CRUST

1 1/3 CUPS	FLOUR	325 ML
1 TBSP	GRANULATED SUGAR	15 ML
3/4 CUP	BUTTER	175 ML

FILLING

2	EGGS	2
1 CUP	BROWN SUGAR	250 ML
1 TSP	VANILLA	5 ML
3 TBSP	FLOUR	45 ML
1 TSP	BAKING POWDER	5 ML
PINCH	SALT	PINCH
1 CUP	SHREDDED COCONUT	250 ML
2/3 CUP	CHOPPED WALNUTS	150 ML
1/4 CUP	SNIPPED GLACÉ CHERRIES	60 ML

BUTTER ICING

1/4 CUP	BUTTER, ROOM TEMPERATURE	60 ML
2 1/2 CUPS	CONFECTIONERS' (ICING) SUGAR	625 ML
3 TBSP	TABLE (18%) CREAM	45 ML

TO MAKE CRUST: PREHEAT OVEN TO 350°F (180°C). COMBINE FLOUR AND SUGAR. CUT IN BUTTER WITH PASTRY BLENDER UNTIL CRUMBLY. PRESS FIRMLY INTO A LIGHTLY GREASED 8-INCH (20 CM) SQUARE PAN. BAKE FOR 20 MINUTES.

TO MAKE FILLING: BEAT EGGS IN A LARGE BOWL, GRADUALLY ADD SUGAR AND VANILLA. MIX FLOUR, BAKING POWDER

AND SALT TOGETHER, THEN ADD TO SUGAR MIXTURE. ADD REMAINING INGREDIENTS. SPREAD OVER CRUST.

RETURN TO OVEN — LOWER TEMPERATURE TO 300°F (150°C). BAKE FOR 25 TO 30 MINUTES, UNTIL TOP IS SET AND LIGHTLY BROWN. COOL.

TO MAKE ICING: BEAT INGREDIENTS TOGETHER AND SPREAD OVER COOLED SQUARE. FREEZES WELL. MAKES 36.

GOLF SCORES ARE DIRECTLY PROPORTIONAL TO THE NUMBER OF WITNESSES.

CRANBERRY SQUARES

ADD THIS GOODIE TO YOUR HOLIDAY BAKING LIST.

CRUST

1/2 CUP	COLD BUTTER	125 ML
1/4 CUP	GRANULATED SUGAR	60 ML
1 CUP	ALL-PURPOSE FLOUR	250 ML

FILLING

1 1/2 CUPS	FROZEN CRANBERRIES	375 ML
1/4 CUP	PACKED BROWN SUGAR	60 ML
2	LARGE EGGS	2
1 CUP	FIRMLY PACKED BROWN SUGAR	250 ML
1 TSP	VANILLA EXTRACT	5 ML
1/3 CUP	ALL-PURPOSE FLOUR	75 ML
1/2 TSP	BAKING POWDER	2 ML
1/4 TSP	SALT	1 ML

TO MAKE CRUST: CUT BUTTER INTO SUGAR AND FLOUR UNTIL CRUMBLY (A FOOD PROCESSOR DOES A DANDY JOB). PAT INTO AN 8-INCH (20 CM) SQUARE PAN. BAKE AT 350°F (180°C) FOR 15 TO 20 MINUTES OR UNTIL GOLDEN.

TO MAKE FILLING: IN A SAUCEPAN, COOK CRANBERRIES (DON'T BOTHER TO THAW) AND 1/4 CUP (60 ML) BROWN SUGAR OVER MEDIUM-LOW HEAT UNTIL BERRIES ARE SOFTENED AND THE SKINS POP, ABOUT 10 MINUTES. COOL. IN A LARGE BOWL, BEAT EGGS AND GRADUALLY ADD BROWN SUGAR. BEAT UNTIL THICKENED. BEAT IN VANILLA. COMBINE DRY INGREDIENTS AND ADD TO EGG MIXTURE. STIR IN COOLED CRANBERRIES AND SPREAD MIXTURE OVER CRUST. BAKE AT 350°F (180°C) FOR 35 TO 40 MINUTES. DON'T OVERBAKE.

LEMON BARS

ANOTHER CLASSIC!

CRUST

1 CUP	FLOUR	250 ML
1/2 CUP	BUTTER	125 ML
1/4 CUP	GRANULATED SUGAR	60 ML
PINCH	SALT	PINCH

LEMON CUSTARD

1 CUP	SUGAR	250 ML
2 TBSP	FLOUR	30 ML
1/4 TSP	BAKING POWDER	1 ML
	ZEST OF 1 LEMON, FINELY GRATED	
	JUICE OF 1 LEMON, 3 TBSP (45 ML)	
2	EGGS, BEATEN	2
	SPRINKLING OF CONFECTIONERS' (ICING) SUGAR	

TO MAKE CRUST: CUT BUTTER INTO DRY INGREDIENTS AND PRESS INTO UNGREASED 9-INCH (23 CM) SQUARE PAN. BAKE AT 350°F (180°C) FOR 20 MINUTES.

TO MAKE CUSTARD: BEAT ALL INGREDIENTS TOGETHER AND POUR OVER CRUST. BAKE AT 350°F (180°C) FOR 25 MINUTES. COOL AND SPRINKLE WITH CONFECTIONERS' SUGAR. CUT INTO BARS. MAKES 24.

IT'S NOT WHO YOU KNOW, IT'S WHOM YOU KNOW.

MAGIC COOKIE BARS

DON'T MAKE THESE IF YOU CAN'T AVOID TEMPTATION — THEY'RE TOO YUMMY.

2 CUPS	CRUSHED CORN FLAKES	500 ML
3 TBSP	GRANULATED SUGAR	45 ML
1/2 CUP	BUTTER	125 ML

MIX INGREDIENTS THOROUGHLY AND PAT INTO A 9-INCH (23 CM) SQUARE PAN.

1 CUP	CHOCOLATE CHIPS	250 ML
1 1/2 CUPS	SHREDDED COCONUT	375 ML
1 CUP	CHOPPED PECANS	250 ML
1	CAN (14 OZ/398 ML) SWEETENED CONDENSED MILK	1

SPRINKLE ABOVE INGREDIENTS OVER FIRST MIXTURE IN ORDER, THEN DRIZZLE CONDENSED MILK OVER ALL. BAKE AT 350°F (180°C) FOR 30 TO 35 MINUTES. MAKES 24.

EVEN THOUGH ANTS ARE ALWAYS AT WORK, ISN'T IT WONDERFUL HOW THEY STILL FIND TIME TO GO TO PICNICS?

NANAIMO BARS

FIRST LAYER

1/2 CUP	BUTTER, MELTED	125 ML
1/4 CUP	BROWN SUGAR	60 ML
3 TBSP	UNSWEETENED COCOA POWDER	45 ML
1	EGG, BEATEN	1
2 CUPS	GRAHAM WAFER CRUMBS	500 ML
1 CUP	FLAKED COCONUT	250 ML
1/2 CUP	CHOPPED WALNUTS	125 ML

SECOND LAYER

2 CUPS	CONFECTIONERS' (ICING) SUGAR	500 ML
1/4 CUP	BUTTER, SOFTENED	60 ML
1/4 CUP	TABLE (18%) CREAM OR MILK	60 ML
2 TBSP	CUSTARD POWDER	30 ML

THIRD LAYER

3	1-OZ (30 G) SQUARES CHOCOLATE (SWEET OR SEMISWEET)	3
1/4 CUP	BUTTER	50 ML

TO MAKE FIRST LAYER: COMBINE INGREDIENTS AND PAT INTO A 9-INCH (23 CM) SQUARE UNGREASED PAN. CHILL FOR 1/2 HOUR.

TO MAKE SECOND LAYER: BEAT ALL INGREDIENTS UNTIL SMOOTH AND FLUFFY. SPREAD CAREFULLY ON TOP OF FIRST LAYER.

TO MAKE THIRD LAYER: MELT CHOCOLATE AND BUTTER TOGETHER. SPREAD OVER SECOND LAYER AND CHILL. CUT INTO SMALL BARS — VERY RICH AND VERY DELICIOUS! MAKES 81.

CAUTION: THIS RECIPE CONTAINS A RAW EGG. IF YOU ARE CONCERNED ABOUT THE FOOD SAFETY OF RAW EGGS, SUBSTITUTE A PASTEURIZED EGG IN THE SHELL OR 1/4 CUP (60 ML) PASTEURIZED LIQUID WHOLE EGGS.

CHOCOLATE RASPBERRY — TRUFFLE SQUARES

DROP DEAD DELICIOUS!

BROWNIE BASE

3	1-OZ (30 G) SQUARES UNSWEETENED CHOCOLATE	3
1/3 CUP	BUTTER	75 ML
1/4 CUP	RASPBERRY JAM	60 ML
2	EGGS	2
1 CUP	GRANULATED SUGAR	250 ML
1 TSP	VANILLA	5 ML
1/2 CUP	FLOUR	125 ML

TOPPING

2 TBSP	HEAVY OR WHIPPING (35%) CREAM	30 ML
2 TBSP	RASPBERRY JAM	30 ML
2 TBSP	BUTTER	30 ML
4	1-OZ (30 G) SQUARES SEMISWEET CHOCOLATE, CHOPPED	4
1 CUP	FRESH RASPBERRIES	250 ML

TO MAKE BASE: PREHEAT OVEN TO 350°F (180°C). LINE AN 8-INCH (20 CM) SQUARE PAN WITH FOIL; GREASE AND SET ASIDE. COMBINE CHOCOLATE, BUTTER AND JAM IN A SAUCEPAN. STIR OVER LOW HEAT UNTIL SMOOTH. REMOVE FROM HEAT. BEAT EGGS IN A LARGE BOWL UNTIL FOAMY. MIX IN SUGAR, VANILLA AND CHOCOLATE MIXTURE. STIR IN FLOUR, JUST UNTIL BLENDED. SPREAD BATTER EVENLY IN PAN AND BAKE FOR 20 TO 35 MINUTES OR UNTIL SET. COOL COMPLETELY IN PAN ON A RACK.

TO MAKE TOPPING: COMBINE, CREAM, JAM AND BUTTER IN A SAUCEPAN. HEAT TO A SIMMER, STIRRING CONSTANTLY UNTIL MELTED. REMOVE FROM HEAT AND ADD CHOCOLATE, STIRRING UNTIL SMOOTH. LET STAND UNTIL COOL BUT STILL SOFT, ABOUT 30 MINUTES. SPREAD TOPPING OVER BROWNIE BASE. IMMEDIATELY TOP WITH RASPBERRIES AND CHILL UNTIL COLD. CUT INTO SMALL SQUARES.

LIGHT TRAVELS FASTER THAN SOUND, WHICH IS WHY SOME PEOPLE APPEAR BRIGHT UNTIL YOU HEAR THEM SPEAK.

FANTASTIC FUDGE BROWNIES

MEN LOVE THEM — SO DO CHILDREN,
(AND MOMS NOT ON DIETS!).

BROWNIES

I CUP	BUTTER	250 ML
2 CUPS	GRANULATED SUGAR	500 ML
1/4 CUP	COCOA POWDER	60 ML
4	EGGS, BEATEN	4
I TSP	VANILLA	5 ML
I CUP	FLOUR	250 ML
I CUP	CHOPPED WALNUTS OR PECANS	250 ML

ICING

2 CUPS	CONFECTIONERS' (ICING) SUGAR	500 ML
2 TBSP	BUTTER	30 ML
2 TBSP	COCOA POWDER	30 ML
2 TBSP	BOILING WATER	30 ML
2 TSP	VANILLA	10 ML

TO MAKE BROWNIES: CREAM TOGETHER BUTTER, SUGAR AND COCOA POWDER. MIX IN BEATEN EGGS AND VANILLA. ADD FLOUR AND STIR. FOLD IN NUTS. BAKE IN A GREASED 13- BY 9-INCH (33 BY 23 CM) PAN AT 350°F (180°C) FOR 40 TO 45 MINUTES. TOP WILL APPEAR TO BE UNDERDONE (FALLS IN MIDDLE), BUT DON'T OVERCOOK. SHOULD BE MOIST AND CHEWY.

TO MAKE ICING: BEAT ALL INGREDIENTS TOGETHER WHILE BROWNIES ARE BAKING. POUR ON TOP AS SOON AS BROWNIES COME OUT OF THE OVEN. IT WILL MELT INTO A SHINY GLAZE.

DESSERTS AND OTHER SWEET TREATS

SPECIAL OCCASIONS DEMAND SPECIAL DESSERTS. HERE WE'VE INCLUDED A FEW OF OUR FAVORITES. SOME ARE A PERFECT LIGHT FINISH TO AN ELABORATE SIT-DOWN MEAL, WHILE OTHERS MAKE A DELIGHTFUL ADDITION TO A BUFFET TABLE.

RASPBERRY PECAN TART WITH SOUR CREAM GLAZE

THIS IS SO EASY — AND SO ELEGANT.
A "WINNER" FOR THE NEXT SPECIAL OCCASION!

FLAKY LEMON PASTRY CRUST

I CUP	ALL-PURPOSE FLOUR	250 ML
1/2 TSP	BAKING POWDER	2 ML
1/4 CUP	GRANULATED SUGAR	60 ML
1/2 CUP	BUTTER	125 ML
I	LARGE EGG	I
I TBSP	GRATED LEMON ZEST	15 ML

FILLING

I CUP	RASPBERRY JAM	250 ML
1/2 CUP	FINELY CHOPPED PECANS	125 ML
1/2 CUP	BUTTER	125 ML
3/4 CUP	GRANULATED SUGAR	175 ML
2	LARGE EGGS	2
I TSP	VANILLA EXTRACT	5 ML
I TBSP	GRATED LEMON ZEST	15 ML
I CUP	FINELY CHOPPED PECANS	250 ML

GLAZE

I TBSP	SOUR CREAM	15 ML
I TSP	VANILLA EXTRACT	5 ML
2/3 CUP	CONFECTIONERS' (ICING) SUGAR	150 ML

TO MAKE CRUST: MIX TOGETHER FLOUR, BAKING POWDER
AND SUGAR. CUT IN BUTTER UNTIL MIXTURE RESEMBLES
COARSE MEAL. BEAT IN THE EGG AND LEMON ZEST UNTIL
JUST BLENDED. DO NOT OVERMIX. PAT DOUGH ONTO THE

BOTTOM OF A GREASED 10-INCH (25 CM) SPRINGFORM PAN AND BAKE AT 350°F (180°C) FOR 25 MINUTES, OR UNTIL TOP IS LIGHTLY BROWNED. ALLOW CRUST TO COOL.

TO MAKE FILLING: STIR TOGETHER RASPBERRY JAM AND $1/2$ CUP (125 ML) PECANS AND SPREAD EVENLY OVER THE CRUST. BEAT BUTTER AND SUGAR UNTIL CREAMY. ADD EGGS, ONE AT A TIME, BEATING WELL AFTER EACH ADDITION. STIR IN VANILLA, LEMON ZEST AND 1 CUP (250 ML) PECANS UNTIL BLENDED. POUR NUT MIXTURE OVER THE JAM. BAKE AT 350°F (180°C) FOR 40 MINUTES OR UNTIL FILLING IS SET. COOL.

TO MAKE GLAZE: STIR TOGETHER SOUR CREAM, VANILLA AND CONFECTIONERS' SUGAR AND DRIZZLE OVER TART. SERVES 8 TO 10 LUCKY PEOPLE!

IN EVERY INSURANCE POLICY, THE BIG PRINT GIVETH AND THE SMALL PRINT TAKETH AWAY.

OLD-FASHIONED BUTTER TARTS

THESE ARE QUICK AND EASY, ESPECIALLY IF YOU PURCHASE THE TART SHELLS.

FILLING

1/3 CUP	BUTTER, MELTED	75 ML
1 1/2 CUPS	BROWN SUGAR	375 ML
3	EGGS	3
1 TSP	GRATED LEMON ZEST	5 ML
1 CUP	CURRANTS	250 ML
1 TSP	VANILLA	5 ML
3	DOZEN UNBAKED TART SHELLS	3

TO MAKE FILLING: IN A MEDIUM BOWL, CREAM BUTTER AND SUGAR. ADD EGGS ONE AT A TIME, BEATING WITH AN ELECTRIC MIXER. STIR IN LEMON ZEST, CURRANTS AND VANILLA.

PREHEAT OVEN TO 375°F (190°C). FILL TART SHELLS AND BAKE FOR 12 TO 15 MINUTES OR UNTIL GOLDEN. MAKES 3 DOZEN TARTS.

HOCKEY IS FIGURE SKATING IN A WAR ZONE.

Lemon Berry Cake (page 266)

Pumpkin Cheesecake (page 267)

Crazy Crunch (page 280)

Christmas Marmalade (page 289)

MINCEMEAT TARTS

8	SHEETS PHYLLO PASTRY, THAWED COOKING SPRAY	8
8 OZ	LIGHT CREAM CHEESE, SOFTENED	250 G
1/2 CUP	CONFECTIONERS' (ICING) SUGAR	125 ML
2 TSP	LIME JUICE	10 ML
1 CUP	MINCEMEAT	250 ML
1/4 CUP	SLIVERED ALMONDS, TOASTED	60 ML

PLACE 1 SHEET OF PHYLLO ON FLAT SURFACE AND LIGHTLY SPRAY WITH COOKING SPRAY. TOP WITH SECOND PHYLLO SHEET, SPRAY AND REPEAT WITH 2 MORE SHEETS. CUT STACKED PHYLLO LENGTHWISE INTO 4 STRIPS; CUT EACH STRIP CROSSWISE INTO 5 PIECES SO THAT YOU HAVE 20 STACKS. PRESS EACH STACK OF PHYLLO INTO EACH OF 20 MINI MUFFIN CUPS TO MAKE TINY TART SHELLS. PREHEAT OVEN TO 350°F (180°C). BAKE 10 TO 12 MINUTES, UNTIL GOLDEN BROWN. REMOVE PAN TO WIRE RACK TO COOL SLIGHTLY. REMOVE TART SHELLS FROM MUFFIN PAN; COOL. REPEAT WITH REMAINING PHYLLO TO MAKE 20 MORE TART SHELLS.

IN SMALL BOWL, BEAT CREAM CHEESE, CONFECTIONERS' SUGAR AND LIME JUICE ON LOW SPEED UNTIL BLENDED. REFRIGERATE UNTIL SERVING TIME.

TO SERVE, SPOON 1 ROUNDED TEASPOON (5 ML) MINCEMEAT INTO EACH TART SHELL AND SPOON CREAM CHEESE MIXTURE ON TOP OF EACH TART. SPRINKLE WITH TOASTED ALMONDS. MAKES 40 TARTS.

EASIER-THAN-APPLE PIE

CRUST

1/2 CUP	BUTTER	125 ML
1 CUP	ALL-PURPOSE FLOUR	250 ML
1/3 CUP	GRANULATED SUGAR	75 ML
1/2 TSP	VANILLA EXTRACT	2 ML

FILLING

1/3 CUP	RASPBERRY JAM	75 ML
8 OZ	CREAM CHEESE	250 G
1/3 CUP	GRANULATED SUGAR	75 ML
1	LARGE EGG	1
1/2 TSP	VANILLA EXTRACT	2 ML
6	APPLES, PEELED, CORED AND SLICED	6
1/3 CUP	GRANULATED SUGAR	75 ML
2 TSP	GROUND CINNAMON	10 ML

TO MAKE CRUST: CUT BUTTER INTO FLOUR (OR BLEND IN A FOOD PROCESSOR), ADD SUGAR AND VANILLA AND MIX WELL. PRESS MIXTURE INTO 9-INCH (23 CM) SPRINGFORM PAN.

TO MAKE FILLING: PREHEAT OVEN TO 450°F (230°C). SPREAD JAM ON TOP OF CRUST. BLEND CREAM CHEESE, SUGAR, EGG AND VANILLA AND POUR EVENLY ON TOP OF JAM. COMBINE APPLES, SUGAR AND CINNAMON AND ARRANGE IN OVERLAPPING PINWHEEL PATTERN ON TOP OF CHEESE MIXTURE. BAKE AT 450°F (230°C) FOR 10 MINUTES. THEN TURN OVEN TO 400°F (200°C) AND BAKE FOR 25 MINUTES. REMOVE THE SIDES WHEN COOL. THIS IS BEST SERVED AT ROOM TEMPERATURE.

AND NOW FOR SOMETHING A LITTLE DIFFERENT:

* SUBSTITUTE APRICOT JAM FOR RASPBERRY JAM IN
  FILLING.

* SUBSTITUTE ALMOND EXTRACT FOR VANILLA IN FILLING.

* SPRINKLE FLAKED ALMONDS ON TOP BEFORE BAKING.

* MELT $\frac{1}{2}$ CUP (125 ML) APRICOT JAM IN MICROWAVE AND
  DRIZZLE OVER TOP AFTER BAKING.

COFFEE BRANDY FREEZE

*A SIMPLY DELICIOUS WAY TO END
AN ELEGANT MEAL. YOU DESERVE IT!*

4 CUPS	COFFEE ICE CREAM	1 L
$\frac{1}{2}$ CUP	BRANDY	125 ML
	SHAVED CHOCOLATE (SEMISWEET)	

SET ICE CREAM OUT TO SOFTEN WHILE YOU CLEAR THE
TABLE. COMBINE ICE CREAM AND BRANDY IN A BLENDER.
BLEND UNTIL ALL LUMPS DISAPPEAR. SERVE IN YOUR
PRETTIEST LONG-STEMMED GLASSES. SHAVE CHOCOLATE
ON TOP AND SERVE. (I SUGGEST YOU HAVE EXTRA
INGREDIENTS ON HAND.) SO SIMPLE AND SOOOO GOOD.
SERVES 4 TO 6.

DON'T CONFUSE AN OPEN MIND WITH ONE THAT'S VACANT.

PUMPKIN PECAN PIE

WE THOUGHT WE'D CALL THIS "PI R SQUARED,"
BUT THEN WE REMEMBERED "PIE ARE ROUND"!

4	EGGS	4
2 CUPS	CANNED OR MASHED COOKED PUMPKIN	500 ML
I CUP	GRANULATED SUGAR	250 ML
1/2 CUP	DARK CORN SYRUP	125 ML
I TSP	VANILLA EXTRACT	5 ML
1/2 TSP	GROUND CINNAMON	2 ML
1/4 TSP	SALT	I ML
I	UNBAKED 9-INCH (23 CM) PIE SHELL	I
I CUP	CHOPPED PECANS	250 ML
I CUP	HEAVY OR WHIPPING (35%) CREAM, WHIPPED (OPTIONAL . . . JUST KIDDING!)	250 ML

BREAK EGGS INTO A LARGE BOWL. BEAT WITH A WIRE
WHISK OR FORK. ADD PUMPKIN, SUGAR, CORN SYRUP,
VANILLA, CINNAMON AND SALT. STIR UNTIL SUGAR IS
DISSOLVED AND INGREDIENTS ARE WELL BLENDED. POUR
INTO PIE SHELL AND SPRINKLE WITH PECANS. BAKE IN
350°F (180°C) OVEN FOR 40 MINUTES OR UNTIL FILLING IS
SET. DELICIOUS AS IS, OR TOPPED WITH WHIPPED CREAM.
SERVES 6 TO 8.

FOR EVERY PERSON WITH A SPARK OF GENIUS,
THERE ARE A HUNDRED WITH IGNITION TROUBLE.

GOOD OLD-FASHIONED GINGERBREAD

FOUR GENERATIONS CAN'T BE WRONG — IT'S DELICIOUS. SERVE WARM WITH WHIPPED CREAM OR LEMON SAUCE.

1/4 CUP	BUTTER	60 ML
1/4 CUP	GRANULATED SUGAR	60 ML
1 TSP	GROUND CINNAMON	5 ML
1 TSP	GROUND GINGER	5 ML
1 TSP	GROUND CLOVES	5 ML
1 TSP	SALT	5 ML
1 TSP	BAKING POWDER	5 ML
1 1/4 CUPS	FLOUR	300 ML
1/2 TSP	BAKING SODA	2 ML
1/2 CUP	MOLASSES	125 ML
1/4 TSP	BAKING SODA	1 ML
3/4 CUP	BOILING WATER	175 ML
1	EGG, BEATEN	1

CREAM TOGETHER BUTTER AND SUGAR. IN A SEPARATE BOWL, MIX CINNAMON, GINGER, CLOVES, SALT, BAKING POWDER AND FLOUR. BEAT BAKING SODA INTO MOLASSES UNTIL FOAMY. ADD TO BUTTER MIXTURE. ADD THE 1/4 TSP (1 ML) OF BAKING SODA TO THE BOILING WATER. ADD THIS ALTERNATELY WITH THE DRY INGREDIENTS TO THE BUTTER-MOLASSES MIXTURE. FOLD IN BEATEN EGG. (THE BATTER WILL BE THIN). POUR INTO GREASED LOAF PAN AND BAKE 30 MINUTES AT 400°F (200°C). SERVES 6 TO 8.

LIGHT CHRISTMAS CAKE

PREPARATION: A THREE-SIZED CHRISTMAS CAKE TIN SET MUST BE LINED, BOTTOMS AND SIDES, WITH BUTTERED BROWN PAPER. CUT THE PAPER TO SIZE. THE NIGHT BEFORE YOU MAKE THIS CAKE, POUR BOILING WATER OVER THE RAISINS, DRAIN AND DRY ON PAPER TOWELING. LEAVE THESE OVERNIGHT. THE FRUIT IN THE RECIPE IS FLOURED WITH HALF THE AMOUNT OF FLOUR CALLED FOR IN THE RECIPE.

3 CUPS	REGULAR FLOUR, SIFTED, DIVIDED	750 ML
1/2 LB	RED GLACÉ CHERRIES	250 G
1/2 LB	GREEN GLACÉ CHERRIES	250 G
1/2 LB	CITRON PEEL	250 G
2	SLICES EACH RED AND GREEN PINEAPPLE, CUT UP	2
2 LBS	BLANCHED SULTANA RAISINS	1 KG
1 1/2 CUPS	GRANULATED SUGAR	375 ML
1 CUP	BUTTER	250 ML
6	EGGS, BEATEN	6
1/2 CUP	ORANGE JUICE	125 ML
	ZEST AND JUICE OF 1 LEMON	
1 TSP	BAKING POWDER	5 ML
1 TSP	SALT	5 ML
1/2 LB	BLANCHED ALMONDS	250 G

USE HALF OF THE FLOUR TO COVER CHERRIES, CITRON PEEL, PINEAPPLE AND WELL-DRIED RAISINS. CREAM SUGAR AND BUTTER, ADD BEATEN EGGS, ORANGE AND LEMON JUICE AND LEMON ZEST. ADD REMAINING FLOUR, BAKING POWDER AND SALT. MIX WELL. ADD FRUIT AND CHOPPED ALMONDS. BAKE AT 275°F (140°C) FOR 2 HOURS. TEST FOR DONENESS. STORE IN A COOL PLACE. MAKES 3 CAKES; EACH SERVES 10.

CHRISTMAS CHERRY CAKE

A DELICIOUS AND NEVER FAIL MOIST WHITE CAKE AND
HALF THE WORK OF A REGULAR CHRISTMAS CAKE!
FREEZES WELL.

1 CUP	BUTTER	250 ML
1 CUP	GRANULATED SUGAR	250 ML
2	EGGS, BEATEN	2
1/2 CUP	ORANGE JUICE	125 ML
2 CUPS	FLOUR	500 ML
1 TSP	BAKING POWDER	5 ML
12 OZ	SULTANA RAISINS	375 G
8 OZ	HALVED RED GLACÉ CHERRIES (OR USE HALF RED AND HALF GREEN CHERRIES)	250 G

CREAM BUTTER AND SUGAR. ADD BEATEN EGGS AND
ORANGE JUICE. SIFT FLOUR AND BAKING POWDER. RESERVE
1/3 CUP (75 ML) OF FLOUR MIXTURE AND TOSS WITH RAISINS
AND CHERRIES (THIS WILL KEEP THEM FROM SINKING
TO THE BOTTOM OF THE CAKE). ADD FLOUR MIXTURE TO
BATTER AND BLEND. ADD FLOURED RAISINS AND CHERRIES
TO DOUGH. BAKE IN A LARGE, GREASED, WAXED PAPER-LINED
LOAF TIN AT 300°F (150°C) FOR 2 1/2 HOURS. DON'T SERVE
UNTIL SEVERAL DAYS OLD. WRAP IN PLASTIC OR FOIL WRAP
AND STORE IN A SEALED TIN. SERVES 16 TO 20.

"LATTE" IS LATIN FOR "YOU PAID TOO MUCH FOR THAT COFFEE."

VICTORIAN ORANGE PEEL CAKE

ALLOW THE FLAVORS TO MELLOW FOR SEVERAL DAYS. DELICIOUSLY MOIST AND FREEZES WELL.

CAKE

	PEEL OF 3 LARGE ORANGES	
1 CUP	RAISINS	250 ML
1 CUP	GRANULATED SUGAR	250 ML
1/2 CUP	BUTTER, ROOM TEMPERATURE	125 ML
2	EGGS	2
3/4 CUP	BUTTERMILK	175 ML
2 CUPS	FLOUR	500 ML
1 TSP	BAKING SODA	5 ML
1/2 TSP	SALT	2 ML
1/2 CUP	CHOPPED WALNUTS	125 ML

ORANGE SYRUP

1 CUP	FRESH ORANGE JUICE	250 ML
1/2 CUP	GRANULATED SUGAR	125 ML
2 TBSP	DARK RUM	30 ML

TO MAKE CAKE: REMOVE WHITE PITH FROM PEEL (IT'S THE BITTER PART). PLACE PEEL AND RAISINS IN PROCESSOR AND MIX UNTIL FINELY CHOPPED. PREHEAT OVEN TO 325°F (160°C). CREAM TOGETHER SUGAR AND BUTTER. ADD EGGS AND BUTTERMILK; MIX THOROUGHLY. MIX FLOUR, BAKING SODA AND SALT; STIR INTO BATTER. MIX IN PEEL, RAISINS AND WALNUTS. POUR INTO A WELL-GREASED 9- OR 10-INCH (23 OR 25 CM) SPRINGFORM PAN AND BAKE 45 TO 50 MINUTES, UNTIL CAKE TESTS DONE.

TO MAKE SYRUP: HEAT ORANGE JUICE, SUGAR AND RUM TOGETHER UNTIL SUGAR IS DISSOLVED.

WHEN CAKE IS DONE, LET STAND 10 MINUTES. REMOVE FROM PAN. RE-INVERT; SLOWLY DRIZZLE SYRUP, A SPOONFUL AT A TIME, OVER CAKE.

PAVLOVA

NEW ZEALAND'S NATIONAL DESSERT.

4	EGG WHITES	4
1 CUP	GRANULATED SUGAR	250 ML
1/2 TSP	VANILLA EXTRACT	2 ML
1 TSP	VINEGAR	5 ML
2 CUPS	HEAVY OR WHIPPING (35%) CREAM	500 ML
	FRESH FRUIT: KIWI, BLUEBERRIES AND STRAWBERRIES ARE PERFECT	
1/2 CUP	TOASTED SLIVERED ALMONDS	125 ML

BEAT EGG WHITES UNTIL SOFT PEAKS FORM. CONTINUE BEATING WHILE ADDING SUGAR SLOWLY, 1 TBSP (15 ML) AT A TIME. ADD VANILLA AND VINEGAR. BEAT UNTIL VERY STIFF. PLACE WAXED OR BROWN PAPER ON A COOKIE SHEET AND SPREAD MIXTURE IN A CIRCLE, SLIGHTLY SMALLER THAN DESIRED SIZE. BAKE FOR 1 HOUR AT 275°F (140°C). TURN OVEN OFF AND LEAVE MERINGUE IN OVEN OVERNIGHT TO DRY. PEEL OFF PAPER. TOP WITH WHIPPED CREAM, FRESH FRUIT AND TOASTED ALMONDS. SERVES 6 TO 8.

CHOCOLATE RASPBERRY TORTE

GOD MADE CHOCOLATE AND THE DEVIL THREW THE
CALORIES IN! THIS TASTES AS GOOD AS IT LOOKS.

CAKE

2 CUPS	ALL-PURPOSE FLOUR	500 ML
2 TSP	BAKING SODA	10 ML
1/2 TSP	SALT	2 ML
1/2 TSP	BAKING POWDER	2 ML
3	SQUARES (EACH 1 OZ/30 G) UNSWEETENED CHOCOLATE	3
1/2 CUP	BUTTER	125 ML
2 CUPS	PACKED BROWN SUGAR	500 ML
3	EGGS	3
1 1/2 TSP	VANILLA EXTRACT	7 ML
3/4 CUP	SOUR CREAM	175 ML
1/2 CUP	STRONG COFFEE	125 ML
1/2 CUP	COFFEE-FLAVORED LIQUEUR (KAHLÚA)	125 ML

FILLING

1 CUP	HEAVY OR WHIPPING (35%) CREAM	250 ML
2 TBSP	CONFECTIONERS' (ICING) SUGAR	30 ML
1	JAR (12 OZ/341 ML) RASPBERRY OR STRAWBERRY JAM	1

FROSTING

1 1/2 CUPS	CHOCOLATE CHIPS	375 ML
3/4 CUP	SOUR CREAM	175 ML
PINCH	SALT	PINCH
	CHOCOLATE CURLS	
	RASPBERRIES OR STRAWBERRIES	

TO MAKE CAKE: PREHEAT OVEN TO 350°F (180°C). GREASE AND FLOUR TWO 9-INCH (23 CM) CAKE PANS. MIX FLOUR, BAKING SODA, SALT AND BAKING POWDER. MELT CHOCOLATE AND LET COOL. IN A LARGE BOWL, BEAT BUTTER, BROWN SUGAR AND EGGS AT HIGH SPEED UNTIL LIGHT AND FLUFFY, ABOUT 5 MINUTES. BEAT IN MELTED CHOCOLATE AND VANILLA. AT LOW SPEED, BEAT IN FLOUR MIXTURE (IN FOURTHS), ALTERNATING WITH SOUR CREAM (IN THIRDS). ADD COFFEE AND LIQUEUR, BLENDING UNTIL SMOOTH. POUR BATTER INTO PANS AND BAKE FOR 30 TO 35 MINUTES OR UNTIL SURFACE SPRINGS BACK. COOL IN PANS FOR 10 MINUTES, THEN REMOVE FROM PANS AND COOL ON WIRE RACKS.

TO MAKE FILLING: BEAT CREAM UNTIL IT BEGINS TO THICKEN. SPRINKLE IN CONFECTIONERS' SUGAR AND BEAT UNTIL STIFF. REFRIGERATE. SLICE CAKE LAYERS IN HALF HORIZONTALLY TO MAKE FOUR LAYERS (CAKE LAYERS CUT MORE EASILY IF FROZEN FIRST). PLACE ONE LAYER, CUT SIDE UP, ON CAKE PLATE. SPREAD WITH 1/2 CUP (125 ML) RASPBERRY JAM AND 1/2 CUP (125 ML) WHIPPED CREAM. REPEAT WITH REMAINING LAYERS, ENDING WITH TOP LAYER CUT SIDE DOWN.

TO MAKE FROSTING: MELT CHOCOLATE CHIPS IN TOP OF DOUBLE BOILER. ADD SOUR CREAM AND SALT AND BEAT UNTIL FROSTING IS CREAMY AND SMOOTH. FROST TOP AND SIDES OF CAKE. GARNISH WITH CHOCOLATE CURLS AND FRESH BERRIES. SERVES 10 TO 12.

TIP: TO MAKE CHOCOLATE CURLS, WARM A GOOD-QUALITY CHOCOLATE BAR TO ROOM TEMPERATURE, THEN USE A VEGETABLE PEELER TO SHAVE OFF CURLS.

CHOCOLATE-MOCHA CHEESECAKE

WHO'D BELIEVE THIS IS LOW-FAT?

16 OZ	LOW-FAT SMALL-CURD COTTAGE CHEESE	500 G
8 OZ	FAT-REDUCED CREAM CHEESE, ROOM TEMPERATURE	250 G
1 CUP	GRANULATED SUGAR	250 ML
1 TBSP	VANILLA	15 ML
2 TSP	INSTANT ESPRESSO POWDER OR INSTANT COFFEE POWDER	10 ML
1/4 TSP	SALT	1 ML
3	LARGE EGGS, ROOM TEMPERATURE	3
5 to 6 TBSP	UNSWEETENED COCOA POWDER	75 to 90 ML
1/4 CUP	GRANULATED SUGAR	60 ML

PREHEAT OVEN TO 350°F (180°C). LINE BOTTOM OF 8-INCH (20 CM) CIRCULAR CAKE PAN OR PIE PLATE AND BUILD SIDES UP TO 2 INCHES (5 CM) WITH PARCHMENT OR BROWN PAPER. SPRAY SIDES WITH VEGETABLE OIL SPRAY.

BLEND COTTAGE CHEESE IN PROCESSOR UNTIL SMOOTH. ADD CHEESE AND MIX WELL. ADD 1 CUP (250 ML) SUGAR, VANILLA, ESPRESSO POWDER AND SALT; BLEND. ADD EGGS AND PROCESS JUST UNTIL SMOOTH. POUR 2 CUPS (500 ML) OF BATTER INTO MEASURING CUP. ADD COCOA POWDER AND 1/4 CUP (60 ML) SUGAR TO BATTER IN PROCESSOR AND BLEND WELL. POUR COCOA BATTER INTO PREPARED PAN. POUR COFFEE BATTER DIRECTLY INTO CENTER OF COCOA BATTER (COFFEE BATTER WILL PUSH COCOA BATTER TO EDGE). RUN A SMALL KNIFE THROUGH BATTERS TO CREATE A MARBLED PATTERN. SET CAKE

PAN INTO A 13- BY 9-INCH (33 BY 23 CM) PAN. POUR
ENOUGH BOILING WATER INTO BAKING PAN TO COME
HALFWAY UP SIDES OF CAKE PAN. SET PAN IN OVEN.
BAKE CAKE UNTIL EDGES JUST BEGIN TO PUFF AND
CRACK AND CENTER IS JUST SET, ABOUT 50 MINUTES.
REMOVE CAKE PAN FROM WATER AND SET ON RACK TO
COOL. COVER CAKE IN PAN WITH PLASTIC WRAP AND
REFRIGERATE FOR ABOUT 6 HOURS. REMOVE WRAP; PUT
PLATE ON TOP OF CAKE PAN AND INVERT. TAP BOTTOM
LIGHTLY TO LOOSEN CAKE FROM PAN. COVER AND
REFRIGERATE. THIS CAN BE MADE AHEAD. SERVES 10 TO 12.

BRANDY MINT CREAM

THIS IS A TERRIFIC DRINK TO SERVE AS A DESSERT.

2 QUARTS	FRENCH VANILLA ICE CREAM	2 L
1/2 CUP	CRÈME DE MENTHE	125 ML
1 CUP	BRANDY	250 ML

LET ICE CREAM SIT AT ROOM TEMPERATURE TO SOFTEN.
WHIRL ALL INGREDIENTS TOGETHER IN A BLENDER. POUR
INTO STEM GLASSES. SERVES 6.

*I TRY TO TAKE ONE DAY AT A TIME, BUT SOMETIMES
SEVERAL DAYS ATTACK ME ALL AT ONCE.*

LEMON BERRY CAKE

18 OZ	UNSWEETENED FROZEN BLUEBERRIES, THAWED	510 G
1	PACKAGE 2-LAYER LEMON CAKE MIX	1
1 CUP	LEMON OR VANILLA YOGURT	250 ML
4	EGGS	4

GLAZE

1 CUP	CONFECTIONERS' (ICING) SUGAR	250 ML
4 TSP	MILK	20 ML

BLUEBERRY SAUCE

1 CUP	GRANULATED SUGAR	250 ML
2 TBSP	CORNSTARCH	25 ML
1 CUP	WATER	250 ML
3 TBSP	LEMON JUICE	45 ML
	WHIPPED CREAM	

RINSE AND DRAIN BERRIES, RESERVING LIQUID. COMBINE CAKE MIX, EGGS AND YOGURT, BEATING 2 MINUTES. FOLD IN HALF OF DRAINED BERRIES. BAKE IN GREASED 10-INCH (25 CM) TUBE OR BUNDT PAN AT 350°F (180°C) FOR 45 MINUTES OR UNTIL DONE. DO NOT INVERT PAN, OR REMOVE, UNTIL CAKE IS COOL. MAKE GLAZE AND DRIZZLE OVER CAKE.

IN PAN, COMBINE SUGAR, CORNSTARCH, THEN THE WATER. BRING TO A BOIL AND COOK 2 MINUTES. ADD BLUEBERRIES AND JUICE. ADDITIONAL CORNSTARCH MAY BE ADDED IF A THICKER SAUCE IS DESIRED.

TO SERVE, REHEAT SAUCE AND POUR OVER CAKE SLICES ON SERVING PLATES, AND ADD A DAB OF WHIPPED CREAM TO EACH SERVING. SERVES 12 TO 16.

PUMPKIN CHEESECAKE

A GRAND FINALE FOR THANKSGIVING DINNER.

GINGER SNAP CRUST

I CUP	CRUSHED GINGER SNAPS	250 ML
3 TBSP	BUTTER, MELTED	45 ML
I TSP	GROUND CINNAMON	5 ML
2 TBSP	BROWN SUGAR	30 ML

FILLING

4	PACKAGES (EACH 8 OZ/250 G) CREAM CHEESE, SOFTENED	4
I$\frac{1}{2}$ CUPS	GRANULATED SUGAR	375 ML
5	EGGS	5
$\frac{1}{4}$ CUP	ALL-PURPOSE FLOUR	60 ML
2 TSP	PUMPKIN PIE SPICE OR EQUAL PARTS GINGER, CINNAMON AND NUTMEG	10 ML
I	CAN (14 OZ/398 ML) PUMPKIN	I
2 TBSP	RUM	30 ML
I CUP	HEAVY OR WHIPPING (35%) CREAM, WHIPPED	250 ML

TO MAKE CRUST: COMBINE INGREDIENTS. LIGHTLY GREASE A 10-INCH (25 CM) SPRINGFORM PAN AND LINE BOTTOM WITH CRUMB MIXTURE. PAT FIRM AND CHILL.

TO MAKE FILLING: PREHEAT OVEN TO 325°F (160°C). BEAT SOFTENED CREAM CHEESE TILL FLUFFY. SLOWLY BEAT IN SUGAR. ADD EGGS, ONE AT A TIME, BEATING WELL AFTER EACH ADDITION. GRADUALLY BEAT IN FLOUR, SPICES, PUMPKIN AND RUM. POUR BATTER OVER CRUST. BAKE FOR I$\frac{1}{2}$ TO I$\frac{3}{4}$ HOURS OR UNTIL FILLING IS SET. COOL FOR AN HOUR. REFRIGERATE SEVERAL HOURS. GARNISH WITH WHIPPED CREAM AND A SPRINKLE OF CINNAMON. SERVES 10 TO 12.

GRANDMA'S CHRISTMAS PUDDING WITH GOLDEN SAUCE

I LB	GROUND SUET	500 G
I CUP	BROWN SUGAR	250 ML
4	LARGE EGGS, WELL BEATEN	4
I LB	CURRANTS	500 G
I LB	DARK RAISINS	500 G
I LB	SULTANA RAISINS	500 G
8 OZ	MIXED PEEL	250 G
I CUP	PEELED AND GRATED CARROTS	250 ML
I CUP	PEELED AND GRATED POTATOES	250 ML
2	APPLES, PEELED AND GRATED	2
2 CUPS	ALL-PURPOSE FLOUR	500 ML
	GRATED ZEST AND JUICE OF I LEMON	
2 CUPS	DRY BREAD CRUMBS	500 ML
I TSP	BAKING SODA	5 ML
2 TSP	GROUND CINNAMON	10 ML
1/2 TSP	GROUND ALLSPICE	2 ML
1/2 TSP	GROUND CLOVES	2 ML
1/2 TSP	SALT	2 ML
I TBSP	LIGHT (FANCY) MOLASSES	15 ML

GOLDEN SAUCE

I CUP	BUTTER	250 ML
2 CUPS	CONFECTIONERS' (ICING) SUGAR	500 ML
1/4 CUP	TABLE (18%) CREAM	60 ML
2	LARGE EGGS, BEATEN	2
PINCH	SALT	PINCH
I TBSP	VANILLA OR WHITE RUM	15 ML

IN A LARGE BOWL OR LARGE ROASTING PAN, BLEND SUET AND SUGAR TOGETHER. ADD EGGS. MIX CURRANTS, RAISINS, PEEL, CARROTS, POTATOES AND APPLES WITH THE FLOUR TO COAT. SPRINKLE WITH LEMON ZEST AND LEMON JUICE. ADD REMAINING INGREDIENTS AND MIX WELL. FILL STERILIZED PINT (500 ML) JARS (OR GREASED COVERED MOLDS) TWO-THIRDS FULL WITH PUDDING MIXTURE. STEAM FOR 3 HOURS. WHEN READY TO SERVE, STEAM FOR $1/2$ HOUR OR HEAT IN MICROWAVE.

TO STEAM: PLACE CONTAINERS ON A TRIVET OR RACK IN A HEAVY KETTLE OVER 1 INCH (2.5 CM) OF BOILING WATER. COVER KETTLE. USE HIGH HEAT TO BEGIN WITH, THEN AS STEAM BEGINS TO ESCAPE, REDUCE HEAT TO LOW FOR REMAINING COOKING TIME. CHECK WATER LEVEL PERIODICALLY AND ADD AS NECESSARY. MAKES 13 PINTS (6.5 L).

TO MAKE SAUCE: COOK ALL INGREDIENTS OVER HOT WATER IN DOUBLE BOILER. BEAT OCCASIONALLY UNTIL THICK AND CREAMY. ALSO A DANDY ADDITION TO ICE CREAM! MAKES ABOUT 2 CUPS (500 ML).

MARRIAGE IS A RELATIONSHIP WHERE ONE PERSON IS ALWAYS RIGHT AND THE OTHER IS THE HUSBAND.

CAJUN BREAD PUDDING WITH RUM SAUCE AND SOFT CREAM

PUDDING

1/3 CUP	BUTTER OR MARGARINE, MELTED	75 ML
16 CUPS	FRENCH BREAD CUBES, DAY OLD, LIGHTLY PACKED	4 L
3	LARGE EGGS	3
1 1/2 CUPS	GRANULATED SUGAR	375 ML
2 TBSP	VANILLA EXTRACT	30 ML
1 TSP	GROUND NUTMEG	5 ML
1 1/2 TSP	GROUND CINNAMON	7 ML
3 CUPS	MILK	750 ML
3/4 CUP	GOLDEN RAISINS	175 ML
1 CUP	CHOPPED TOASTED PECANS	250 ML

RUM SAUCE

1 CUP	BUTTER OR MARGARINE	250 ML
1 1/2 CUPS	GRANULATED SUGAR	375 ML
2	LARGE EGGS, BEATEN UNTIL FROTHY	2
1/4 to 1/2 CUP	DARK RUM	60 to 125 ML

SOFT CREAM

2 CUPS	HEAVY OR WHIPPING (35%) CREAM	500 ML
1/3 CUP	CONFECTIONERS' (ICING) SUGAR	75 ML
1 TBSP	VANILLA EXTRACT	15 ML
2 TBSP	BRANDY	30 ML
2 TBSP	FRANGELICO LIQUEUR	30 ML
1/4 CUP	SOUR CREAM	60 ML

TO MAKE PUDDING: POUR A SMALL AMOUNT OF THE MELTED BUTTER IN A 13- BY 9-INCH (33 BY 23 CM) PAN AND SWIRL AROUND TO COVER BOTTOM AND SIDES. PLACE

BREAD CUBES IN PAN. IN A LARGE BOWL, BEAT EGGS AND SUGAR UNTIL THICKENED (3 TO 4 MINUTES). ADD VANILLA, NUTMEG, CINNAMON AND MILK PLUS RESERVED BUTTER. BEAT AT LOW SPEED TO COMBINE. STIR IN RAISINS AND PECANS. POUR OVER BREAD. STIR TO EVENLY DISTRIBUTE RAISINS AND NUTS. ALLOW BREAD TO ABSORB ALL LIQUID (30 TO 45 MINUTES). PRESS BREAD DOWN OFTEN TO COVER ALL CUBES. PREHEAT OVEN TO 350°F (180°C). BAKE UNTIL CRUSTY AND GOLDEN BROWN (45 TO 60 MINUTES). COOL TO LUKEWARM AND SLICE INTO SQUARES.

TO MAKE RUM SAUCE: CREAM BUTTER AND SUGAR UNTIL LIGHT AND FLUFFY. PUT IN TOP OF A DOUBLE BOILER OVER SIMMERING WATER. COOK 20 MINUTES, WHISKING OFTEN. IN A BOWL, WHISK 2 TBSP (30 ML) BUTTER-SUGAR MIXTURE INTO BEATEN EGGS, THEN WHISK IN 2 TBSP (30 ML) MORE. NOW, WHISK EGG MIXTURE INTO BUTTER-SUGAR MIXTURE. COOK OVER SIMMERING WATER 4 TO 5 MINUTES, WHISKING CONSTANTLY. COOL SLIGHTLY. WHISK IN RUM. (BY NOW YOU'RE PROBABLY ALL WHISKED OUT — TASTE THE SAUCE AND YOU'LL KNOW IT WAS WORTH IT!)

TO MAKE SOFT CREAM: CHILL BEATERS AND A MEDIUM-SIZED BOWL UNTIL VERY COLD. BEAT INGREDIENTS ON MEDIUM-HIGH UNTIL SOFT PEAKS FORM (3 TO 4 MINUTES). DO NOT OVERBEAT. COVER TIGHTLY AND REFRIGERATE UNTIL SERVED.

TO SERVE: ON INDIVIDUAL PLATES, PLACE A SPOONFUL OF WARM RUM SAUCE, A SQUARE OF PUDDING AND A LARGE DOLLOP OF SOFT CREAM. SERVES 12 TO 14.

LITTLE STICKY TOFFEE PUDDINGS

1 CUP	WATER	250 ML
1/2 TSP	VANILLA	2 ML
1/2 TSP	BAKING SODA	2 ML
1 CUP	DRIED CRANBERRIES	250 ML
3/4 CUP	BUTTER	175 ML
2/3 CUP	GRANULATED SUGAR	150 ML
2	EGGS	2
1 CUP	FLOUR	250 ML
1/4 TSP	BAKING POWDER	1 ML

TOFFEE SAUCE

1 CUP	BROWN SUGAR	250 ML
1/2 CUP	BUTTER	125 ML
1/2 CUP	HEAVY OR WHIPPING (35%) CREAM	125 ML

BUTTER EIGHT 4-OZ (125 ML) RAMEKINS. BRING WATER TO A BOIL; ADD VANILLA AND BAKING SODA. ADD CRANBERRIES; SET ASIDE TO COOL. CREAM BUTTER AND SUGAR UNTIL LIGHT AND FLUFFY. LIGHTLY BEAT EGGS AND GRADUALLY ADD TO BUTTER MIXTURE IN THREE STAGES. SIFT FLOUR AND BAKING POWDER TOGETHER; GENTLY FOLD INTO BATTER. FOLD CRANBERRY MIXTURE INTO BATTER. PORTION INTO RAMEKINS AND BAKE AT 350°F (180°C) FOR 25 MINUTES.

TO MAKE TOFFEE SAUCE: COMBINE INGREDIENTS IN SAUCEPAN; STIR OVER LOW HEAT UNTIL SUGAR IS DISSOLVED. SIMMER UNTIL THICKENED. TO SERVE, REMOVE PUDDINGS FROM RAMEKINS BY RUNNING A KNIFE AROUND EDGE. INVERT ON PLATE AND DRIZZLE WITH WARM TOFFEE SAUCE. SERVES 8.

CHILLED LEMON SOUFFLÉ

THIS SIMPLE CITRUS SOUFFLÉ
HITS THE SPOT AFTER A SPICY MEAL.

1 TBSP	UNFLAVORED GELATIN (1 PACKAGE)	15 ML
1/4 CUP	COLD WATER	60 ML
4	EGGS, SEPARATED	4
1 CUP	GRANULATED SUGAR	250 ML
1/2 CUP	FRESHLY SQUEEZED LEMON JUICE	125 ML
1 1/2 TBSP	GRATED LEMON ZEST	22 ML
1 CUP	HEAVY OR WHIPPING (35%) CREAM	250 ML

PLACE GELATIN IN WATER AND SET ASIDE TO SOFTEN. IN A HEAVY SAUCEPAN, OVER LOW HEAT, WHISK THE EGG YOLKS UNTIL SMOOTH. WHISK IN THE SUGAR, LEMON JUICE AND ZEST. COOK, STIRRING, UNTIL SLIGHTLY THICKENED, ABOUT 10 MINUTES. STIR IN SOFTENED GELATIN AND COOK UNTIL DISSOLVED, 1 TO 2 MINUTES. POUR INTO LARGE MIXING BOWL AND ALLOW TO COOL. WHIP CREAM UNTIL SOFT PEAKS FORM; DO NOT OVERBEAT. FOLD WHIPPED CREAM INTO CHILLED LEMON MIXTURE UNTIL BLENDED. BEAT EGG WHITES UNTIL STIFF BUT NOT DRY. FOLD INTO LEMON-CREAM MIXTURE. SPOON MIXTURE INTO A GLASS DISH AND REFRIGERATE UNTIL SET — ABOUT 2 HOURS. SERVES 6 TO 8.

NOTE: THIS RECIPE CONTAINS RAW EGG WHITES. IF YOU ARE CONCERNED ABOUT THE FOOD SAFETY OF RAW EGGS, USE PASTEURIZED EGGS IN THE SHELL.

FROZEN LEMON PUFF

GUARANTEED RAVES AND A GREAT MAKE-AHEAD.

5	LARGE EGGS (SEPARATE 3 AND RESERVE WHITES)	5
3/4 CUP	LEMON JUICE	175 ML
I CUP	GRANULATED SUGAR	250 ML
2 CUPS	HEAVY OR WHIPPING (35%) CREAM	500 ML
	VANILLA WAFERS TO COVER BOTTOM AND SIDES OF PAN	
DASH	CREAM OF TARTAR	DASH
1/4 CUP	CONFECTIONERS' (ICING) SUGAR	60 ML

MIX 2 EGGS AND 3 EGG YOLKS, LEMON JUICE AND SUGAR TOGETHER IN THE TOP OF A DOUBLE BOILER AND COOK UNTIL THICK, STIRRING CONSTANTLY. COOL. WHIP THE CREAM AND FOLD INTO LEMON MIXTURE. LINE SIDES AND BOTTOM OF A 9-INCH (23 CM) SPRINGFORM PAN WITH VANILLA WAFERS. POUR LEMON MIXTURE INTO THE PAN. BEAT THE 3 EGG WHITES UNTIL FOAMY. ADD CREAM OF TARTAR AND CONFECTIONERS' SUGAR AND BEAT UNTIL PEAKS ARE STIFF. SPREAD ON THE LEMON MIXTURE AND BROWN UNDER THE BROILER. (WATCH CAREFULLY!) COVER WITH FOIL, MAKING SURE IT DOESN'T TOUCH THE MERINGUE. FREEZE 8 HOURS OR MORE. REMOVE FROM FREEZER (TAKING FOIL OFF IMMEDIATELY) AT LEAST 1 1/2 HOURS BEFORE SERVING. SERVES 10 TO 12.

FOOD GIFTS

NOTHING SAYS "HAPPY HOLIDAYS" MORE SINCERELY
THAN A GIFT OF MADE-FROM-SCRATCH FOOD. WHILE
PRESERVES ARE ALWAYS WELCOME, YOU CAN ALSO FILL A
PRESERVING JAR WITH SEASONED NUTS, OR A TISSUE-LINED
BOX WITH HOMEMADE TOFFEE OR ANOTHER CANDY-TYPE
TREAT, TO RING IN THE SEASON WITH GOOD CHEER.

HOT ROASTED NUTS

FOR A HOLIDAY GIFT, MAKE UP A BATCH OR TWO OF
THESE YUMMY NUTS AND PACKAGE IN PRETTY JARS.
IF WELL SEALED, THE NUTS WILL KEEP FOR 10 DAYS.

SALTY ALMONDS WITH THYME

2 CUPS	UNBLANCHED ALMONDS	500 ML
$1/2$ TSP	FRESHLY GROUND WHITE PEPPER	2 ML
1 TBSP	FINE SEA SALT (OR TO TASTE)	15 ML
2 TBSP	EXTRA VIRGIN OLIVE OIL	30 ML
2 TBSP	FRESH THYME LEAVES	30 ML

IN A SMALL (MAXIMUM $3^1/_2$-QUART) SLOW COOKER,
COMBINE ALMONDS AND WHITE PEPPER. COVER AND COOK
ON HIGH FOR $1^1/_2$ HOURS, STIRRING EVERY 30 MINUTES,
UNTIL NUTS ARE NICELY TOASTED. IN A BOWL, COMBINE
SALT, OLIVE OIL AND THYME. ADD TO SLOW COOKER AND
STIR THOROUGHLY TO COMBINE. SPOON MIXTURE INTO
A SMALL SERVING BOWL AND SERVE HOT OR LET COOL.
MAKES ABOUT 2 CUPS (500 ML).

TIP: SEA SALT IS AVAILABLE IN MOST SUPERMARKETS. IT
IS MUCH SWEETER THAN TABLE SALT AND IS ESSENTIAL
FOR THESE RECIPES, AS TABLE SALT WOULD IMPART AN
UNPLEASANT ACRID TASTE TO THE NUTS.

BUTTERY PEANUTS

2 CUPS	RAW PEANUTS (SEE TIP, OPPOSITE)	500 ML
$1/4$ CUP	MELTED BUTTER	60 ML
2 TSP	FINE SEA SALT	10 ML

IN A SMALL (MAXIMUM $3^1/_2$-QUART) SLOW COOKER,
COMBINE PEANUTS AND BUTTER. COVER AND COOK ON

HIGH FOR 2 TO 2½ HOURS, STIRRING OCCASIONALLY, UNTIL PEANUTS ARE NICELY ROASTED. DRAIN ON PAPER TOWELS. PLACE IN A BOWL, SPRINKLE WITH SALT AND STIR TO COMBINE. MAKES ABOUT 2 CUPS (500 ML).

TIP: USE PEANUTS WITH SKINS ON OR BUY THEM PEELED, DEPENDING UPON YOUR PREFERENCE. BOTH WORK WELL IN THIS RECIPE.

SPICY CASHEWS

2 CUPS	RAW CASHEWS	500 ML
I TSP	CHILI POWDER	5 ML
1/2 TSP	CAYENNE PEPPER	2 ML
1/4 TSP	GROUND CINNAMON	I ML
2 TSP	FINE SEA SALT	IO ML
I TBSP	EXTRA VIRGIN OLIVE OIL	I5 ML

IN A SMALL (MAXIMUM 3½-QUART) SLOW COOKER, COMBINE CASHEWS, CHILI POWDER, CAYENNE AND CINNAMON. STIR TO COMBINE THOROUGHLY. COVER AND COOK ON HIGH FOR 1½ HOURS, STIRRING EVERY 30 MINUTES, UNTIL NUTS ARE NICELY TOASTED. IN A SMALL BOWL, COMBINE SEA SALT AND OLIVE OIL. ADD TO SLOW COOKER AND STIR TO THOROUGHLY COMBINE. TRANSFER MIXTURE TO A SERVING BOWL AND SERVE HOT OR LET COOL. MAKES ABOUT 2 CUPS (500 ML).

CANDIED ALMONDS

1/4 CUP	WATER	60 ML
1/2 CUP	SUGAR	125 ML
1 CUP	ALMONDS (OR PECANS)	250 ML

PLACE INGREDIENTS IN CAST IRON FRYING PAN. (THIS RECIPE DOUBLED FITS WELL INTO A 10-INCH (25 CM) PAN.)

COOK ABOUT 10 MINUTES, STIRRING CONSTANTLY WITH WOODEN SPOON. MIXTURE WILL BECOME POWDERY WHITE, THEN GLAZE WILL BEGIN.

KEEP STIRRING UNTIL NUTS ARE COVERED WITH THE GLAZE. TURN OUT ON BREADBOARD AND SEPARATE — BE CAREFUL AS NUTS ARE VERY HOT. MAKES 1 CUP (250 ML).

THESE MAKE NICE CHRISTMAS GIFTS IN LITTLE BOWLS OR JARS.

A HUSBAND IS SOMEONE WHO CAN GUESS WHAT HIS WIFE IS GOING TO SAY BEFORE SHE REPEATS IT.

SPICED PECANS

A GREAT GIFTABLE.

2 CUPS	PECAN HALVES	500 ML
1 1/2 TBSP	BUTTER	22 ML
1 TSP	SALT	5 ML
2 TSP	SOY SAUCE	10 ML
1/4 TSP	HOT PEPPER SAUCE	1 ML

PREHEAT OVEN TO 300°F (150°C). PLACE PECANS ON
A BAKING SHEET. MELT BUTTER AND ADD REMAINING
INGREDIENTS. POUR OVER PECANS. BAKE 15 MINUTES. STIR
AND TOSS DURING COOKING TIME. COOL AND DIG IN —
YUMMY! MAKES 2 CUPS (500 ML).

CARAMELIZED WALNUTS

1	EGG WHITE	1
1 TSP	COLD WATER	5 ML
1 LB	SHELLED WHOLE WALNUTS	500 G
1 CUP	BROWN SUGAR	250 ML
1/4 TSP	SALT	1 ML

BEAT EGG WHITE AND WATER UNTIL FROTHY. ADD WALNUTS
AND STIR UNTIL WELL COATED. COMBINE SUGAR AND SALT
AND COVER WALNUTS. BAKE 1 HOUR AT 225°F (110°C) ON A
GREASED COOKIE SHEET. STIR EVERY 15 MINUTES. MAKES
ABOUT 2 1/2 CUPS (625 ML).

CRAZY CRUNCH

PUT THIS IN FANCY JARS AND GIVE IT AS A LITTLE EXTRA AT CHRISTMAS TIME.

2 QUARTS	POPPED POPCORN	2 L
1 1/3 CUPS	PECANS	325 ML
2/3 CUP	ALMONDS	150 ML
1 1/3 CUPS	GRANULATED SUGAR	325 ML
1 TSP	VANILLA	5 ML
1 CUP	MARGARINE	250 ML
1/2 CUP	CORN SYRUP	125 ML

MIX POPCORN, PECANS AND ALMONDS ON A COOKIE SHEET. COMBINE SUGAR, VANILLA, MARGARINE AND SYRUP IN A PAN. BOIL 10 TO 15 MINUTES OR TO A LIGHT CARAMEL COLOR. POUR OVER CORN, PECANS AND ALMONDS. MIX WELL. SPREAD TO DRY. MAKES ABOUT 10 CUPS (2.5 L).

NOVEL NUTS

1	EGG WHITE	1
1 TSP	COLD WATER	5 ML
1 LB	LARGE PECAN HALVES	500 G
1/2 CUP	GRANULATED SUGAR	125 ML
1/4 TSP	SALT	1 ML
1/2 TSP	GROUND CINNAMON	2 ML
SPRINKLE	FRESHLY GROUND NUTMEG	SPRINKLE

BEAT EGG WHITE AND WATER UNTIL FROTHY. ADD PECANS
AND MIX UNTIL WELL COATED. COMBINE SUGAR, SALT,
CINNAMON AND NUTMEG. ADD TO PECAN MIXTURE. BAKE
1 HOUR AT 225°F (110°C) ON BUTTERED COOKIE SHEET,
STIRRING EVERY 15 MINUTES. THESE KEEP WELL IN A
COVERED CONTAINER AND MAKE A LOVELY HOSTESS GIFT.
MAKES ABOUT 2 1/2 CUPS (625 ML).

*I WENT TO THE OPERA ONCE, BUT I DIDN'T ENJOY IT.
I COULDN'T EVEN TELL WHO WON.*

MAGIC MIXED NUTS

THESE SWEET AND SPICY NUTS JUST PLAIN DISAPPEAR!

2	EGG WHITES	2
4 CUPS	UNSALTED NUTS: CASHEWS,	1 L
	ALMONDS, PECANS AND HAZELNUTS	
1/2 CUP	GRANULATED SUGAR	125 ML
1 TSP	GROUND CINNAMON	5 ML
1 TSP	CAYENNE PEPPER	5 ML
1/2 TSP	SALT	2 ML

PREHEAT OVEN TO 325°F (160°C). PLACE EGG WHITES IN A LARGE BOWL. WHISK JUST UNTIL FOAMY. STIR IN NUTS UNTIL COATED. COMBINE SUGAR WITH CINNAMON, CAYENNE PEPPER AND SALT. POUR OVER NUTS AND TOSS UNTIL COATED. SPREAD EVENLY ON GREASED COOKIE SHEETS AND BAKE 20 TO 25 MINUTES, STIRRING FREQUENTLY. COOL AND STORE IN SEALED CONTAINERS. MAKES 4 CUPS (1 L).

BEING POLITICALLY CORRECT MEANS ALWAYS HAVING TO SAY YOU'RE SORRY.

NUTS AND BOLTS

FOR THOSE WHO ARE MECHANICALLY DECLINED.
AND JUST ABOUT ANYONE ELSE!

1 LB	BUTTER	500 G
2 TBSP	WORCESTERSHIRE SAUCE	30 ML
1 TBSP	GARLIC POWDER	15 ML
1½ TSP	ONION SALT	7 ML
1½ TSP	CELERY SALT	7 ML
4 CUPS	CHEERIOS	1 L
4 CUPS	LIFE CEREAL	1 L
4 CUPS	SHREDDIES OR WHEAT CHEX	1 L
2	BOXES (EACH 16 OZ/454 G) PRETZELS	2
2 CUPS	PEANUTS, SALTED (IF YOU INSIST)	500 ML
1	BOX (5½ OZ/150 G) BUGLES	1
1	BOX (8 OZ/250 G) CHEESE NIPS OR CHEESE BITES	1

PREHEAT OVEN TO 250°F (120°C). PLACE BUTTER IN A VERY LARGE ROASTER. PLACE IN OVEN TO MELT WHILE OVEN IS PREHEATING. REMOVE ROASTER AND ADD SPICES; STIR. ADD REMAINING INGREDIENTS, MIXING WELL TO COAT EVENLY WITH BUTTER MIXTURE. BAKE FOR 1½ HOURS. STIR AND TURN EVERY 30 MINUTES. MAKES ABOUT 24 CUPS (6 L).

CRANBERRY PISTACHIO BARK

A FOOLPROOF CANDY FOR CHRISTMAS GIFT-GIVING.

1 LB	GOOD-QUALITY WHITE CHOCOLATE	500 G
1 CUP	DRIED CRANBERRIES	250 ML
1 CUP	SHELLED PISTACHIOS	250 ML
	BE SURE AND BUY EXTRA — YOU'LL	
	HAVE TO BRIBE THE PISTACHIO SHELLER!	

MELT CHOCOLATE IN THE TOP OF A DOUBLE BOILER. LET COOL TO ROOM TEMPERATURE. ROAST PISTACHIOS AT 350°F (180°C) FOR 5 TO 7 MINUTES. SET ASIDE TO COOL.

STIR CRANBERRIES AND PISTACHIOS INTO MELTED CHOCOLATE. POUR ONTO FOIL-LINED 15- BY 10-INCH (38 BY 25 CM) RIMMED BAKING SHEET. REFRIGERATE FOR AT LEAST 1 HOUR, THEN BREAK INTO PIECES. *MAKES ABOUT 1½ POUNDS (750 G).*

PEPPERMINT BRITTLE

2 LBS	WHITE CHOCOLATE (BULK IS BEST)	1 KG
1 to 1½ CUPS	CRUSHED CANDY CANES	250 to 375 ML

LINE A 15- BY 10-INCH (38 BY 25 CM) RIMMED BAKING SHEET WITH HEAVY-DUTY FOIL. BREAK UP CHOCOLATE AND MELT OVER LOW HEAT IN A SAUCEPAN. BE VERY CAREFUL NOT TO BURN. ADD CRUSHED CANDY TO CHOCOLATE AND POUR INTO PAN AND CHILL UNTIL SET (ABOUT 1 HOUR). BREAK INTO PIECES BY SLAMMING PAN ON COUNTER.

MICROWAVE PEANUT BRITTLE

TRAVELS WELL AND MAKES A GREAT GIFT.

1 CUP	SALTED PEANUTS, PECANS OR CASHEWS	250 ML
1 CUP	GRANULATED SUGAR	250 ML
1/2 CUP	CORN SYRUP	125 ML
PINCH	SALT	PINCH
1 TSP	BUTTER	5 ML
1 TSP	VANILLA EXTRACT	5 ML
1 TSP	BAKING SODA	5 ML

STIR FIRST FOUR INGREDIENTS TOGETHER IN AN 8-CUP (2 L) MEASURING CUP OR VERY LARGE MICROWAVE-SAFE BOWL. COOK ON HIGH FOR 3 TO 4 MINUTES. STIR WELL. COOK FOR 4 MORE MINUTES. STIR IN BUTTER AND VANILLA. COOK FOR 1 MINUTE MORE. ADD BAKING SODA AND GENTLY STIR UNTIL LIGHT AND FOAMY. SPREAD MIXTURE QUICKLY ON LIGHTLY GREASED COOKIE SHEET. COOL FOR AN HOUR. BREAK INTO PIECES. MAKES ABOUT 3 DOZEN PIECES.

NEVER BUY A CAR YOU CAN'T PUSH.

TURTLES

THESE ARE BETTER THAN STORE-BOUGHT!

50	CARAMELS, UNWRAPPED	50
2 TBSP	HALF-AND-HALF (10%) CREAM	30 ML
1½ LBS	GOOD-QUALITY MILK CHOCOLATE	750 ML
150	WHOLE PECANS	150

PLACE CARAMELS IN FREEZER FOR ½ HOUR — WRAPPERS COME OFF IN A FLASH! MELT CARAMELS OVER LOW HEAT AND ADD CREAM. IN A DOUBLE BOILER, MELT CHOCOLATE TO A SMOOTH CONSISTENCY. LINE A COOKIE SHEET WITH WAXED PAPER. TO MAKE EACH TURTLE, PLACE 3 PECANS ON THE COOKIE SHEET IN A "Y" SHAPE, OR IF THE PECANS ARE LARGE, 2 ON THE BOTTOM AND 1 SITTING ON TOP. TURTLES SHOULD BE 1 TO 2 INCHES (2.5 TO 5 CM) APART. SPOON 1 TSP (5 ML) OF CARAMEL MIXTURE OVER THE TOP OF THE PECANS. PLACE IN FREEZER FOR 15 MINUTES. PICK UP A TURTLE WITH A FORK AND SUBMERGE IN MELTED CHOCOLATE. HOLD ABOVE PAN UNTIL IT STOPS DRIPPING AND REPLACE ON THE WAXED PAPER–LINED COOKIE SHEET. LET TURTLES SET IN REFRIGERATOR. STORE IN AN AIRTIGHT CONTAINER AND KEEP IN A COOL PLACE. MAKES 50 TURTLES.

VENI, VIDI, VISA: I CAME, I SAW, I SHOPPED.

XMAS TOFFEE

*YOUR KIDS WILL LOVE HELPING YOU — FOR
THE FIRST 3 MINUTES! SOFT CHEWY CANDIES.*

1 LB	BUTTER	500 G
4 CUPS	GRANULATED SUGAR	1 L
1	10-OZ (284 ML) CAN SWEETENED CONDENSED MILK	1
1	16-OZ (454 ML) BOTTLE GOLDEN CORN SYRUP	1

MIX ALL INGREDIENTS IN LARGE SAUCEPAN. GRADUALLY
BRING TO BOIL. COOK 20 TO 30 MINUTES, STIRRING
CONSTANTLY, TO SOFT BALL STAGE. (USE CANDY
THERMOMETER.) POUR ONTO 2 WELL-BUTTERED RIMMED
BAKING SHEETS. WHEN SET, CUT INTO SMALL PIECES AND
WRAP IN WAXED PAPER — TWISTING BOTH ENDS CLOSED.
MAKES 20 DOZEN.

TIGER BUTTER

1 LB	GOOD-QUALITY WHITE CHOCOLATE	500 G
3/4 CUP	PEANUT BUTTER	175 ML
2 OZ	GOOD-QUALITY DARK CHOCOLATE	60 G

MELT WHITE CHOCOLATE AND PEANUT BUTTER IN
MICROWAVE OR DOUBLE BOILER UNTIL SMOOTH. (DON'T
LET IT SCORCH!) POUR ONTO RIMMED BAKING SHEET LINED
WITH WAXED PAPER. MELT DARK CHOCOLATE AND DRIZZLE
OVER PEANUT BUTTER MIXTURE. SWIRL WITH A KNIFE.
REFRIGERATE TO SET. CUT OR BREAK INTO PIECES.

GREEN TOMATO MINCEMEAT

ALL YOU NEED IS A LARGE POT AND A DAY AT HOME. THE AROMA IS WONDERFUL AND YOUR TARTS WILL BE TOO.

3 CUPS	FINELY CHOPPED GREEN TOMATOES	750 ML
3 CUPS	FINELY CHOPPED PEELED TART APPLES	750 ML
1/2 CUP	GROUND SUET	125 ML
2 CUPS	BROWN SUGAR	500 ML
1 1/2 CUPS	CURRANTS	375 ML
1 1/2 CUPS	RAISINS	375 ML
1/2 CUP	CHOPPED MIXED PEEL	125 ML
6 TBSP	WHITE VINEGAR	90 ML
2 TBSP	LEMON JUICE	30 ML
1/2 TSP	GROUND CLOVES	2 ML
1/2 TSP	GROUND ALLSPICE	2 ML
1 1/2 TSP	GROUND CINNAMON	7 ML
1 TSP	SALT	5 ML
	RUM TO TASTE (OPTIONAL)	

COVER TOMATOES WITH COLD WATER. BRING TO A BOIL AND DRAIN. REPEAT TWICE MORE, DISCARDING THE WATER EACH TIME. DRAIN WELL. ADD REMAINING INGREDIENTS EXCEPT RUM. BRING TO BOIL, REDUCE HEAT AND SIMMER, UNCOVERED, UNTIL MIXTURE THICKENS, AT LEAST 2 HOURS. ADD RUM. POUR INTO STERILIZED JARS AND STORE IN THE REFRIGERATOR FOR UP TO 3 WEEKS. MAKES ABOUT 4 PINT (500 ML) JARS.

NOTE: THIS MAKES A LARGE BATCH, BUT ISN'T SAFE FOR BOILING WATER CANNING AND SHOULD BE EATEN WITHIN 3 WEEKS, SO GIVE SOME AWAY TO FRIENDS FOR THEM TO ENJOY.

CHRISTMAS MARMALADE

A FRIEND ONCE LEFT THIS ON MY DOORSTEP CHRISTMAS EVE (IT WAS A WARM NIGHT!) AND I'VE MADE IT EVER SINCE. WHY NOT MAKE A BATCH FOR YOUR FRIENDS?

3	MEDIUM ORANGES	3
2	LEMONS	2
1½ CUPS	COLD WATER	375 ML
1	BOTTLE (6 OZ/170 ML) PRESERVED GINGER	1
6 CUPS	GRANULATED SUGAR	1.5 L
1	BOTTLE (6 OZ/170 ML) MARASCHINO CHERRIES, DRAINED AND CHOPPED (ADD EXTRA GREEN CHERRIES AS WELL — COLORFUL!)	1
1	POUCH LIQUID PECTIN	1

WASH ORANGES AND LEMONS. SLICE PAPER THIN. DISCARD SEEDS. PUT INTO LARGE KETTLE. ADD WATER AND BRING TO A BOIL. TURN DOWN HEAT, COVER AND SIMMER ABOUT 30 MINUTES, UNTIL RINDS ARE TENDER AND TRANSPARENT. STIR OCCASIONALLY. DRAIN GINGER, SAVING SYRUP. CHOP GINGER FINELY. ADD SUGAR, CHOPPED GINGER, GINGER SYRUP AND CHERRIES TO ORANGE-LEMON MIXTURE. TURN HEAT TO HIGH AND BRING TO A FULL, ROLLING BOIL, STIRRING CONSTANTLY. BOIL HARD 1 MINUTE. REMOVE FROM HEAT AND STIR IN PECTIN. CONTINUE STIRRING AND SKIMMING FOR 5 MINUTES. LADLE INTO HOT, STERILIZED JARS, LEAVING ¼ INCH (0.5 CM) HEADSPACE. WIPE RIMS AND SEAL WITH TWO-PIECE CANNING LIDS. PROCESS IN A BOILING WATER CANNER FOR 5 MINUTES. CHECK SEALS AND REFRIGERATE ANY JARS THAT ARE NOT SEALED.

MAKES ABOUT TEN 8-OZ (250 ML) JARS.

CRANBERRY PEAR CHUTNEY

THIS CHUTNEY IS PACKED WITH WONDERFUL FLAVORS.

2 CUPS	WATER	500 ML
1 CUP	RAISINS	250 ML
2 CUPS	GRANULATED SUGAR	500 ML
2 TBSP	WHITE WINE VINEGAR	30 ML
1 CUP	ORANGE JUICE	250 ML
2 TBSP	GRATED ORANGE ZEST	30 ML
2 TBSP	SLIVERED GINGERROOT	30 ML
6 CUPS	CRANBERRIES, FRESH OR FROZEN	1.5 L
2	PEARS, PEELED, CORED, CHOPPED	2
1 CUP	TOASTED SLIVERED ALMONDS	250 ML

BOIL WATER AND ADD RAISINS. REMOVE FROM HEAT AND LET STAND 20 MINUTES. DRAIN, RESERVING $\frac{1}{2}$ CUP (125 ML) LIQUID. ADD SUGAR AND VINEGAR TO RAISIN WATER. HEAT IN SAUCEPAN UNTIL SUGAR DISSOLVES. INCREASE HEAT AND BOIL, WITHOUT STIRRING, UNTIL SYRUP TURNS GOLDEN BROWN, ABOUT 15 MINUTES. ADD ORANGE JUICE, ZEST, GINGER AND CRANBERRIES AND COOK ABOUT 10 MINUTES. STIR IN RAISINS, PEARS AND ALMONDS. POUR INTO STERILIZED JARS AND KEEP REFRIGERATED. MAKES ABOUT 6 CUPS (1.5 L).

THE MEEK SHALL INHERIT THE EARTH,
BUT NOT ITS MINERAL RIGHTS.

HOT PEPPER ORANGE CHUTNEY

ALL YOU NEED IS SOME CRACKERS AND CREAM CHEESE
AND YOU HAVE A NICE TANGY APPETIZER. GIFTABLE!

8	LARGE ORANGES	8
3 CUPS	CHOPPED RED BELL PEPPER	750 ML
1/2 CUP	CHOPPED JALAPEÑO PEPPERS	125 ML
1 CUP	CHOPPED ONION	250 ML
1 CUP	RAISINS	250 ML
1 CUP	MIXED PEEL	250 ML
1 1/2 CUPS	WHITE WINE VINEGAR	375 ML
2 CUPS	BROWN SUGAR	500 ML
1/4 TSP	CAYENNE PEPPER	1 ML
1 TSP	GROUND CINNAMON	5 ML
1/2 TSP	GROUND NUTMEG	2 ML

PEEL ALL BUT 3 ORANGES. SLICE THE 3 UNPEELED
ORANGES THINLY AND CUT EACH SLICE IN HALF. CUT
PEELED ORANGES IN 1/2-INCH (1 CM) CHUNKS. PLACE ALL
INGREDIENTS IN A LARGE POT OVER MEDIUM-HIGH HEAT
AND BRING TO A BOIL. REDUCE HEAT AND SIMMER UNTIL
THICKENED. LADLE INTO HOT, STERILIZED JARS, LEAVING
1/2 INCH (1 CM) HEADSPACE. WIPE RIMS AND SEAL WITH
TWO-PIECE CANNING LIDS. PROCESS IN A BOILING WATER
CANNER FOR 15 MINUTES. CHECK SEALS AND REFRIGERATE
ANY JARS THAT ARE NOT SEALED. MAKES TWELVE 8-OZ
(250 ML) JARS.

CONTRIBUTING AUTHORS

The Best of Bridge Publishing Ltd.
The Best of the Best and More
Recipes from this book are found on pages 20, 56 (bottom), 59 (top), 76, 142, 161, 191, 195, 197, 210 (top), 238, 260, 264, 273, 282, 284 (top) and 290.

The Best of Bridge Publishing Ltd.
The Rest of the Best and More
Recipes from this book are found on pages 67, 182, 196, 208, 237, 246, 252 and 272.

The Best of Bridge Publishing Ltd. with Chef Vincent Parkinson
A Year of the Best
A recipe from this book is found on page 88.

Karen Brimacombe, Mary Halpen, Helen Miles, Valerie Robinson and Joan Wilson
The Complete Best of Bridge Cookbooks, Volume 1
Recipes from this book are found on pages 12, 16, 18, 21, 23, 35, 36, 42, 44, 49, 51, 59 (bottom), 62, 65, 68–70, 74 (top), 75, 81 (top), 83–85, 92, 94, 96–99, 101 (bottom), 103–7, 112–16, 119, 124, 125, 143–46, 152, 153, 164, 166, 168, 180, 181, 184, 190, 192–94, 198, 200, 202–4, 207, 214, 220, 225, 230 (both), 231 (top), 232, 234, 235 (top), 240, 243–45, 248, 255, 257, 258, 259, 265, 266, 278–81 and 289.

Karen Brimacombe, Mary Halpen, Helen Miles, Valerie Robinson and Joan Wilson
The Complete Best of Bridge Cookbooks, Volume 2
Recipes from this book are found on pages 11, 13, 17, 19, 26, 29, 32, 34, 40, 41, 45, 53, 56 (top), 66, 71–73, 74 (bottom), 78–80, 82, 90, 185–88, 199, 201, 209, 210 (bottom), 215, 233, 236, 239, 256, 261, 262, 267, 283 and 285.

Karen Brimacombe, Mary Halpen, Helen Miles, Valerie Robinson and Joan Wilson
The Complete Best of Bridge Cookbooks, Volume 3
Recipes from this book are found on pages 10, 22, 28, 43, 46–48, 50, 52, 54, 58, 64 (both), 81 (bottom), 89, 91, 93, 138, 139, 147, 162, 165, 170, 189, 205, 231 (bottom), 235 (bottom), 242, 250, 253, 254, 268, 270, 274, 284 (bottom), 286, 287 (both), 288 and 291.

Johanna Burkhard
500 Best Comfort Food Recipes
Recipes from this book are found on pages 14, 30, 100, 102, 108, 110, 120, 121, 122, 148, 154, 157, 158, 172, 174, 178, 206 and 221.

Judith Finlayson
A recipe by this author, developed for this book, is found on page 160.

Judith Finlayson
125 Best Rotisserie Oven Recipes
Recipes from this book are found on pages 216, 218, 222, 224, 226 and 228.

Judith Finlayson
150 Best Slow Cooker Recipes, Second Edition
Recipes from this book are found on pages 57, 60, 63, 126, 128, 130, 134, 136 and 276.

Judith Finlayson
175 Essential Slow Cooker Classics
A recipe from this book is found on page 140.

Judith Finlayson
The Complete Gluten-Free Whole Grains Cookbook
A recipe from this book is found on page 212.

Judith Finlayson
Delicious & Dependable Slow Cooker Recipes
A recipe from this book is found on page 176.

Judith Finlayson
Slow Cooker Comfort Food
Recipes from this book are found on pages 24 and 38.

Library and Archives Canada Cataloguing in Publication

Best of Bridge holiday classics : 225 recipes for special occasions.

Includes index.
ISBN 978-0-7788-0487-1 (hardcover wire-o binding)

1. Holiday cooking. 2. Cookbooks. I. Best of Bridge Publishing Ltd, author

TX739.B47 2014   641.5'68   C2014-903339-7

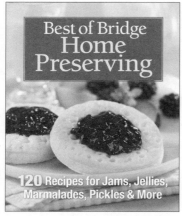

More Great Books
from Robert Rose

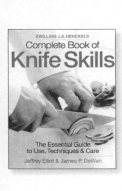

Bestsellers

- The Juicing Bible, Second Edition
  by Pat Crocker
- The Complete Coconut Cookbook
  by Camilla V. Saulsbury
- 175 Best Babycakes™ Cake Pop Maker Recipes
  by Kathy Moore and Roxanne Wyss
- Eat Raw, Eat Well
  by Douglas McNish
- The Smoothies Bible, Second Edition
  by Pat Crocker
- The Food Substitutions Bible, Second Edition
  by David Joachim
- Zwilling J.A. Henckels Complete Book of Knife Skills
  by Jeffrey Elliot and James P. DeWan

Appliance Bestsellers

- 225 Best Pressure Cooker Recipes
  by Cinda Chavich
- 200 Best Panini Recipes
  by Tiffany Collins
- 125 Best Indoor Grill Recipes
  by Ilana Simon
- The Convection Oven Bible
  by Linda Stephen
- The Fondue Bible
  by Ilana Simon

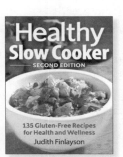

- Easy Everyday Slow Cooker Recipes
  by Donna-Marie Pye
- The 150 Best Slow Cooker Recipes, Second Edition
  by Judith Finlayson
- The Vegetarian Slow Cooker
  by Judith Finlayson
- The Healthy Slow Cooker, Second Edition
  by Judith Finlayson
- Slow Cooker Winners
  by Donna-Marie Pye
- Canada's Slow Cooker Winners
  by Donna-Marie Pye
- 150 Best Breakfast Sandwich Maker Recipes
  by Jennifer Williams
- 300 Best Rice Cooker Recipes
  by Katie Chin
- 650 Best Food Processor Recipes
  by George Geary and Judith Finlayson
- The Mixer Bible, Third Edition
  by Meredith Deeds and Carla Snyder
- 300 Best Bread Machine Recipes
  by Donna Washburn and Heather Butt
- 300 Best Canadian Bread Machine Recipes
  by Donna Washburn and Heather Butt

Baking Bestsellers

- Sensational Buttercream Decorating
  by Carey Madden
- 150 Best Gluten-Free Muffin Recipes
  by Camilla V. Saulsbury
- Piece of Cake!
  by Camilla V. Saulsbury
- The Cheesecake Bible
  by George Geary
- Complete Cake Mix Magic
  by Jill Snider
- 750 Best Muffin Recipes
  by Camilla V. Saulsbury
- 200 Fast & Easy Artisan Breads
  by Judith Fertig

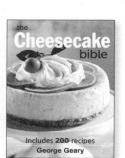

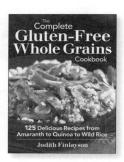

- Complete Gluten-Free Cookbook
  by Donna Washburn and Heather Butt
- 250 Gluten-Free Favorites
  by Donna Washburn and Heather Butt
- Complete Gluten-Free Diet & Nutrition Guide
  by Alexandra Anca and Theresa Santandrea-Cull
- The Complete Gluten-Free Whole Grains Cookbook
  by Judith Finlayson
- The Vegetarian Kitchen Table Cookbook
  by Igor Brotto and Olivier Guiriec

Healthy Cooking Bestsellers

- Canada's Diabetes Meals for Good Health, Second Edition
  by Karen Graham
- Diabetes Meals for Good Health, Second Edition
  by Karen Graham
- 5 Easy Steps to Healthy Cooking
  by Camilla V. Saulsbury
- 350 Best Vegan Recipes
  by Deb Roussou
- The Vegan Cook's Bible
  by Pat Crocker
- The Gluten-Free Baking Book
  by Donna Washburn and Heather Butt

Health Bestsellers

- ASD: The Complete Autism Spectrum Disorder Health & Diet Guide
  by R. Garth Smith, Susan Hannah and Elke Sengmueller
- The Complete Arthritis Health, Diet Guide & Cookbook
  by Kim Arrey with Dr. Michael R. Starr
- The Complete Weight-Loss Surgery Guide & Diet Program
  by Sue Ekserci with Dr. Laz Klein
- The PCOS Health & Nutrition Guide
  by Dr. Jillian Stansbury with Dr. Sheila Mitchell

For more great books, see previous pages

Robert ROSE

Visit us at www.robertrose.ca